Evidence Based Clinical Supervision

This book is dedicated to my father, Alec Milne.
Like a good supervisor, he taught me to value
both evidence and experience.

Evidence-Based Clinical Supervision

Principles and Practice

Derek Milne

The British Psychological Society

BPS Blackwell

This edition first published 2009 by the British Psychological Society and Blackwell Publishing Ltd
© 2009 Derek Milne

BPS Blackwell is an imprint of Blackwell Publishing, which was acquired by John Wiley & Sons in February 2007. Blackwell's publishing program has been merged with Wiley's global Scientific, Technical, and Medical business to form Wiley-Blackwell.

Registered Office
John Wiley & Sons Ltd, The Atrium, Southern Gate, Chichester, West Sussex, PO19 8SQ, UK

Editorial Offices
350 Main Street, Malden, MA 02148-5020, USA
9600 Garsington Road, Oxford, OX4 2DQ, UK
The Atrium, Southern Gate, Chichester, West Sussex, PO19 8SQ, UK

For details of our global editorial offices, for customer services, and for information about how to apply for permission to reuse the copyright material in this book please see our website at www.wiley.com/wiley-blackwell.

The right of Derek Milne to be identified as the author of this work has been asserted in accordance with the Copyright, Designs and Patents Act 1988.

Library of Congress Cataloging-in-Publication Data

PB: Milne, Derek, 1949–
   Evidence-based clinical supervision : principles and practice / Derek Milne.
      p. cm.
   Includes bibliographical references and index.
   ISBN 978-1-4051-5849-7 (pbk. : alk. paper) 1. Mental health personnel–Supervision of. I. Title.
   RC440.8.M55 2009
   616.89'023–dc22

                                          2008044182

A catalogue record for this book is available from the British Library.

Set in 10.5/13pt Minion
by SPi Publisher Services, Pondicherry, India
Printed and bound in Malaysia by KHL Printing Co Sdn Bhd

The British Psychological Society's free Research Digest e-mail service rounds up the latest research and relates it to your syllabus in a user-friendly way. To subscribe go to www.researchdigest.org.uk or send a blank e-mail to subscribe-rd@lists.bps.org.uk.

1   2009

Contents

Preface

One of the fascinating aspects of writing this book on Evidence-Based Clinical Supervision (EBCS) has been to experience the interplay between theory and practice in clinical supervision at a personal level, as if writing this book was one great big learning exercise. This came about because I adopted the evidence-based practice framework, a broad approach to problem-solving which required me to repeatedly adopt alternating and rather different ways of understanding supervision. As a result, I spent a year revolving around an extensive experiential learning cycle, during the time that was devoted to preparing this book. Much of this period was occupied with discussions with experts in clinical supervision, in order to develop guidelines and to continue my own research programme. But there was also the protracted process of studying relevant theories and research findings in a particularly systematic way, whilst preparing and submitting some of the articles that are embedded within this book for peer review, in relation to publishing in scientific journals. This personal journey of discovery can be seen explicitly in some passages of the book (e.g. in Chapters 3 and 9), where my grasp of similar approaches, such as cognitive-behaviour therapy (CBT) supervision, challenged my assumption that EBCS was a distinct approach. Ultimately, I reasoned that EBCS was sufficiently distinctive to merit its own brand name. For example, by comparison with CBT supervision, EBCS has a wider range of theoretical roots, entails working explicitly with the supervisee's emotional material, draws systematic analogies with related literatures (especially staff development and therapy process–outcome research), and has broader objectives than CBT (e.g. educational goals, especially the development of 'capability'). I appreciated that these apparent distinctions may simply be differences of emphasis, as there would appear to be nothing in EBCS that is fundamentally contrary to CBT supervision. But careful scrutiny of the evidence from observations of CBT supervision and surveys of CBT supervisors indicated that EBS really was different (Milne, 2008a). By the end of my year's adventure, I came to view EBCS as subsuming CBT supervision, as well as a range of related supervision models. This is largely due to its integrative, 'bigger picture' approach (i.e. seeking out the core psychological and social factors within supervision, based on a fairly general search). Indeed, the original title for this book was The Psychology of Supervision. Thus, I believe that EBCS is unique, but affords a suitable way of revitalising CBT and related approaches to clinical supervision (i.e. modern professional practice; applied science).

The book aims to provide clinical supervisors, and those who support them, with the best-available evidence to guide their work (which is assumed to be primarily CBT in Britain), as practised within the mental health field. This includes empirical knowledge derived from the latest research, and guidance from expert consensus. Such material addresses the 'restorative' and 'normative' functions of supervision, but priority is given to the supervisor's 'formative' or educative role. The resultant material was also sifted and sorted by drawing on my 25 years of relevant experience, moderated by regular interaction with colleagues with a similar investment in developing supervision (at conferences, workshops, etc). This includes the detailed feedback I received from the referees and editors of scientific and professional journals, as a result of submitting much of the original material in this book as research papers for peer review. Taken together, these aims and methods are intended to address a paradox in the supervision field. This is that, despite its manifest importance, supervision is a sorely neglected topic. As Watkins (1997) has put it, 'something does not compute' (p.604). This paradox has been a spur to my work, as reported in this book.

Based on this evidence-based process of attempting to make things compute, Chapter 1 reviews how supervision has been defined to date, offering a more rigorous definition, derived from a systematic review of 24 recent studies of effective clinical supervision. I describe this particular review approach, the best-evidence synthesis (and continue to draw on it in subsequent chapters). I also question the conventional historical account, which identifies Freud as the first to explicitly utilise and report clinical supervision. Rather, applying the definition of supervision precisely and delving into pre-Freudian history, it seems to me that the ancient Greeks got there first (again!). Chapter 2 summarises the main types of models (conceptual frameworks) that are intended to help us understand supervision. They are mainly ones that are either based explicitly on therapies (where CBT is a strong example), or on developmental models, or are supervision-specific ones. In Chapter 3, I draw on these models to propose my own EBS approach, which (following a critical review) then colours the remainder of the book. The important role of the learning alliance in supervision is recognised in Chapter 4, alongside some challenges to its creation and maintenance (i.e. the 'rupture and repair' cycle; power dynamics). The first of my four EBCS guidelines is introduced here. These guidelines were designed following the National Institute of Clinical Excellence (NICE) methodology, but revised as necessary to make the approach as relevant as possible to supervision (what we termed the NICE(R) guideline development procedure). Over a hundred clinical supervisors and tutors helped to refine these guidelines. Chapter 5 sets out the supervision cycle, namely: conducting a learning needs assessment; negotiating the objectives (learning contract); utilising different methods of supervision; and evaluating progress. Three EBCS guidelines are introduced in this chapter, as it is the heart of routine supervision. All four guidelines are part of the EBCS training manual, which is accessible from www.wiley.com/go/milne. The EBCS model has been represented physically as a tandem, according to which reasoning the front wheel of the bike is controlled by the supervisor. This then casts the rear wheel (and the back seat) as the supervisee's province, set out as the Kolb (1984) experiential learning cycle. Chapter 6 details this cyclical process, furnishing supportive evidence and illustrating how supervisees are essential collaborators in the business of supervision. But this tandem duo are insufficient to develop and maintain effective supervision within complex workplace systems, so Chapter 7 reviews the ways in which supervision can be supported, especially through the dominant intervention of supervisor training. Chapter 8 returns to the task of evaluation, offering the 'fidelity framework' as a coherent, step-wise way to view and practise the evaluation of supervision. Implementation issues are also addressed, in order to increase the likelihood that evaluation serves a useful purpose. In the ninth and concluding chapter I tease out the main principles of EBCS, adding reflective commentaries where there is unfinished business, such as the overlap between EBCS and CBT supervision, and I offer a specification for career-long supervision.

The method I've used to tackle these chapters has also been CBT-compatible, as in adopting the evidence-based practice model (Roth & Fonagy, 1996), then using it as a framework to guide a process of scholarly review, featuring:

- critically analysing and constructively re-synthesising the research literature;
- integrating research findings with knowledge from textbooks and from formal consensus statements by experts;
- relating this knowledge-base to the contexts in which supervision occurs (e.g. organisational and professional influences on supervision);
- reviewing the nature and effectiveness of supervisor training and support arrangements;
- comparing closely related approaches to supervision; and
- auditing the fidelity of supervision, and evaluating its results.

This method enabled me to draw out numerous practical implications, and to summarise a comprehensive approach to supervision as an applied psychological science. As a result, I believe that this book is original yet accessible, detailed yet coherent, critical yet constructive. It offers a rounded rationale and a systematic guide for evidence-based supervision, and, more generally, it offers a way of making the vital business of supervision 'compute' (Watkins, 1997). I hope that you will also enjoy the experience of discovery, as you read the book.

Acknowledgements

As already touched on, the parallel between the experience of writing this book and the experience of supervision appears strong to me: I have grappled with some suitably challenging and perplexing material, learning much along the way, and have been supported and guided by those who have written about supervision (in texts, journal papers and consensus statements). I have also had the benefit of receiving encouragement and feedback from numerous colleagues, locally and nationally. I am grateful to the main local allies for their interest (Roger Paxton, Chris Dunkerley, Tonia Culloty, Chiara Lombardo, Colin Westerman, Dominique Keegan, Ian A. James, Caroline Leck, Nasim Choudhri, Alia Sheikh, John Ormrod, Helen Aylott, Peter Armstrong and Mark Freeston). Nationally, I have felt aided and influenced by Dave Green's DROSS group (i.e. the Development and Recognition of Supervisory Skills initiative, based in Northern England, latterly rechristened STAR), by those colleagues who write about supervision (Joyce Scaife and Graham Sloan), and by my Clinical Tutor colleagues within the Group of Trainers in Clinical Psychology (GTiCP). I am grateful to them for their collaboration and their encouragement to reflect on supervision as a serious academic topic, and especially for their help in developing the guidelines on EBCS (and please note that many additional individuals have their input acknowledged within the EBCS training manual, available from the www.wiley.com/go/milne. But perhaps the greatest regular impetus has been the stimulating interaction that arose through the EBS consultancy that I provided to my international colleague, Californian Robert Reiser, during the year when I was writing this book. This fortnightly engagement in listening to and discussing tapes of his ongoing supervision provided a vital practical dimension to the book, enlivening the theoretical information that I was trying to process. As a consequence of this quasi-supervisory experience, I felt energised and supported, and learnt much about this young but essential field of professional practice.

Learning is one thing, producing the goods quite another, and so I must also acknowledge the massive assistance received from the secretarial staff at the Newcastle Doctorate in Clinical Psychology programme (Karen Clark, Kathryn Mark, Barbara Mellors and Lynne Armstrong); I am also grateful to Amy Lievesley, for acting as my 'production assistant' (i.e. obtaining articles and checking the manuscript), and Judy Preece (graphic artist, Newcastle University), for drawing many of the figures in the book. Assistance also took the form of grants from the Higher Education Academy (Psychology Network) and the British Psychological Society (Division of Clinical Psychology).

Finally, I must say a heartfelt thanks to my partner, Jan Little, for her steadfast and warm support, and to my daughter, Kirsty, for her unstinting encouragement and unfaltering belief. I hope that all these great people will see in this book some worthwhile return for their help.

Derek Milne
Morpeth
Northumberland
1 March 2008

About the author

Professor Derek Milne (B.Sc., M.Sc., Dip.Clin.Psych., Ph.D., C. Psychol., FBPS) is a Consultant Clinical Psychologist with Northumberland, Tyne & Wear NHS Trust, and Director of the Doctorate in Clinical Psychology at Newcastle University. His previous experience includes 12 years as a Clinical Tutor at both Newcastle and Leeds Universities. Prior to this he also gained valuable experience in the roles of clinical supervisor, teacher, tennis coach, sport psychologist, mentor, and as an action researcher (on staff development generally, focusing on clinical supervision latterly). Since 1979 he has published six books and over 150 scientific and professional papers, many on staff development and supervision.

1

Recognising Supervision

Introduction

Sitting squarely at the crossroads between professional development and professional practice, clinical supervision cries out for study and enhancement. It ensures safe and effective practice (Falender & Shafranske, 2004), maximises the outcomes for clients (Krasner *et al.*, 1998; Holloway & Neufeldt, 1995), offers support for supervisees (Russell & Petrie, 1994) and represents the foremost method (Holloway & Poulin, 1995) and most critical part (Watkins, 1997) of teaching clinical skills to mental health practitioners. Duly perceived as the main influence on clinical practice amongst qualified staff and their trainees (Lucock *et al.*, 2006), it also helps to address the growing emphasis on clinical accountability (Wampold & Holloway, 1997), is required for the accreditation of initial professional training (e.g. British Psychological Society (BPS), 2002), is necessary for continuing professional development and regulation (e.g. British Association of Behavioural and Cognitive Psychotherapists (BABCP), see Latham, 2006), and is an accepted defence against litigation (Knapp & Vandecreek, 1997). Not surprising, then, that the Department of Health (1998) should regard effective staff training that subsumes supervision as one of the 'ten essential shared capabilities' of mental health practitioners (Department of Health, 2004). Although a welcome acknowledgement, this important role has actually been long recognised, as indicated in the Hippocratic oath ('… I will keep this oath and … him who taught me this art equally dear to me as my parents …').

Yet, in spite of its critical and highly valued role, the development of supervisors has long been a neglected research area, one that has 'generated only a modicum of research' (Holloway & Poulin, 1995, p.245), research that has been judged inadequate scientifically (Ellis *et al.*, 1996). Russell and

Petrie (1994, p.27) find this neglect 'alarming', and Watkins (1997) noted how this neglect simply 'does not compute' (p.604) with the important role supervision plays in professional life.

It should not be surprising, then, to learn that supervision models do not correspond to the complexities of professional practice (Cleary & Freeman, 2006), and that the adequacy of supervision has been rated as 'very poor' in 20–30 per cent of cases, according to a national enquiry concerning junior doctors in the UK (see Olsen & Neale, 2005). In the presence of such damning views, and in the absence of a well-developed toolkit of psychometrically sound instruments, concerns that the practice of clinical supervision may generally be poor are difficult to dispel (Binder, 1993; Worthington, 1987). To illustrate the validity of such concerns, a rigorous $N=1$ observational analysis of an experienced cognitive-behaviour therapy (CBT) supervisor raised questions about his competence, despite being accredited by at least two organisations (Milne & James, 2002).

The Evidence-based Approach to Clinical Supervision (EBCS)

In order to address some of these concerns, and to provide a fresh, systematic and topical approach, the present book describes an evidence-based approach to supervision (EBCS). EBCS is similar to 'Best Evidence Medical Education' (Harden *et al.*, 1999), as both treat professional development in a systematic way, based on the highest-quality, most relevant research. It differs most markedly from intensively personal (humanistic) approaches, which assert, for instance, that 'good supervision, like love … cannot be taught' (Hawkins & Shohet, 1989, p.157).

The theoretical foundation of EBCS is 'experiential learning', as summarised by Kolb many years ago (1984), but still endorsed within the mental health professions currently (e.g. the BABCP, see Lewis, 2005; British Psychological Society, 2003). This is appropriate, as clinical supervision is primarily a form of experiential learning (Carroll, 2007). According to this experiential learning model, supervisees acquire competence by learning from experience, through a necessary combination of four learning modes: reflection; conceptualisation (thinking); planning; and concrete experience (feeling and doing). According to this view, professional competence is achieved most efficiently when the supervisee is given regular opportunities to use all four modes. Drawing on this theory and on the research literature, it appears that the supervisor needs to use a range of methods to succeed in enabling the learner to utilise these different modes (Milne & James, 2000). To restate this in traditional behavioural terms, supervisors are initially judged competent and effective when their supervision draws on such methods, and when this successively serves the function of facilitating this kind of experiential learning in their supervisees (i.e. a functional definition of competence). Additionally, supervision should also be judged in terms of its influence on the work of the supervisees, characteristically the development of their therapy and its clinical effectiveness. Chapter 8 elaborates this argument. Two studies have indicated the value of this model for the development of supervision, utilising an observational tool called Teachers' PETS (Process Evaluation of Training and Supervision: Milne *et al.*, 2002; Milne & James, 2002). In summary, according to this EBCS model, effective and competent supervision will be characterised by the use of a range of supervision methods (e.g. collaborative goal-setting), ones which increase the supervisees' use of the four learning modes (i.e. a structural and a functional definition of effective supervision, respectively), and consequently their capacity to work competently, safely and effectively.

EBCS is therefore a specialised aspect of evidence-based practice (EBP, see Roth, Fonagy & Parry, 1996), now a hot issue in health services, and part of an international effort to ensure that patients have access to the best-available care. For example, in the USA the American Psychological Association has developed a policy for EBP, and international scientific journals that are published there have carried special issues to foster understanding and to promote EBP (e.g. see Thorn, 2007). Figure 3.4 (Chapter 3) sets out the EBP framework, adapted only slightly by replacing 'therapy' with 'supervision'. This framework helps to clarify how the different factors that we should consider in relation to supervision can be brought together successfully (e.g. the relationship between research findings and professional consensus on what represents best practice). The EBCS framework underpins this book, as summarised shortly under the 'Aims' section below, and is detailed in Chapter 3. The extent to which EBCS can be described as 'evidence-based' is discussed in the final chapter.

The Significance of Supervision

The regular media attention to examples of professional misconduct provides a powerful reminder of the importance of supervision within EBP.

The 'Bristol case' is an illustration, a case in which unusually high death rates amongst infants following two types of heart surgery led to doctors being struck off the medical register. The enquiry dramatically highlighted how the traditional trust placed in doctors needs to be replaced by systems for monitoring competence and for providing relevant training, amongst other things (such as effective quality-control procedures within professionals' organisations, Smith, 1998). Supervision would logically form a central part of that training, and should draw on any monitoring data.

Unfortunately for the public's protection, supervision is a neglected research topic, despite considerable investment. In the UK alone, the Department of Health spent about £2 billion per year on the training of clinical staff (Department of Health, 2000). In 2007 the investment was described as 'huge' (Department of Health, 2007, p.3). Although only a small part of this is likely to relate to the training of supervisors, supervision is surely the major form of continuing professional development (CPD) for clinical staff and therefore the greatest investment that healthcare providers like the National Health Service (NHS) make in staff support and development. This investment was justified within a modernisation agenda in which the development of the workforce was emphasised (e.g. see *A First Class Service*, Department of Health, 1998). Over time, the UK government's interest in CPD has become increasingly specific, detailing its nature, content and process (see Gray, 2006, for a thorough review of these policy refinements). A case in point is supervision, which needs to be regular and to be available to all staff as it can 'ensure a high quality of practice' and 'will encourage reflective practice', at least in relation to the psychological therapies (Department of Health, 2004, p.35). More generally, 'recognising the importance of supervision and reflective practice' (p.18) became one of 'the ten essential capabilities' (Department of Health, 2004a), and a core national standard was that 'clinical care and treatment are carried out under supervision' (Department of Health, 2004b, p.29). Latterly, the contract specification for training clinical psychologists in the UK (which presumably applies equally to all staff groups) added that this should be 'effective' supervision, developed through CPD (Section 2.1). This is consistent with recent policy guidance on initial training and CPD, which indicates a major shift in contracting and monitoring by stressing, for instance, the need for all training to be 'of high quality' (p.26), within a system that raises the importance of training to be 'core business' (Department of Health, 2007, p.27). As a result of investing heavily, the NHS expects staff to be motivated, confident and skilled, so that they can provide appropriate care, treatment and support to patients throughout their careers (Department of Health, 2007).

Apart from the explicit functions it serves, such as ensuring safe and effective clinical practice (see the next chapter for a full breakdown of these functions), supervision is also significant in terms of attracting new recruits (Lavender & Thompson, 2000), affording job satisfaction (Milne, 1991), providing status and enhanced pay, helping therapists in managing their caseloads, and as part of the natural career development of professionals (e.g. when the passing on of skills to develop junior colleagues becomes particularly satisfying – the business of generativity). Therefore, although there are concerns about the generally poor quality of research on supervision, there is a markedly greater emphasis on the importance of supervision, both in developing initial competence (so that trainees become qualified as independent practitioners), and as a major way to ensure CPD. This book attempts to redress this striking imbalance by highlighting a seam of better research, which, linked to resources such as professional consensus and transferable knowledge (see Chapter 3 for a full rationale), can provide a satisfactory knowledge-base for the current implementation of policy directives. But next I want to try to understand how we got to the present situation: how did supervision become so valued, despite being so poorly understood? How can we make sense of the present significance of supervision, in terms of the past? The next section takes a brief look at the early forms of supervision, based on some literature relating to the mental health field.

The History of Supervision

Given the widespread use of the apprenticeship approach in society, exemplified by the learning of a trade or profession from a more skilled practitioner or employer, it seems likely that supervision has been practised since ancient times. How else would those with the necessary skills and the responsibility for providing specialist services ensure that they had a skilled workforce, one that was doing their work to the required standard? I suspect that certain aspects of this apprenticeship relationship persist to this day. Even such seemingly extreme examples as the training of a monk suggest some continuity across the social spectrum. Consider a historical account of the Zen Buddhist approach to training (Suzuki, 1934). Just like modern trainees, apprentices routinely experienced rejection on first attempting to gain access to training. Those who persisted were subjected to initial episodes of humiliation and then hard labour, before gaining the requisite experience to graduate. This is eerily like the modern student's experience, with (for example) hundreds of rejected applicants for clinical psychology training (humiliation), then three years of training (labour), not to mention the hard labour entailed in accruing the necessary voluntary work experience, Assistantships, and other arduous aspects of the journey to even stand a chance of commencing the journey to professional 'enlightenment'.

This mystical illustration is perhaps not as perverse as you might imagine, since psychotherapy was traditionally regarded as mystical and therefore not amenable to such practical methods as observation (Baker *et al.*, 1990). It was only in 1957 that Carl Rogers moved training 'out of the realm of the mysterious to the realm of the observable and trainable, by making audiotape recordings of sessions' (Baker *et al.*, 1990, p.357). This evolved into the systematic approach known as micro-counselling (see Baker *et al.*, 1990, for a summary). Psychoanalytic supervision relied heavily on the apprenticeship system 'from the very beginning' (DeBell, 1963, p.546), and the use of training clinics in psychology in general goes back at least to the late 19th century, when Witmer (1907) utilised case-based instruction. Shakow (2007) dates the emergence of proper psychological clinics from Witmer's time, noting that 'with respect to training, there was a consistent recognition of the importance of providing systematic education in applied psychology and supplying facilities to psychologists, educators, and other students for study in the practical setting. Courses, demonstrations, and practicum facilities in the clinical field for the study of exceptional children were a regular part of the programme' (p.2). Shakow believed that Witmer's early emphasis on training led universities to establish clinics and formal training courses. He noted that, by the time of a survey reported in 1914 (but referring to practices some time prior), there were 26 university clinics, and many related courses, in the USA. However, according to Shakow (2007), training remained generally unsystematic, relying on individual trainees to organise their own programme of professional development. In America, it was not until 1945 that training in clinical psychology was formalised into university-based, four-year PhD programmes. Seemingly for the first time, clinical supervision was a clearly specified requirement within this training programme: students were first to receive teaching, then to acquire clinical skills in diagnosis and therapy under 'close individual supervision' (Shakow, 2007, p.7).

It is not clear from this account whether or not anything like our current conception of supervision was implemented. Therefore, it is often recounted that the first recorded example of supervision in the mental health field occurred with Freud's treatment of Little Hans (Freud, 1909). Hans had developed a fear that one of the large horses he saw pulling coaches past his home might bite him. Freud began to work on Little Hans's phobia through the boy's father, Max Graf. Freud utilised suggestion and didactic instruction in supervising Max Graf, who actually delivered the treatment to Hans (Jacobs *et al.*, 1995). This account is cited by Bernard and Goodyear (2004), who go on to quote Frawley-O'Dea and Sarnat (2001) who noted that 'Freud was the first supervisor and thus represents the archetypal supervisor … in his model of supervision he combined a positivistic stance … with a personal insistence on maintaining a position as the ultimate arbiter of truth, knowledge, and power' (p.17). However, this example is problematic, as working clinically through a non-professional like a parent represents consultancy or indirect therapy, rather than supervision (see the Definition section below), so I suggest that we need to look elsewhere for the first recorded example of supervision.

Freud's dogmatism in supervision is reminiscent of primitive psychotherapy and quackery (Lawrence, 1910), to which we now turn for an insight into the true origins of supervision. According to Lawrence's many accounts of quackery, instilling confidence in the healer is an essential first step. Drawing on Lawrence's review of ancient mental health practice, I wish to suggest that Freud was far from being the first mental health supervisor. In ancient Greece, temples were the first hospitals, and priests were the first physicians. Just as Freud used his authority to create the conditions for change, so in ancient Greece various mystic rites took place in order to influence a patient's imagination. With a resemblance to the modern health hydro, ancient Greek temples had a regime of practical therapies (though the details differed, including such things as baths, friction of the skin and a strict diet). This treatment occurred in places carefully chosen for their 'healthful environment' (p.79), just like the ensuing Victorian psychiatric hospital in the UK. The mythological god of healing, Asclepius, like Freud after him, interpreted the dreams of the Grecian pilgrims in search of health, as, at that time, it was believed this afforded the proper cure for an ailment. In turn, 'the interpretation of these dreams and the revelation to the patient of their alleged meaning was entrusted to a priest, who served as an intermediary between Asclepius and the patient' (Lawrence, 1910, p.98). Adding to my supposition that these priests were the first known therapists and that Asclepius was therefore the first recorded supervisor, Lawrence (1910) records that Asclepius, far from being a god, was in fact an historic personage. He transmitted his professional knowledge to the priests, who were versed in medical understanding. Lawrence records that for centuries the most famous Grecian physicians were members of this order, and that Hippocrates (often considered to be the father of modern medicine) is said to be 17th in direct descent from Asclepius. Other parallels with modern mental healthcare are cited, including how the records of cures were inscribed upon the walls of the temple, perhaps representing the first written case studies? However, my assumption that Asclepius was the first clinical supervisor is challenged by studying Wikipedia (visited on 8 October 2007). According to the information on Greek mythology there, Asclepius in turn apparently acquired the art of healing from Chiron, a kind and great healer who was highly regarded as a tutor. Asclepius was therefore a disciple of Chiron's, and so I now propose that Chiron was the first-ever clinical supervisor.

The significance of a supervisor's personality and general self-presentation is echoed within Jackson's (1999) history of psychological healing. He notes, in a far more favourable vein, how Hippocrates recorded that physicians might use various measures to gain the patient's confidence: 'these included appearance and dress, manner (serious and humane), way of life (regular and reliable), just conduct, control of himself, and social adeptness' (p.40).

To my knowledge, the first clear-cut example of clinical supervision in recent times dates from the 19th century, when social workers guided the work of volunteers within charity organisation societies, where moral treatments were provided to the poor (Harkness & Poertner, 1989). Many decades on, it appears that Freud's formal involvement in supervision began in his Zurich clinic in 1902, when a group of physicians studied analysis with him at regular meetings (Kovacs, 1936). Indeed, it appears that the need for a personal analysis of the therapist began to appear within these study circles. According to Kovacs, Freud 'noted certain disturbing factors, which proved a great hindrance to harmonious co-operation, and he began to surmise that this disharmony was mainly due to the unresolved psychic conflicts of his fellow workers' (p.347). The first international conference took place in 1908, including a report on this Zurich clinic. This had been founded by Bleuler, and was the first place where psychoanalysis was officially taught and practised (Kovacs, 1936). The main methods of supervision at the time were guided reading of the current psychoanalytical literature, plus word association tests, designed to give the trainee analyst a first-hand experience of the unconscious. It soon became established that, for psychoanalysis to be successful, the therapist first needs to undergo psychoanalysis. By 1922, it was further established that 'only those persons should be authorised to practise psychoanalysis who, as well as taking a theoretical course of training, had submitted to a training analysis conducted by an analyst approved by the Society at the time. A training committee was set up within each Society for the purpose of organising a system of training' (Kovacs, 1936, p.25). The training analysis was based on the supervisee analysing one or two patients, under the supervision of an experienced colleague. This was believed to develop the 'right attitude' towards patients, and to help in the acquisition of techniques.

Therefore, it does appear that the apprentice system has been relied on heavily since the ancient Greek approach. In summary, 'almost from the beginning of organised teaching, supervision has been accorded an important place in the training programme' (DeBell, 1963, p.546). According to DeBell, the essential method of apprenticeship amongst healthcare professionals was to use case material to draw out relationships between theoretical concepts and the specific practicalities of a case. Supervisors reportedly used the methods of feedback, self-disclosure, didactic teaching, encouragement, reflection on material, and the translation of the case into relevant theory. Other methods included confrontation and clarification, in order to formulate the case from the supervisee's written notes of therapy (process notes), and work on the supervisee's account of therapy within the subsequent supervisory hour (especially the use of interpretations, Bibring, 1937). At that time, a total of 150 hours was regarded as the minimum for effective supervision. The goal was to enable a less experienced therapist to become effective in the task of benefiting patients (DeBell, 1963).

To place this in context, research on therapy is dated from the end of the Second World War, with research on supervision appearing in the 1950s (Bernard & Goodyear, 2004). I next bring this review up to date, drawing carefully on the research available at the start of the 21st century to address another important building-block for supervision, its current definition.

The Definition of Clinical Supervision

As a complex intervention, it is not surprising that supervision is defined in a variety of ways. For instance, in the UK it has been defined within the

NHS as: 'A formal process of professional support and learning which enables practitioners to develop knowledge and competence, assume responsibility for their own practice, and enhance consumer protection and safety of care in complex situations' (Department of Health, 1993, p.1). The most widely cited definition of clinical supervision, popular in the USA, is the one provided by Bernard and Goodyear (2004). According to them, supervision is: '… an intervention provided by a more senior member of a profession to a more junior member or members of that same profession. This relationship is evaluative, extends over time, and has the simultaneous purposes of enhancing the professional function of the more junior person(s), monitoring the quality of professional services offered to the clients, she, he, or they see, and serving as a gatekeeper for those who are to enter the particular profession' (p.8). The evidence that this definition is widely embraced in the USA at least is indicated by its unchallenged use within a consensus statement (Falender *et al.*, 2004) and in the *Handbook of Psychotherapy Supervision* (Watkins, 1997).

However, numerous prior reviews have noted that these definitions of supervision are problematic (e.g. Lyth, 2000; Hansebo & Kihlgren, 2004). Additionally, surveys of practitioners indicate that they are unclear over the nature and purposes of supervision (e.g. Lister & Crisp, 2005). The popular Bernard and Goodyear (2004) definition appears problematic on several counts. In terms of specificity, it is unclear quite what constitutes the 'intervention'; it fails to recognise that supervision may be provided across professional boundaries; and there is no emphasis on the importance of the supervisory relationship. For these kinds of reasons, I conducted a systematic review in order to develop an empirical definition of clinical supervision (Milne, 2007). In the first part of that review I examined the logical requirements of a sound definition, then I looked hard at a carefully selected sample of successful supervision studies. These steps are now summarised.

Logical basis for a definition

According to philosophy and general scientific convention, a definition needs to state the precise, essential meaning for a word or a concept in a way that makes it distinct (*Concise Oxford English Dictionary* (COED), 2004). I refer to this as the 'precision' criterion. Precision can be enhanced by drawing out comparisons and citing examples, in order to distinguish one concept from another. A clear instance in the case of supervision is attempting to draw out meaningful boundaries between supervision and closely related concepts, such as 'therapy', 'coaching' or 'mentoring'. To illustrate, coaching has been defined as the provision of technical assistance, in order to model, simulate and practise, with corrective feedback, so as to improve the transfer of learning to the workplace (Joyce & Showers, 2002). These features are part of supervision too, so the distinction would appear to be that supervision subsumes coaching, as supervision has additional features and functions. Similarly, there are aspects of therapy and mentoring in supervision, such as the emphasis on the relationship and on reflection, respectively. However, there are important distinctions between these concepts and supervision, in terms of such aspects as the formal authority required to supervise, and the formal evaluative ('summative') function of supervision.

This discussion indicates that we also need 'specification', namely a detailed description of the elements that make up the concept of supervision (COED, 2004). Within research, the term 'hypothesis validity' defines the extent to which a study accurately relates different concepts to the development of hypotheses, and to the way that these are tested and the results interpreted (Wampold *et al.*, 1990). That is, according to theory-driven research, the sequence is first to adopt a theoretical model of a concept like supervision, then to specify which panels (also known as boxes or variables) within the model are the subject of a particular investigation, and what relationships are predicted between these panels. The next task is to suitably operationalise the key relationships in the model, so that appropriate forms of measurement are planned. If one applies these steps to the Bernard and Goodyear (2004) definition, one can see the kinds of difficulty that arise. In particular, it is highly possible that we can have what Wampold *et al.* (1990) called 'inconsequential', 'ambiguous', or 'non-congruent' elements within a definition.

To emphasise this point, consider the summary provided in Table 1.1. This sets out the concept of a supervisory 'intervention' following the specification provided within six illustrative texts on clinical supervision. It can be seen that none of these textbooks actually identified the same variables when they came to specify the supervision intervention. That is, although there was precision (different concepts or elements of supervision were noted, such as the basis of supervision being the relationship), there was a lack of consistent specification of such elements of supervision. Such a fundamental lack of consensus makes the whole foundation on which research and practice might be based insecure and indefinite: Just what is 'clinical supervision'?

Table 1.1 Testing some textbook definitions of 'clinical supervision'

Criteria for an empirical definition of 'supervision'	Textbooks					
	1 Bernard & Goodyear (1992)	2 Fall & Sutton (2004)	3 Falender & Shafranske (2004)	4 Hart (1982)	5 Hawkins & Shohet (1989)	6 Loganbill et al. (1982)
A Operationalised?						
1. Senior person	✓	✓	×	✓	×	✓
2. Relationship based	×	×	✓	×	✓	✓
3. Educational	×	✓	✓	✓	✓	×
4. Longitudinal	✓	×	×	×	×	×
5. Evaluative	✓	✓	✓	✓	×	×
6. Quality control (protects clients, et al.)	✓	✓	✓	×	×	×
7. Gate keeping role	✓	✓	×	×	×	×
8. Objectivity of role	×	✓	×	×	×	×
9. Supportive	×	×	×	×	×	×
10. Experienced person	×	✓	✓	×	×	×

11. Develops competence	✓	✓	✓	✓	✓	✓
12. Science-informed	x	x	✓	✓	x	x
13. Develops confidence	x	x	✓	✓	x	x
B Measured?						
14. Defined in observable terms	x	x	x	x	x	x
15. Instrument/s specified/exist	x	x	x	x	x	x
16. Conducted assessment	x	x	x	x	x	x
C Supported (by evidence)?						
17. Consensus claimed (e.g. 'widely accepted')	x	x	x	x	x	x
18. Cites corroborating literature (e.g. a text or review paper)	x	x	x	x	x	x
19. Notes at least one empirical study as supporting definition	x	x	x	x	x	x

NB: This assessment is based on the part of the text that explicitly presents the authors' definition of clinical supervision. It is acknowledged that some or all of these criteria may be met elsewhere in the text. Also, criteria judged to be subsumed by the above categories have not been detailed. For example, in Falender and Shafranske (2004) various ways of 'educating' and 'developing confidence' are noted (e.g. instruction and modelling), which are subsumed under these broad categories.

In addition, Table 1.1 presents a disappointing picture in relation to whether or not the variables that each of these six books specified within their definition of supervision were actually capable of being measured, or indeed were actually measured. This brings me to my third logical requirement of a sound definition, called 'operationalisation'. For instance, none of these authors noted an instrument that might measure their definition of supervision. This is unfortunate, as an instrument will tend to limit a concept to some critical parameters, enabling supervisors to see more clearly what is meant when an author uses the term supervision. Also, vague definitions do not enable researchers to manipulate or measure a loosely bounded, murky concept. What is needed is a statement of supervision in a form that enables sensitive measurement to occur. Additionally, an operational definition enables one to state valid hypotheses, and it guides us in manipulating the independent variable (supervision) with fidelity. Reliable manipulation of supervision is then possible, a key element in enabling the intervention to be specified in a manual and administered in a consistent, replicable way (Barker *et al.*, 2002). In turn, such careful operationalisation allows us to determine whether supervision is indeed being delivered as it is specified in a manual (termed variously an adherence, audit, or fidelity check). It also allows the subsequent outcomes to be attributed in a precise way to that intervention, assuming a suitable research design. The concept of intervention fidelity is helpful at this point, as it distinguishes usefully between five aspects of a properly specified intervention (Borelli *et al.*, 2005). This concept will be discussed and illustrated with supervision research in Chapter 8.

In sum, not only is the Bernard and Goodyear (2004) definition problematic in a number of respects, but a representative group of textbooks do nothing to improve this sorry state of affairs. By way of verifying my own position, consider the view reached by Ellis *et al.* (1996). They conducted a systematic review of 144 empirical studies of clinical supervision, concluding that hypothesis validity was not properly specified within this body of literature. They also noted that this poor precision and vague or absent specification meant that supervision cannot be manualised or replicated. In turn, this hampers the interpretation of results from research, and the teasing out of practice implications.

The fourth and last of the necessary conditions for an empirical definition of supervision is that it has received clear support from empirical research: that there exists some persuasive information that helps to justify a given definition. Unfortunately, none of the texts in Table 1.1 satisfied any of the three evidential criteria. For example, no mention is given to supportive studies. I refer to this as the 'corroboration' criterion: something that confirms or gives support to a concept (COED, 2004). Logically, a definition could in principle meet the earlier three criteria (i.e. be precise, specified and operationalised), yet lack an evidence-base. Systematic reviews like the one by Ellis *et al.* (1996) address this criterion directly. Indeed, this is surely the most firmly established of the four criteria for an operational definition, as it is customary for textbooks and review papers to give systematic attention to the available evidence-base.

If we apply these four tests to Bernard and Goodyear's (2004) definition, it can be seen that it falls short on every count: the intervention is not defined precisely (e.g. is it primarily restorative, formative or normative?), no measurement instrument is indicated, and no evidence is furnished to support their definition. Similarly, other popular definitions fail one or more of these tests. It is surely time to tackle this impediment to good supervisory research and practice.

An improved definition of clinical supervision

However, the texts noted in Table 1.1, together with definitions provided by professional bodies and by the NHS, do give us a full range of concepts with which to fashion an improved definition of supervision. This builds on the Bernard and Goodyear (2004) definition, largely in order to try to maintain continuity with the general consensus on what constitutes supervision. On this basis, the following is an improved definition (the tests of a definition are noted in bold):

> The formal provision, by approved supervisors, of a relationship-based education and training that is work-focused and which manages, supports, develops and evaluates the work of colleague/s (**precision**). It therefore differs from related activities, such as mentoring and therapy, by incorporating an evaluative component (**precision by differentiation**) and by being obligatory. The main methods that supervisors use are corrective feedback on the supervisees' performance, teaching, and collaborative goal-setting (**specification**). The objectives of supervision are 'normative' (e.g. case management and quality control issues), 'restorative' (e.g. encouraging emotional experiencing and processing) and 'formative' (e.g. maintaining and facilitating the supervisees' competence,

capability and general effectiveness) (**specification by identifying the functions served**). These objectives could be measured by current instruments (e.g. 'Teachers' PETS': Milne *et al.*, 2002; **operationalisation**).

This definition is supported by recent reviews of the empirical literature (e.g. Watkins, 1997; Falender & Shafranske, 2004), and by a consensus statement (Falender *et al.*, 2004; **corroboration**). This empirical definition not only integrates the main current options (i.e. Bernard & Goodyear, 2004; Department of Health, 1993; Proctor, 1992; Watkins, 1997), but also embraces various supervision formats, professions, therapeutic orientations and stages of provision (pre-qualification and CPD). It excludes staff training, consultancy, performance management, mentoring, coaching, and other variations on the supervision theme that do not satisfy the above definition.

Testing this definition: a systematic review

In order to test the working definition produced above from logical and general scientific criteria, a systematic review was conducted. This adopted the 'best evidence synthesis' approach (Petticrew & Roberts, 2006) to examine a body of literature so as to extract helpful seams of good practice. This stands in stark contrast to reviews that attempt to scrutinise all studies within an area, regardless of considerations like their rigour or effectiveness (e.g. Ellis & Ladany, 1997). In the example that follows, the aim was to test whether this working definition was sufficiently precise to capture the definitions that were used explicitly or implicitly in the selected sample of empirical studies, and was specified and operationalised in ways that also corresponded with these studies (i.e. a carefully selected group of 24 research papers in which clinical supervision was studied within interpretable designs, and where it had proved successful: see Milne, 2007 for details). Lastly, I wanted to see whether the findings from these 24 studies corroborated the working definition. It should be borne in mind that one of the criteria used to select these 24 studies was that the supervision had proved successful (as defined by the authors and supported by the findings: outcomes included the learning of the supervisee, the transfer of that learning to therapy, or other aspects of the supervisee's work). This therefore provided a very practical test of the working definition.

I found that explicit definitions were largely absent within these 24 studies: only six papers specified what they meant by clinical supervision (25 per cent of the sample). Five of these papers specified at least two methods and one function of the supervision as manipulated in their studies, but none of the authors differentiated this definition from closely related educational activities (like mentoring). It was therefore concluded that this literature corroborated the working definition as far as it went, but was basically inadequate to provide a proper test.

The next test was to examine how this body of scientific literature specified its supervision intervention. It was found that 23 of the 24 studies specified some of the variables making up their supervision manipulation, and these agreed with those in the working definition. There was, however, an absence of any reference to the normative or restorative functions of supervision, and so the working definition above should be amended accordingly to represent a strict empirical definition, at least for research purposes. However, given the slightly broader aims of this book (see below), these functions will be retained for present purposes.

Sixteen (67 per cent) of the 24 studies measured all or most of the variables specified within their application of supervision. The measures used were consistent with the outline in the working definition. For example, Fleming *et al.* (1996) measured the competence of the four supervisors in their study using a nine-item observational checklist (e.g. assessing 'participative goal-setting' and 'provides feedback').

Lastly, in order to assess corroboration for the working definition, a simple, seven-point, summary rating was made across all 24 studies, in order to gain a general sense of their effectiveness. A value of 2.4 for supervisees (i.e. the amount of learning for the therapist) and 2.3 for patients (clinical outcomes) indicated that these studies were generally very successful, equivalent to an 80 per cent and 77 per cent effectiveness of supervision score, respectively. Overall, these systematic review data indicate that supervision, as per the working definition, is associated with positive outcomes, giving it empirical support. In conclusion, having passed these various tests, the working definition will be accepted as the definition of clinical supervision used within this book.

Aims of This Book

In order to build on this empirical definition and to redress the imbalance between research and policy noted earlier, this book will collate the best available evidence on clinical supervision (referred to simply as 'supervision' from now on) in order to aid our understanding of what it is and how it works, so that research and practice can benefit, and so that policy can be translated into practical intervention. Unlike prior reviews, I add original material (e.g. instruments for measuring key aspects of supervision, and a manual for training supervisors), and, unlike most other textbooks, this book will provide a critical, scholarly and evidence-based review of this vital activity as it stands at the start of the 21st century. As a result, the basic psychological principles and practices will be clarified in a searching yet constructive way, so that we can understand and apply CBT and related forms of supervision more effectively. Although the focus is on 1:1 supervision, other formats will be discussed, such as group and peer-consultation arrangements. Also, the prime emphasis is on the supervision of the clinician's caseload, although I also attend to the traditional concern with the clinician's wellbeing. This foundation for improved supervision practice is fostered by presenting and elaborating some supervision guidelines, part of that manual for training new supervisors (Milne, 2007a). Another neglected aspect of the training of supervisors, and of routine supervision, is the emotional dimension. There is a 'tyranny of niceness' (Fleming *et al.*, 2007) that can suffocate supervision, dampening down in particular the exploration and effective use of emotional experiences in supervision. Therefore, due weight will be given to developing supervision by attending to the relevant thoughts, feelings and behaviours.

Although you may already sense that psychological emphasis coming through, this book is written for all those involved in supervision, not just psychologists, and not just supervisees or those who train supervisors. The emphasis is on isolating the basic, essential ingredients of effective supervision, drawing primarily from the relevant research literatures, so as to provide a useful account of supervision. This information should therefore be relevant to everyone involved in supervision (and not just to supervisors in the mental health field, though that is the assumption). As a result, there are also implications for supervisees, researchers, commissioners, programme reviewers, patients and others with an interest in supervision. Reflecting these stakeholders, and using the evidence-based practice framework, the material in this book will also be influenced by professional consensus, national guidelines and local audits, not to mention my regular involvement in supervision for the past 25 years, most of it within a major training programme. Relevant neighbouring literatures will also be used to strengthen the evidence-base and the theoretical awareness, particularly material from the staff training and psychotherapy fields. This, then, is psychologically informed supervision for the evidence-based practitioner and for the modern healthcare organisation. Supervision will be regarded as a complex intervention and treated with long-overdue rigour, as a core part of the business of delivering high-quality health services.

Plan for the Book

The remaining eight chapters are suitably businesslike, stressing informed action within a coherently structured, logical approach. To summarise, Chapter 2 outlines a basic, evidence-based model of the factors that govern supervision, and Chapter 3 goes on to reconstruct an experiential model. Recognising the importance of the relationship between the supervisor and the supervisee (typically a therapist) is far from novel, but it merits serious attention. Therefore, I review recent work on this interpersonal professional 'alliance' in Chapter 4, where I introduce the first of four guidelines. These early chapters prepare us to address the technical tasks faced by supervisors, and Chapter 5 sets these out as the 'supervision cycle'. Drawing on the staff training literature, supervision is regarded as a closely related series of activities: assessment of the supervisee's learning needs; collaborative goal-setting; applying methods to facilitate learning; and evaluation. Further guidelines on these topics are introduced. Chapter 6 then mirrors this emphasis on the supervisor by giving attention to the part played by the supervisee, a strangely neglected player in most published accounts of supervision. I detail how supervisees can be understood to learn from their experience through supervision, affording a psychological map of the unfolding journey of professional development. Related to this understanding, some instruments with which to capture this process are noted (to be discussed in Chapter 8, alongside a wider summary of the available tools and associated issues). Chapter 7 notes the need to ensure that professionals are properly supported in their emotionally demanding work. This aspect of supervision has been called the 'restorative' or 'supportive' function, complementing the 'formative' focus of Chapters 5 and 6. Here I will deal with the various practical arrangements that need to be addressed by those who appoint, support and guide supervisors, such as regular peer support groups and training workshops. The final chapter (9) draws together the essential principles and implied practices covered above. This summary provides the basis to relate supervision (as discussed in the preceding chapters) to the wider workplace and to the professional context. Similarly, the professional affiliation of the supervisor (and other factors) will be considered, including how supervision needs to change through the professional's career.

In summary, this book offers you an experienced guide's version of supervision as an applied psychological science, in a way that is intended to show how supervisors can integrate theory and practice in this vital professional activity, within the current healthcare context (especially the NHS).

Summary

Supervision is belatedly receiving the attention it deserves, given its pivotal role in professional development and in the maintenance of competent, ethical practice. But there is an awkward gulf between the aspirations that are expressed in the policies of national bodies such as the BABCP and the material that is available to develop supervision. Therefore, this book draws on the evidence-based practice framework to set out a systematic, scholarly and constructive approach, called evidence-based clinical supervision (EBCS). Using techniques such as the 'best evidence synthesis' to review the core literature and the results of professional consensus building, EBCS affords a contemporary approach to competent supervision practice, a stimulus to research, and a promising way to bridge the theory–practice gulf.

An illustration of this scholarly, constructive style was the critical attention given to how we define supervision. It was argued that the most popular definition is seriously flawed, and a more logically coherent and evidence-based revision was provided. This specifies what supervision entails, how it can be measured and what it is known to achieve. A brief glimpse of the available history of supervision, aided by some speculation regarding ancient history, suggested that the apprenticeship model has a considerable pedigree.

2

Understanding Supervision

Introduction

In order to make sense of the complex intervention known as clinical supervision, authors have produced a bewildering range of theoretical models. These models set out the different variables that are required to explain their preferred understanding of supervision. In addition, models suggest how these variables relate to one another. Typically, a general theory may be drawn on to provide a coherent framework for the specifics of a supervision model. For example, the most popular type of supervision model is based on lifespan development theory. It draws on our understanding of how humans grow and mature, so that the developmental model of supervision can then introduce key concepts from the general theory, like 'stages, phases and tasks'. The theory suggests that, in addressing life's tasks successfully, we stimulate progression from one phase of growth to another (see, for example, Kaufman & Schwartz, 2003). When applied in relation to supervision, this general theory encourages us to assume some lawful pattern in how supervisees become competent professionals, and to attend to stages, phases and tasks in their continuing development.

A major alternative to the developmental model of supervision is those that simply extend the concepts and practices of therapy to the business of supervision. This systematic use of an analogy is thought to be one of the main guides that professionals use in their supervision. A strong example is the cognitive-behavioural therapy (CBT) model, which explicitly extends key concepts used in therapy to propose how supervision should be conducted (e.g. utilising processes such as collaboration and guided discovery: Padesky, 1996). I will refer to these as therapy models.

Thirdly, there are models that propose altogether different constructions of supervision, going beyond developmental prototypes and therapy extensions to introduce unique accounts, the so-called supervision-specific models.

Finally, it should be acknowledged that there are approaches to supervision that dispense with the need for theoretical models altogether, adopting instead a pragmatic approach. From surveys, it appears that the most popular model of all is simply drawing on how one was supervised during one's own training (Falender & Shafranske, 2004). Another pragmatic example is outcome-oriented supervision (Worthen & Lambert, 2007), which advocates tracking clinical outcomes as the way to understand and practise supervision. On this logic, good supervision is supervision that produces results. Such data serve as systematic feedback to therapists, to let them know how they are succeeding, together with suggestions about possible interventions (especially for patients who are failing to benefit from therapy). And to conclude, we should acknowledge that some eclectic mixture of these models is a further option, one that after all appears popular in conducting therapy, as in bolting one or more of these pragmatic options together, or blending this with an explicit theoretical model, to augment it in a congruent, personally meaningful way. For example, CBT supervision is developed naturally by incorporating an outcome emphasis, combined with its other guiding principles. However, this chapter will focus on the most professionally appropriate options, namely the developmental, therapy-specific and unique models.

Chapter Plan and Objectives

In order to develop a better understanding of clinical supervision, this chapter will first go back a step, to clarify what is generally meant by a psychological model. This will draw on basic reasoning and philosophical premises (as per Chapter 1), in order to define the criteria by which the above models can be best grasped and assessed.

Having clarified the nature and parameters of a model, I will next summarise the developmental, therapy and specific models. Part of this synthesis will entail mapping the models against a basic training model, so as to clarify where they place their emphasis and what they omit or minimise. In this way I will be trying to establish a basic model of supervision, one that clarifies the essential factors and processes. Given that one of the criteria for a model is the degree to which evidence is available to support or refute it, this essential model will also be evidence-based. The choice of the term 'essential' is deliberately chosen to draw out the idea of a distillation of the best ingredients from these models (the essence), to recognise the growing pressure to be able to justify one's methods in relation to the evidence (having a rationale or justification), and to convey the idea that having such a model to guide one's practice is vital ('nothing as practical as a good theory'). Having constructed an essential model (see Milne, Aylott, Fitzpatrick *et al.*, 2008, for more background), this will then be critiqued against some of these criteria for a good model. It will be suggested that, although there are a wide and helpful range of concepts and relationships within the existing modelling of clinical supervision, some significant deficiencies remain (e.g. the lack of a sufficiently detailed account of how development occurs within supervision to permit the systematic training of supervisors). This critical review therefore collates what is known and suggests some explicit requirements for further model-building, which are then addressed in the next chapter (at which stage the criteria for a good model will be applied more carefully). The present chapter closes with a discussion of some emergent issues.

Theoretical Models

We draw on theoretical models throughout our clinical and professional practice, because models are helpful devices for gaining an improved understanding of phenomena. Models can be mechanical, like the DNA double helix, mathematical (like some representations of memory functioning), or conceptual, where variables and their relationship are depicted in words and diagrams (Warr, 1980). CBT has adopted the latter approach, epitomised by the diagrammatic formulation of the basic cognitive therapy model (see, for example, Liese & Beck, 1997, p.116). A model therefore provides us with the basic elements (variables) that we require to make sense of something, like the schemas, triggers and automatic thoughts in the CBT model. These are then arranged into some kind of order, so that the way that they interact is clear (for example, by the sequencing of these variables within the diagram, and the use of directional arrows in CBT). Some of these variables and processes (represented by the arrows) may be common to several models. In the case of supervision, it appears that all models include variables like a relationship variable (often specified as a learning alliance), some techniques to promote reflection and development in the supervisee, and some evaluative work to clarify whether supervision is progressing in the right direction. However, to complicate matters, the different models will select different terms. For example, a supervision model based firmly on a particular therapy, like CBT, should have an appropriately distinctive (i.e. internally consistent) idea of the nature of variables like the learning alliance, as in stressing the importance of guided discovery in defining the shared goals of supervision. In a good model, such specifications will distinguish approaches like CBT from the way that the psychodynamic model (for instance) treats the alliance. As we saw in Chapter 1, the recent history of supervision has actually been dominated by the psychodynamic model. This approach required the supervisee to undertake a personal analysis, as the individual's personality might otherwise influence the learning alliance in ways that were deemed to be unhelpful. By contrast, the CBT model generally discounts the presence of unconscious influences in the alliance, viewing the relationship in terms of such basic factors as warmth, empathy, trust and rapport (Padesky, 1996). This illustrates how the same broad concept needs to be framed within a given theory. In addition to these theoretically shaped core concepts, the different models of supervision introduce additional variables, in an effort to provide a satisfactory explanation of the operation of supervision. These will be detailed shortly.

Therefore, a model of supervision needs to satisfy a number of criteria, and to pass some long-established tests before it can be granted the status of a model (by comparison, drawing on a framework, or some hunches that derive from clinical experience, is preliminary to a model). The criteria for a model are that it offers a theoretically grounded (i.e. logically plausible) analysis of the elements required to explain how supervision should be practised, how such practices come to operate (i.e. mechanisms or processes of change), and the kinds of outcomes that are prioritised. In addition, a sound model of supervision is a tentative theory, an internally consistent proposition regarding the explicit relationships between variables (i.e. precise assertions, with proper elaboration), one that is expressed in a way that is amenable to scientific analysis (i.e. falsifiable, for example through suggesting new hypotheses, and through being quantifiable). This implies the need for elegance or parsimony in the expression of the essential ingredients. Additional criteria are that models should have a focus (a delimited, bounded area of application); be justified by supportive evidence; aid understanding (e.g. by indicating how change occurs); and have action implications (Popper, 1972; Warr, 1980). Such criteria allow different models to be contrasted and evaluated on logical, scientific and practical grounds, so that we can decide objectively whether some models are 'better' than others (because they satisfy more of these criteria, or 'correspond better to the facts': Popper, 1972, p.232; and thereby enable practitioners to improve their understanding and practice).

These criteria will next be used in relation to the three broad types of model that are popular in supervision. This critical review process will enable us to judge the strengths and weaknesses of the respective models, leading to the view that none are wholly satisfactory. This provides the rationale for a fresh synthesis and extension of these models, the subject of the next chapter.

The Developmental Model of Clinical Supervision

According to this model, supervision is an example of lifespan development, namely 'the description, explanation and optimisation of … individual change … from birth to death' (Sugarman, 1986, p.2). The assumptions that underpin this optimisation process are that the potential for development extends throughout the lifespan; that there is no specific route that development must or should take; that development occurs on a number of different fronts; and that the individual and the environment influence each other – there is a reciprocal relationship between a changing being and a changing context. Sugarman's (1986) account remains contemporary, as these assumptions are reflected in more recent summaries of the developmental perspective. Although using different terms for the same concepts (i.e. plasticity, diversity, relationism and temporality, respectively), Lerner (1998) has underscored Sugarman's (1986) assumptions. According to these assumptions, the essential message for supervisors is to adopt a stance in which the potential for change always exists, recognising that it will occur at multiple levels, within a complex system (relationism). The system will have change as an inevitable and necessary feature, promoting development (temporality or 'historical embeddedness'). As a result of individual differences in the supervisor and the supervisee, a dynamic interaction arises that drives development (Lerner, 1998).

In terms of the moment-to-moment process that enables development to occur, the model takes the view that, fundamentally, development hinges on selective adaptation. This involves three essential activities: the selection of courses of action, based on option-appraisal relative to one's goals; the active use of coping strategies; and the selection of optimal environments, so as to optimise the attainment of these goals and what is referred to as 'compensation', namely responding to the unfolding situation so as to adjust coping and effort in a way that minimises losses and maximises success (Baltes *et al.*, 1998).

Let's now apply these assumptions from the general developmental theory to supervision. A classic example in supervision is the work of Heppner and Roehlke (1984) on the stages of supervisee development. They studied counsellor supervisees over a two-year period, in order to analyse the change process, focusing on how supervisees judged effective supervision over time. Beginners valued support and simple concrete skills-enhancement work. But later in their development they appreciated more attention to understanding the basis for their actions (e.g. conceptualisation skills, such as the formulation of cases). Only after two to three years of training were the supervisees interested in personal issues, developing their individual approaches, and other 'meta' issues. As a result of this kind of analysis, the different stages can be defined according to the developmental model (the following breakdown is from Hess, 1987):

Stage 1 (inception): This features insecurity and considerable dependency on the supervisor, with an onus on defining the role and building relationships, so that competence is demonstrated to an adequate level.

Stage 2 (skill development): At this point there is a shift to an apprenticeship model, and a greater involvement of the supervisee in identifying goals and selecting strategies.

Stage 3 (consolidation): Now supervisees are developing what is termed a 'therapeutic personality' – they are beginning to specialise, and to show some confidence in their practice.

Stage 4 (mutuality): The supervisee can next begin to demonstrate some creativity, working with increasing independence and relating to the supervisor in terms of a 'mutual consultation among equals'. Collegiality succeeds the apprentice status.

Heppner and Roehlke's (1984) analysis was based on the self-reported frequency of developmentally critical instances over training for beginning

($N = 15$), advanced ($N = 14$) and Doctoral intern trainees ($N = 12$), and it illustrated these stages. For example, whereas no personal issues were noted by beginners, the Doctoral interns reported these to be frequent. Conversely, competence issues decreased over time, ceasing to be a significant incident for the Doctoral interns.

Perhaps the best-known contemporary developmental model within clinical supervision is the integrated developmental model (IDM; Stoltenberg & Delworth, 1987; Stoltenberg & McNeill, 1997). Characteristically for this model, different levels of development are delineated, in which 'level 1' (unfortunately no label is offered for these levels) involves supervisees having a primary focus on themselves, particularly their need to develop skills whilst managing their performance anxiety and evaluation apprehension. By 'level 2', skills are developing and anxiety and apprehension are decreasing. As a result, awareness of the other (the client, primarily) can emerge, allowing empathy and understanding to blossom. But some destabilisation (i.e. temporary loss of confidence and competence) is a feature of level 2, as motivation is more variable and some confusion and ambivalence predominate. Equally, there is variability in the supervisees' need for autonomy, including swings from inappropriate independence to excessive dependence. 'Level 3' represents the successful resolution of the issues of level 2 and, by this stage (benchmarked against the third year of initial professional training), motivation stabilises and the supervisee develops appropriately autonomous and individualised role performance with an acceptable degree of insight.

In order to depict these levels with what they regard to be the necessary complexity, their account covers assessment, intervention, ethical practice, and other dimensions of professional activity for each of the above three levels of development. This is because there needs to be a degree of specificity to enable an adequate assessment of the supervisee's developmental level. Thus, for example, a level 1 supervisee will tend to try to apply diagnostic categories and assess clients strictly 'by the book', looking for a fit between general theory and practice. By level 2 the focus will shift towards a more personal account of the client, although there may be a lack of understanding of how diagnostic labels affect the client and others with whom the supervisee needs to communicate. By level 3 the supervisee is thought to develop a much better-grounded grasp of the options for assessment, and to use things like diagnostic categories more flexibly, depending on factors such as the setting and the client (Stoltenberg & McNeill, 1997).

This model will be evaluated later, after the other two popular models have been described.

Therapy-based Models of Clinical Supervision

Accounts of supervision that are based on therapy draw an explicit analogy between the critical assumptions and practices within therapy and supervision. Probably the dominant example of this analogy is the importance accorded to the therapeutic or 'working' relationship. The following are considered to be 'demonstrably effective' relationship variables in therapy by the American Psychological Association Task Force (APA; Norcross, 2001):

- therapeutic alliance;
- cohesion (in group therapy);
- empathy;
- goal consensus and collaboration;
- dealing with resistance;
- addressing functional impairments.

In addition to these demonstrably effective relationship variables, the APA task force listed a further seven variables that were promising and 'probably effective' relationship variables:

- positive regard;
- congruence/genuineness;
- feedback;
- repair of alliance ruptures;
- self-disclosure;
- management of counter-transference;
- quality of relational interpretations.

By contrast, it was thought that there was insufficient research to judge whether customising therapy for the following characteristics of the patient would improve outcome: attachment style; gender; ethnicity; religion and spirituality; preferences; and personality disorders.

Linking several of these variables together within an explanatory, evidence-based model, Norcross (2002) defined the therapeutic relationship in terms of 'the feelings and attitudes that therapists and clients have toward one another, and the manner in which these are expressed' (p.7). He proposed that the relationship was 'like a diamond, composed of multiple, interconnected facets' (p.8).

Some therapy-based models of clinical supervision apply such thinking and research directly, as in CBT supervision. For example, Liese and Beck (1997) note that the 'therapeutic relationship is *highly* important in cognitive therapy' (p.119, italics in original), featuring a collaborative stance. According to them, the relationship can become a central focus in therapy if necessary, and therapists will naturally pay attention to the interpersonal processes that occur (even including transference and counter-transference: Safran & Segal, 1990). This kind of link between the therapy and its supervision is made strongly by Padesky (1996), who stated that 'cognitive therapy supervision parallels the therapy itself' (p.281), and that 'the same processes and methods that characterise the therapy can be used to teach and supervise therapists' (p.289). As noted by Padesky (1996), Beck's initial manual for CBT (Beck *et al.*, 1979) had a chapter on the necessity of a positive therapeutic relationship, founded on warmth, empathy and genuineness. There was also an acknowledgement of difficulties in the relationship, and a discussion of transference and counter-transference issues. Therefore, according to Padesky (1996), competent cognitive therapists were always expected to be able to develop and sustain effective therapeutic relationships.

The working relationship (usually referred to as the 'learning alliance' in supervision) is only one example of a direct parallel being made between therapy and supervision. Perhaps the clearest and most thorough explication of the link between CBT and its supervision is a table provided by Liese and Beck (1997) in the *Handbook of Psychotherapy Supervision* (Watkins, 1997). This table (8.1 on p.121) helpfully provides a direct comparison of nine steps that characterise CBT, showing the equivalent step within supervision. To illustrate, the first step in CBT is agenda-setting, followed by a mood check and bridging with previous therapy sessions. The parallel steps in supervision are check-in, agenda-setting and bridge from previous supervision session. Equally strong parallel steps continue through to the final one which is, in both instances, eliciting feedback (throughout the session, and at the end). Interest in the supervisory relationship has continued within the CBT tradition (e.g. the rupture and repair cycle: Safran & Muran, 2000).

Other therapies also stress the importance of the relationship or alliance in supervision. This is most pronounced within the psychoanalytic tradition, where the supervisor is first trained as a psychoanalyst, based on the completion of a didactic programme, the analysis of several patients under the supervision of a senior analyst, and then through the candidate's personal therapy (Dewald, 1997). These traditional three elements in the development of a psychoanalytic supervisor are expected to be synthesised and applied within therapy. But, by contrast with CBT, it would appear that there are fewer parallels between therapy and supervision, as Dewald (1997) notes that 'most psychoanalytic supervisors consider supervision to be a process in some ways similar and in other ways quite different from therapeutic psychoanalysis' (p.33). Similarities include the need for an alliance and a place of comfort and safety, to promote open and honest interaction. Also, the needs of the patient/supervisee are important and take priority within the alliance. Other analogies within psychoanalysis include the recognition of the need for empathic recognition and acceptance (of some of the issues and conflicts experienced by the supervisee/patient) and transference/counter-transference phenomena (these may be drawn to the attention of a supervisee, though these would conventionally be addressed within the private analysis). In short, such is the overlap between therapy and supervision that it has traditionally been assumed that 'if one were a skilled analyst one would be able to do skilled supervision' (p.41). However, it is now being recognised that, whilst some analysts may be effective, others will have difficulty communicating concepts in an effective way as a teacher, necessitating some training.

Therefore, both CBT-based and psychoanalysis-based supervision treat the relationship as necessary for effective supervision, and both import concepts and practices directly from therapy for use in supervision. But, reflecting the need for internal consistency, in psychoanalysis the relationship that develops is a relatively intense, long-term and significant component (Dewald, 1997, p.43).

Another major therapy model is based on systems reasoning. Within the systemic model there is also a close correspondence between the therapy and supervision, referred to as an 'isomorphic translation' (Rigazio-DiGilio *et al.*, 1997, p.224). Supervisees are seen as developing a complex, recursive pattern which requires a highly personalised approach. Within this developmental path, supervision is seen as a 'co-constructive process', meaning that a dialectic relationship between the supervisor and supervisee needs to emerge. In Holloway's (1997) systems approach the relationship 'is the container of dynamic process in which the supervisor and the supervisee negotiate a personal way of utilising the structure of power and involvement that accommodates the trainee's progression of learning. This structure becomes the basis for the process by which the trainee will acquire knowledge and skills – the empowerment of the trainee' (p.251).

Although there is a difference of emphasis amongst these rather different therapies, the integrative model of supervision (which appears at the end of this section of the *Handbook of Psychotherapy Supervision*: Watkins, 1997) regards nurturing the supervisory relationship as one of the 'cardinal principles' of integrative supervision (Norcross & Halgin, 1997, p.208). They note that the therapeutic relationship has long been regarded as a primary curative factor in therapy, so conclude that 'it does not involve a great leap of understanding to perceive the supervisory relationship as being comparably important in fostering growth in clinical trainees' (p.212). Not surprisingly, this integrative model also draws parallels between therapy and supervision. Like good therapists, 'good supervisors are those who use appropriate teaching, goal-setting and feedback; they tend to be seen as supportive, non-critical individuals who respect their supervisees' (p.212). According to the integrative model, some of the same methods that are used to promote the therapeutic relationship are appropriate in supervision, with caveats. In this sense, the supervisor should aim to be supportive and use interpersonal techniques, so that the supervisee feels supported, understood and well educated. The aim is ultimately to reduce the inherent power imbalance, working towards an empathic and collaborative relationship in which insecurities, disagreements and alternatives can be discussed.

Other Commonalities Between Therapies and Supervision

Whilst the relationship or alliance features prominently in all accounts of supervision, we have already seen that there can be a considerable extension of the other therapeutic methods to supervision. Indeed, an interesting corollary becomes the question of the boundaries between therapy and supervision. In order to capture both the commonalities and these limits, Table 2.1 summarises how the main therapeutic orientations explicitly transfer methods to supervision, but also where they place the limits, or make modifications to these extensions.

As Table 2.1 indicates, whilst both supervision and therapy would emphasise agenda-setting in the case of CBT (patient and the supervisee

Table 2.1 Examples of the overlaps and distinctions between therapy and supervision

Therapy (source reference)	Identical (therapy and supervision are isomorphic/ indistinguishable)	Modified for supervision (exclusions/extensions)
CBT (Liese & Beck, 1997)	• Agenda-setting (patient and supervisee contribute items) • Feedback (elicited throughout and at end)	• Focus (on patient, i.e. excluding the supervisee as the 'patient' as an agenda item) • Includes formal (standard documentation) and summative evaluation (pass/ fail judgement)
Psychoanalysis (Dewald, 1997)	• Goal of accessing internal experiences and functioning (e.g. counter-transference) • Building a working alliance (to provide comfort and safety, so promoting open and honest interaction)	• Boundary – but only access experiences specific to impaired learning in supervision. Personal issues of supervisee to be addressed within the separate personal analysis
Systemic (Rigazio-DiGilio *et al.*, 1997)	• Assumed that change/ development is an individual but co-constructed journey, complex, holistic and recursive in nature	• This assumption is a topic for explicit, educational discussion in supervision (e.g. impact of culture and ability on use of model)
Integrative/ Eclectic (Norcross & Halgin, 1997)	• An eclectic blend of methods should be used pragmatically (i.e. in response to the patients/supervisees needs at the time) • Evaluation of outcomes	• Methods like 'case discussion conferences' are presumably excluded from therapy; as are the roles of 'lecturer, teacher & collegial peer'. Also, the adequacy of supervision is 'typically assumed, rather than verified' (p.214)

are active collaborators, contributing agenda items), this would be limited to what the therapist/supervisor deemed to be an appropriate focus. In this sense, the supervisee would not normally be permitted to include their personal functioning or personal growth as an agenda topic. Similarly, whilst feedback is integral to both, only the supervisee would expect to have their performance recorded on standard documentation forms that emanate from a local training programme, and to have that performance judged in terms of whether or not it was up to a required standard. Other examples include the goals and the importance of the alliance. All of these examples are taken for convenience and ready comparability from the *Handbook of Psychotherapy Supervision* (Watkins, 1997). However, a defining characteristic of the supervision models summarised in Table 2.1 (and of others that draw on therapy for their inspiration) is that these methods transfer to supervision, and to a large extent. That is, far more unites the two areas of practice than divides them, and locating examples bounding or limiting the extension of therapeutic methods to supervision is relatively difficult. Personally, I agree with this explicit use of reasoning by analogy, because it is a useful skill when addressing new problems (itself a common topic in supervision), and it is also a highly professional way to think about how activities that may seem distinct are actually better understood as different points on related continua (see Milne, 2007b for a detailed justification for utilising analogies).

Supervision-specific Models

Social role models

A social role model specifies the roles that a supervisor performs, together with the associated functions (Beinart, 2004). They are basically pragmatic, placing little explicit emphasis on a governing theory. For example, according to a popular model, the supervisor partly plays the manager role, serving a 'normative' set of functions (e.g. ensuring that paperwork is completed and that the organisation's procedures are followed). This is complemented by the therapist role, in which the supervisor performs a 'restorative' function (providing support and care to the therapist), and the teacher role (carrying out the 'formative' function, in which the supervisee is educated and trained: Kadushin, 1976; Proctor, 1988). A fourth role that has been defined is that of consultant, someone who allows supervisees to share responsibility for their development, to become a resource, whilst encouraging supervisees to take responsibility and to trust their own ability to resolve work issues (Bernard, 1997). In playing the consultant role, the supervisor will encourage discussion of different options (e.g. different therapeutic possibilities) and encourage reflection on the pros and cons of different options. Another consultant activity would be to encourage the conceptualisation of work problems, and to work on the emotional aspects of such work.

Another major role that has been delineated is that of evaluator or monitor (Bernard & Goodyear, 2004). Holloway (1997) also emphasises the task of working on the professional role, including emotional awareness and self-evaluation. As do several authors, she generates a matrix to show how these different tasks relate to roles, trainee factors, client factors and organisational or contextual factors. Holloway (1997) refers to her model as a dynamic one, in which her Systems Approach to Supervision (SAS) provides a frame of reference that allows supervisors to perform their roles systematically. The model is also meant to be pan-theoretical and practical, highlighting the work that needs to be done, pivoting around the quality of the supervisory relationship, with the familiar objective of enabling the supervisee to become competent. These broad roles can be subdivided and expressed in terms of the behaviours that make up the larger roles. For example, the teacher role can be based on instruction, advice, modelling, and so forth (see Holloway, 1995, for an explication).

Whilst the dominant role categorisation of teacher, therapist and manager appears to survive empirical scrutiny, for example withstanding factor analytic testing (Winstanley, 2000), the role of consultant and these other subsidiary roles (consultant, evaluator, monitor) do not appear to be as well defined (see Bernard & Goodyear, 2004, for a critical review).

Supervision task models

The social roles (and the different styles or orientations that supervisors use to perform them) necessarily link to the related tasks of supervision. This is because one's orientation dictates that certain activities have priority, as in a CBT supervisor adopting the formative role and a task-orientated style in order to develop an agenda collaboratively. Because of these important links to a different theoretical framework, these supervision-specific models are not subsumed under the developmental model, although the notion of 'tasks' is also commonly used within that approach.

Examples of these task-orientated models include Bernard's discrimination model (1997), in which the three topics of 'interventions, conceptualisation and personalisation' are emphasised. The focus of intervention concerns discussion of all aspects of therapy, such as attempts to greet, empathise, confront or interpret within therapy. Conceptualisation refers to the efforts that the supervisee makes in therapy (or their other work) to make theoretical sense of phenomena and to generate predictions or hypotheses. In supervision this becomes a joint activity and is referred to as the conceptualisation task. Finally, the supervisee's functioning as an individual makes up the personalisation focus (including their personality, culture and other individual differences). This latter category would also subsume professional behaviour or personal professional development, namely aspects of ethical functioning and the interface between the individual and their professional persona (Gillmer & Marckus, 2003).

For Hawkins and Shohet (2000) there are seven distinguishable topics or 'modes' within supervision. These are the content of therapy, the strategies and interventions used within therapy, the therapeutic relationship, the therapist's process (i.e. phenomena such as counter-transference and parallel processes), the supervisor's own processes (including reactions to the supervisee), the supervisor–client relationship (e.g. attending to fantasies the supervisor and client may have about one another), and the wider context (i.e. attention to the professional community and other aspects of the environment which relate to the supervisee, like the service organisation in which they both operate). This longer list of tasks can be seen to overlap closely with, and essentially extend, those within Bernard's discrimination model (1997), subdividing some activities like therapy, and providing a much clearer account of the context within which this would be addressed. According to Hawkins and Shohet (2000), good supervision involves the use of all seven modes over time (i.e. not necessarily occurring in every single supervision session). They suggest that the use of the different modes should be related to considerations such as the developmental stage or readiness of the supervisee for the different modes. But, as a general rule, they suggest starting with mode 1 (focusing on therapy with the client and the details of each session's work). With growing sophistication in the supervisee, they believe that the other modes become more prevalent and appropriate (echoing the developmental model material presented earlier). Other considerations are the nature of the work being undertaken, the quality of the alliance between supervisor and supervisee (especially openness and trust), and the respective styles of the parties (e.g. learning style and cultural background). Although they do not furnish any empirical data, they are strongly of the view that all seven modes are necessary for successful supervision: 'we have become increasingly convinced that to carry out effective supervision … it is necessary for the supervisor to be able to use all seven modes of supervision' (p.87).

These task models can, in turn, merge with process and functional models. For example, consider the work of Shanfield *et al.* (1989). They trained raters to use the Psychotherapy Supervision Inventory to reliably distinguish the different styles of 34 supervisors who worked with supervisees whose style was held constant. Supervisors judged to be excellent used a lot of empathy to enable supervisees to detail their therapy work, attended to the emotional accompaniments that the supervisees experienced, and focused their remarks on the clinical material that was provided, in order to help the supervisee to understand the patient (Shanfield *et al.*, 1993).

Functional models

One way of clarifying these diverse models and their numerous dimensions is to distil them down to their core functions. Clarity about one's functions as a supervisor can greatly enable decisions about the most appropriate topics, styles, and so on (a truth from biology: 'form follows function'). As touched on a moment ago, Holloway's SAS model (1997) identifies five supervisory functions, those of monitoring/evaluating, advising/instructing, modelling, consulting, and supporting/sharing. She offers a matrix to show how these functions would be related to different tasks and the other dimensions of her model. For example, the supervisee's experience and the client's problems combine in a dynamic process, in which the seven different dimensions of her SAS model 'mutually influence one another and are highly inter-related' (p.250). The SAS delineation incorporates the traditional Kadushin (1976) breakdown, in terms of the normative, formative and restorative functions, adding detail on how development can be supported (i.e. the modelling and consulting functions). Combined with the above tasks, a supervisor's efforts to fulfil these five primary functions represent supervision 'process' to Holloway (1997).

Despite the multitude of tasks, roles and functions, they can be brought into a relatively clear focus by working back from the primary purposes of supervision, including the provision of safe and ethical therapy, and the development of competence and capability in the supervisee. Other functions, labelled 'outcomes' and 'tasks' in Figure 2.1, are set out to illustrate how the different levels of supervisory function can be thought to contribute to these primary purposes. This analysis of the functions of supervision

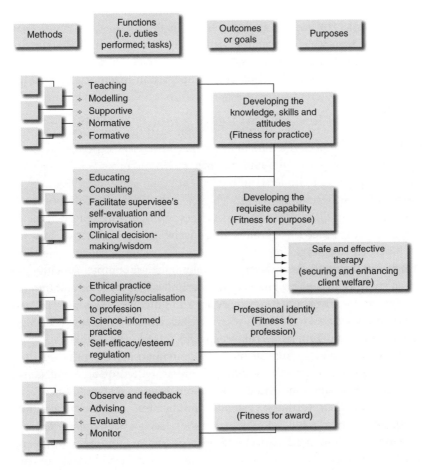

| Methods | Functions (I.e. duties performed; tasks) | Outcomes or goals | Purposes |

Figure 2.1 A thematic summary of the related functions of supervision

is based on collating illustrative material in the supervision literature (Bernard & Goodyear, 2004; Binder & Strupp, 1997; Falender & Shafranske, 2004; Ladany *et al.*, 2005; Holloway, 1997; Lambert & Ogles, 1997). This wealth of material was then organised around the four kinds of broad educational outcomes (i.e. the second-order themes) that are identified by the Quality Assurance Agency (QAA; 2005). This has everyday parallels in how individual and collective behaviour is organised as a hierarchy. For example, a university has the purpose of generating knowledge that is relevant to society, which is pursued primarily through the functions of teaching and research, with specific outcomes (such as training health practitioners to be fit for practice). A popular analogy can be made with the *Canterbury Tales*, in which Chaucer's characters can be thought of as quite distinctive, yet to share a common destination.

Critical Review and Requirements for Progress

Developmental models

In their favour, developmental models such as the IDS are intuitively appealing, as we naturally tend to view supervisees as progressing along a developmental path. Indeed, it is hard to conceive of an alternative way for competence to emerge ('osmosis' and 'magic' have been cynical suggestions offered in the past!). Also, developmental models are compatible with (and even incorporated within) most other accounts of supervision, and they are helpful in thinking about how supervisor and supervisee can jointly address the issues associated with supervision (e.g. balancing support with challenge; addressing evaluation issues constructively).

However, although authors such as Stoltenberg have conducted their own affirmative reviews of the available literature (Stoltenberg, McNeill & Crethar, 1994), other more neutral reviewers have been less convinced. For instance, in their textbook, Falender and Shafranske (2004) note that empirical support for developmental models has not been obtained, as the literature is a 'methodological morass' (p.15). And the exhaustive and meticulous systematic review by Ellis and Ladany (1997) similarly concluded that the rigour of the relevant research was 'sub-standard' (p.493). They concluded that the central premises of the developmental model remained untested. These impartial reviews question the empirical support for the developmental model. Furthermore, there are theoretical concerns that the model is fundamentally simplistic and vague (Russell *et al.*, 1984). In model criteria terms, there is a lack of 'elaboration'. Another long-standing criticism, dating from Worthington's (1987) early review of 16 developmental models, is that little explication is offered as to how transitions are made between the different stages of development (i.e. weak 'causal precision'). Other weaknesses of this approach include the reliance on self-report and experience (time served) as the way in which development is operationalised (Bernard & Goodyear, 2004: i.e. poor 'assumptions').

These concerns make one question the strong conclusion from the Stoltenberg *et al.* (1994) review, namely that 'evidence appears solid for developmental changes across training levels' (p.419). In summary, whilst the developmental model makes intuitive sense and provides a useful basis for organising supervision (i.e. good 'heuristic value'), even advocates of the developmental approach conclude that a more precise theory is required if we are to clarify how specific thoughts, feelings and behaviours, occurring at the different developmental stages, predict patterns of development (Watkins, 1997). It is Watkins' view that we require a much clearer focus on the actual behaviours of both supervisors and supervisees, over specified developmental passages and incorporating superior methodologies, if we are to realise the promise of developmental models.

Therapy models

Turning to the therapy-based models, it is evident that much overlap can be defined between a therapy and its supervision. This is indicated by Table 2.1, and by the emphatic quotes cited above (from the proponents of particular therapies). Adopting one's preferred therapy model as one's model of clinical supervision has considerable advantages. One automatically imports a coherent, acceptable and well-understood model to the complex business of supervision (as shown earlier by the explicit 'compatibility' of the CBT models of therapy and supervision). Also, one similarly imports well-honed skills, in relation to the different methods that are shared by supervision and the specific therapy (i.e. the 'action implications'). However, a challenge for every therapy-based model is to be clear about the boundaries of this extension to supervision (i.e. 'focus' issues). This is touched on in Table 2.1, and indicates the nature of the challenge, but in routine supervisory practice such grey areas will become an important and, at times, a vexatious issue.

If we adopt the traditional distinction between the normative, formative and restorative functions of supervision (Kadushin, 1976; Proctor, 1988), then we can illustrate some of these difficulties. In normative terms we should acknowledge that there are important power differences between therapy and supervision: whilst the client can opt out of therapy, the supervisee is normally obliged to remain in supervision (Bernard & Goodyear, 2004; Newman, 1998). This involuntary or mandatory aspect is typically most evident in pre-qualification supervision, and although more experienced practitioners may exercise more choice over their supervisor and the content/ methods of supervision, the different professional bodies and the supervisee's employers tend to require career-long supervision. This power difference can have a significant differential impact within supervision, negating therapy-based approaches. For example, there are no precedents in therapy for the situation where a supervisor might insist that a supervisee discontinues something that is judged to be inappropriate, or for the possible sequel, a disciplinary or course continuation (progress) episode. It follows that within this rather differently charged environment there arise various thoughts, feelings and behaviours that would be unusual in therapy. This includes negative aspects, like professional rivalry and deception ('faking good' in relation to evaluation), and positive ones like informal collegiality (which tends to characterise established supervisory relationships, but which would be inappropriate in therapy).

In terms of the formative function of supervision, these examples touch on the important distinction around the presence of evaluation: whilst both supervisors and therapists are supposed to routinely evaluate their work, in the case of supervision the instruments and procedural details (e.g. the frequency of assessments, and who is privy to the information) are dictated by the local training programme (pre-qualification), or by the profession (post-qualification: CPD), and to an extent that usually exceeds national (e.g. managed care) or employer requirements. Also, in supervision the competence of the professional providing the service is an explicit focus, which is rarely a criterion (outside of some research trials) in therapy. Given the summative function of evaluation, this can lead to supervisors being 'blacklisted' by training programmes to an extent that seems far more common than their being 'struck off' by their profession or 'fired' by their employer, for reasons of incompetence.

Finally, from the restorative perspective, therapy techniques are inappropriate in supervision when they represent treatment for the supervisee's personal functioning or growth, because these should not be part of the contract between supervisor and supervisee, and are not part of the expectations that authorising organisations have of supervision. Rather, supervision is primarily an educational enterprise, focusing on the therapy that is provided, rather than the therapist who provides it. This is not to say that there are not therapeutic elements and features within appropriately focused supervision (e.g. the non-specific factors, such as warmth and concreteness), but rather that the boundaries between these activities need to be monitored and maintained. To quote Watkins (1997), 'supervision may have its therapeutic elements, but it is primarily education' (p.606). This is a boundary that is also acknowledged within the psychodynamic tradition, through its use of a separate arrangement for personal issues (i.e. the training analysis), and through the clarification of the goals of supervision: '... the typical supervisor applies psychodynamic clinical theories and methods usually associated with therapy to achieve the educational goals of supervision' (Binder & Strupp, 1997, p.45).

Overall, however, there is much to commend the reasoned, cautious transfer of therapy to supervision, and it is perhaps because of the extensive and highly plausible parallels between the two professional activities that using therapeutic thinking is one of the two most popular models of supervision (competing with that of supervising as one was supervised).

Specific models

Task models have been criticised on the grounds that they omit key activities. For example, in her review of the different models, Beinart (2004) points out that the discrimination model (Bernard & Goodyear, 1992) fails to take account of evaluation as part of the supervisor's role, and also gives little attention to relationship qualities.

In general terms, these models are probably better described as frameworks or practical schemes for organising supervision. This is because they tend to lack any theoretical basis, deriving instead from experience and expert consensus on what is important (e.g. topics for the agenda; awareness of roles, contexts and systems). Whilst this will make them serviceable (i.e. high on the 'action implications' criterion), and perhaps particularly appealing to the novice supervisor (given their concreteness, and their 'compatibility' with their existing understanding), there appear to be no carefully developed guidelines or manuals that set out such things as how supervisors should behave, or how they should be trained. This omission (poor intervention 'elaboration') is tackled in Chapter 5 (supervision methods). Without a clear, written statement about what a model is meant to include, research on its effectiveness is severely hampered. For example, there is the real risk that outcome evaluations are fatally flawed by the lack of specificity as to what the particular 'supervision' process should look like (i.e. weak intervention 'fidelity': Borelli *et al.*, 2005). This may seem obvious, but it is surprising how few outcome evaluations even describe their intervention in outline terms, far less provide data on what actually happened within the study (i.e. 'quantification' is absent). Such process-outcome evaluations are necessary if a specific model is to move forward. Chapter 8 picks up this issue, describing ways to pursue these and related types of evaluation.

Another kind of problem with specific models is that the absence of a guiding theory makes such pragmatic approaches of limited value (e.g. in not having some core principles or understanding that can be deployed in complex, novel or difficult situations). By contrast, a supervisor who is working from a therapy model will have the option of considering an issue from that guiding theory. For example, CBT suggests how one might address difficulties in forming and maintaining an effective working alliance, because this is also a common issue in therapy (see Chapter 4 for details).

Their limited, rather concrete level of generality is a further concern, as it fails to suggest exactly how the functions of supervision are achieved (i.e. low 'causal explanation'), the ways in which they might be researched are unclear (i.e. 'assumptions' about the most appropriate research methods do not follow from the framework), and, in particular, it is not obvious which predictions follow (i.e. they have limited 'potential').

I want to close this critical review by mapping these three broad types of supervision model onto one that is derived from the staff development literature. This represents a critical evaluation of all three models. If they are sound, they should surely address the majority of themes within the comparably well-developed field of staff training.

An Essential, Staff Development Model of Supervision (Being a Critical Reflection on All Three Broad Models)

A helpful framework against which now to map the three supervisory models is the model of staff training and development (e.g. Colquitt *et al.*, 2000; Goldstein, 1993). This allows us to draw on a highly relevant neighbouring literature in order to specify the essential variables that logically should be in a general supervision model, at least as far as the formative/educational function of supervision is concerned. Figure 2.2 depicts this model, showing a classic conceptual model made up of boxes or panels (i.e. the variables) and arrows linking these variables (i.e. the causal mechanisms or generative processes by which the variables influence each other, to promote development).

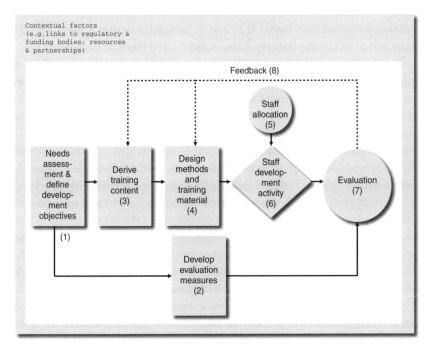

Figure 2.2 The essential model of staff development

According to this general model, supervision can be understood as requiring: a process of needs assessment, so that learning objectives can be specified (panel 1 in Figure 2.2); the development of instruments to measure and evaluate the extent to which these objectives have been achieved; the designing of a syllabus or programme of activity, and a related design effort to specify the supervisory methods and supporting materials that are indicated. Once this work has been done, the supervisory activity can commence with suitably allocated supervisees (panels 6 and 5 in Figure 2.2, respectively). As indicated in a partial way within Figure 2.2, each of these panels or variables should be linked to one another by feedback loops. This provides the essential means by which the supervision system can adapt to its changing context, and monitor the supervisee's development. Lastly, as indicated by the heading 'contextual factors', the eight defined elements that make up this general supervision model need to be considered within such contextual considerations as the workplace environment, and the resources that exist to support supervision (e.g. private rooms; recording and playback equipment). Each of these variables, by definition, can take on a range of values and are multidimensional. For example, 'staff allocation' (panel 5 in Figure 2.2) can in turn be described through such dimensions as the supervisee's personality (including their conscientiousness or anxiety), their age, their confidence and cognitive ability, and their motivation to learn (Colquitt *et al.*, 2000). In their review, Colquitt *et al.* (2000) reported that each of these dimensions has been found to be associated with learning outcomes and the transfer of that learning to the workplace. Similarly, the context that surrounds the variables in Figure 2.2 includes the dimensions of organisational climate, the support provided by managers, and peer support (Colquitt *et al.*, 2000). In ideal practice, this model would operate in the following way: the recruitment of staff would focus on applicants with the requisite personality, ability and motivation; they would work within a supportive organisation; the organisation would work collaboratively with that individual to design and deliver an appropriate development pathway; given peer support, appropriate supervision and other development input, the model assumes that a range of learning outcomes can be achieved, to be evaluated in terms of such dimensions as the supervisee's reactions to supervision and their acquisition of relevant skills. The extent to which these become part of that individual's job performance represents the degree to which supervision has resulted in successful transfer to the workplace (technically referred to as generalisation, across time and settings).

How do the three models we've just considered map onto this essential one? In general terms, pretty much everything that is specified within the essential model is present to some extent within the three models discussed earlier. However, the degree to which the nine different variables are emphasised (treating 'context' as the ninth factor) understandably varies. For instance, the systemic approach (as per the SAS model) perhaps gives most emphasis to this supervision context, whereas the developmental one would lay greater stress on the individual characteristics of the supervisee. Therefore, in a general sense, it seems that these three models duly reflect the staff development one (which, it is only fair to note, is itself open to the criticism that it places relatively little emphasis on the restorative or normative functions of supervision).

In summary, I believe that the essential model of supervision set out in Figure 2.2 can be thought of as compatible with the three broad supervision models that we've considered, capturing at least the core variables and processes that are necessary to understand supervision. However, more elaborate models are needed, such as the one developed by Colquitt *et al.*

(2000) to account better for staff development. In this sense, I will treat the essential model as the basis for reformulating supervision, the task of the next chapter.

Discussion

It has been said that supervision 'can be as complex and challenging as … therapy itself' (Liese & Beck, 1997, p.114) and this brief overview of the different models within clinical supervision surely emphasises that view. Indeed, logically one might argue that it is even more complex than therapy itself, because it subsumes it (in terms of treating the therapy, necessarily overlaying therapist issues such as personal professional development). One could reasonably argue that, amongst the challenges faced by mental health professionals, supervision is second only to organisational change in complexity.

I have tried to ensure that this complexity has been duly reflected in this chapter, as even my relatively superficial analysis of the different supervision models indicates the wide variety of theories and concepts that drive equally diverse notions of the roles, tasks and methods of supervision. If one simply thinks about the therapy-based supervision models then there are surely hundreds of variations on the supervision theme, given that there are hundreds of different therapies. Add to this the individual differences, theoretical orientations and styles, not to mention the preferences, fads and hang-ups that individual supervisors have, and then multiply that by the emphasis within different training programmes, and one can begin to envisage the complexity of the supervision business!

But perhaps this complexity (which violates some of the criteria for a good model, such as parsimony and falsifiability) can be whittled down to a more concise, elegant model of supervision? After all, the history of science is replete with instances where hugely complex phenomena are ultimately reduced to their essence through research (e.g. the incredible diversity of Earth's organisms ultimately being comprehensible by reference to natural selection, or explicating the innumerable individual differences between us humans through a few chemicals composing DNA, elements so rudimentary that they were initially overlooked). The essential model is an example of how this might eventually be achieved in relation to supervision, although of course we have a long way to go yet, awaiting much more and much better research, and the timely arrival of our own Darwin, Watson or Crick.

In addition to recognising the daunting complexity of supervision, there are other reasons to feel uncomfortable about the current status of supervision. For instance, applying the criterion of empirical support, these popular models do not appear particularly promising. For instance, Ellis and Ladany's (1997) systematic review found that one of the most widely cited approaches, the integrated developmental model (IDM; Stoltenberg & Delworth, 1987), 'has not been adequately tested and no tentative inferences seem justifiable given the poor rigour of the two studies' (p.480). Ellis and Ladany (1997) opined that their review of the developmental model led to 'disheartening' (p.482) conclusions (e.g. because significant difficulties had not been resolved in relation to hypothesis validity, and there has been a heavy reliance on cross-sectional research to test the longitudinal inferences that are integral to a developmental model). A second issue that they raised, and which applies to all three models, is that of fidelity: it is rare for researchers to demonstrate objectively that supervisors are adhering to the given model, as opposed to studies which provide outcome data purportedly showing that their model was successful. A number of studies of the fidelity of therapists and supervisors bear out this caution, and I have certainly found this to be an issue in my own collaborative research (e.g. Milne & James, 2002). Such over-simplification is unlikely to give supervision the complex modelling needed for its full comprehension or successful implementation. What we require are carefully specified models of the kind that allow measurement of precisely how different supervisory activities or relationship qualities relate to specific changes in the supervisee (Gonsalvez *et al.*, 2002). There is a need to focus on the actual behaviours of supervisors and supervisees, in their context (Watkins, 1997).

These and other criticisms lead us smoothly into the next chapter, which puts forward a partial solution to several of these issues. In order to provide a general working model and a fresh point of reference, I will again draw on the staff training literature for more building-blocks, to add to the essential model of supervision. This tactic (another example of reasoning by analogy) is used explicitly because it allows us to draw on a closely related but surprisingly distinct literature. Like Darwin in the geographically distinct Galápagos Islands, such points of comparison can prove illuminating. In particular, I will try to show how this essential model can be developed by drawing on the best of the above supervision models, becoming an integrative and (through further careful scrutiny of the research literature) evidence-based model. I believe that this is the kind of model that is required to take supervision further down its own developmental path.

3

Reframing Supervision

Introduction

As noted in the last chapter, the many models of clinical supervision are impressively strong on imagination, but worryingly weak when subjected to careful evaluation. Of particular relevance to this present chapter is a fundamental weakness, shared by many of the models discussed in the preceding chapter, which is the general lack of conceptual rigour. Although there is a strong tendency to judge research and theory on the basis of the outcomes (e.g. statistically significant findings that support a theory), research needs to start with careful reasoning, as in utilising clear concepts, acknowledged assumptions and proper arguments (Machado & Silva, 2007). In general, the models that were summarised in Chapter 2 do not withstand such basic logical tests. For instance, there is a lack of internal consistency, and insufficient elaboration to make a model useful and testable (Warr, 1980). As a result, the models lack the degree of precision needed for supervisors to know what to do in specific situations, and it also means that research work is hampered. Specifically, this imprecision compromises the hypothesis validity of research (Wampold & Holloway, 1997), in the sense of making it difficult to set out hypotheses that are based on the model, and which are appropriately explicit and relevant. According to a review of 144 studies of clinical supervision conducted up to 1993, it was judged that at least 80 per cent of these studies had poor conceptualisation (i.e. inconsequential or ambiguous hypotheses: Ellis *et al.*, 1996). To overcome these difficulties, Ellis and colleagues (1996) suggested that future research would be better served by an explicit model that defines the constructs that are involved, so that appropriately clear hypotheses can be explicated and tested.

Of course, this kind of priority and detail is also a great help to those who practise supervision, as it specifies exactly which variables are thought to be important and how they are thought to interact. This relates to another criticism of current models, namely that they are not sufficiently complex to reflect the realities that envelop supervision in typical service settings. Because models are typically set out in rather general terms, for example with only a few interacting variables, those with an awareness of the business of delivering supervision in the 'real world' believe that these models fail to recognise its inherent complexity (Watkins, 1995; Worthington, 1987). In addition to recognising the complex work environments in which supervisors work, there is also a need for models to clarify the way that moment-to-moment interactions are supposed to unfold. Models need to state what it is that supervisors are supposed to be doing within the process of a supervision session, and the anticipated effects that this will have on the supervisee.

Given these concerns about current models, one option is to abandon them in favour of a more pragmatic approach, one that simply builds on experience and consensus to test a limited number of ideas in the practice setting. An example is the outcome-orientated approach, in which the focus is on guiding therapy through corrective feedback, based on the therapists' clinical effectiveness (Harmon *et al.*, 2007). But this sort of theory-free approach seems fraught with difficulty. For one thing, it is inconceivable that supervisors could somehow empty their minds of theory whilst engaged in their professional duties. But even were that possible, reliance on simple technologies like feedback would fail to furnish supervisors with the intellectual basis to solve new problems in the present. Also, the history of science indicates that conceptual analysis is required to develop and test knowledge (Machado & Silva, 2007). In this sense, abandoning models appears problematic, making the issue one of trying harder to establish which factors are critical to supervision in its complex context (e.g. in relation to the generalisation of supervision to routine work like therapy).

Therefore, the assumption made in this book is that an appropriate model is the proper basis for taking forward both research and practice in supervision. But this needs to be evaluated with vigour, within complex settings (i.e. naturalistically), if it is to develop the requisite specificity and practice relevance. This approach, called theory-based evaluation (Chen, 1990), can provide the necessary balance. As Falender and Shafranske (2004, p.232) put it: 'An empirical, evidence-based, theoretical foundation is required.' Having a sound theory is, of course, something that many educationalists have advocated for many a long year. In his classic book, *Experience and Education*,

Dewey (1938) described the need for a model in these terms (I have substituted the term supervision for education): 'the issue is not one model or another, but what is worthy of the name supervision. The basic question concerns the nature of supervision, pure and simple. We shall make surer and faster progress when we devote ourselves to finding out just what supervision is – and what conditions have to be satisfied in order that supervision may be a reality, and not a name or a slogan. We need a sound philosophy' (pp.90–91). This, then, is the goal of this chapter: what is a sound philosophy, one that overcomes these difficulties with current models?

In order to address this challenging question, the remainder of this chapter recounts my work on the evidence-based approach to clinical supervision. As I will illustrate shortly, this includes drawing very carefully on the existing evidence in order to set out the important variables, and to try to indicate how they interact. As a result, an experiential learning model of supervision will be articulated. In order to address the traditional problems over imprecision, this model will be presented in a variety of ways (i.e. graphically and metaphorically), to maximise its comprehension and precise application (to research or practice).

This conceptualisation work is just the beginning of the scientific journey, and will lead into the manualisation of the approach ('implementation'). This is another important step, one that allows practitioners and researchers to see exactly how the model might be applied. But before the intervention we need to have 'operationalisation', namely a stage in which we specify how the model is to be measured. In order to address this additional scientific requirement, a number of processes and outcomes will be specified from the evidence-based clinical supervision model, and an instrument described for the measurement task. In the final phase of this research agenda, evidence bearing on the 'evaluation' of this model in routine practice will be presented. Based on this analysis, the final part of this chapter will be a critical review of this EBCS model.

Conceptualising Supervision

A basic model of supervision

I have already described the 'best evidence synthesis' approach to the literature review in Chapter 1, in working up an empirical definition of clinical supervision. It will be recalled that this approach focuses on a carefully selected sample of key papers (i.e. research that is highly relevant to the question at hand). These selected papers are then scrutinised thoroughly, in a consistent way, in order to help us clarify what is known (and remains to be found out) about something. This is the basic systematic review method (Petticrew & Roberts, 2006), a cornerstone of EBCS. This best-evidence synthesis approach was therefore repeated so that an evidence-based model of supervision could be clarified (for more detail, see Milne, Aylott, Fitzpatrick *et al.*, 2008). That is, we took studies of supervision that had occurred in naturalistic work settings and which had been successful, as in achieving their intended educational and clinical outcomes. In this way, we aimed to distil out a range of variables and interactions that had proved successful in the recent past into a crystallisation of how supervision could be understood inductively at least for pragmatic purposes. We found 24 such evaluations, most of them coming from the learning disability field, but involving a range of professional groups. These studies had used a wide range of instruments to assess the effectiveness of supervision, including supervisees' reactions, measures of the supervisees' learning, and the transfer of such learning to therapy. Most of these studies were drawn from residential settings, and the key variables manipulated through supervision were feedback, support and instruction. We used a coding manual to review these 24 papers, looking for three fundamental kinds of information. In order to address the need for a more complex model of supervision, we summarised the 'moderator' variables noted in these studies. A moderator is a background factor that effects the direction and/or strength of the relationship between an independent and a dependent variable (Barron & Kenny, 1986; Kraemer *et al.*, 2002). Thus, the way that feedback or instruction is used might be moderated in one study by local history, by the personalities of these involved, or by the physical environment in which supervision takes place. These factors are usually subsumed under the term 'context', meaning that there is assumed to be a system within which supervision occurs. Indeed, several nested layers of systems are assumed, including primarily the social and physical ones, and these are thought to be evolving and influencing one another over time (Reis *et al.*, 2000). These authors quote Capra (1996) as observing that: 'Throughout the living world we find living systems nesting within other living systems' (p.28). A familiar example of this kind of nesting is the relationship between the 'common factors' of therapy, such as the alliance, which is understood to operate independently of the specific, technical aspects of a therapy (e.g. 'guided discovery' in CBT: see

Nathan *et al.*, 2000). Another term for this nesting relationship is that of 'coupling' – the idea that all variables are continually linked and mutually interactive (Thelen & Smith, 1998). In supervision a major example concerns the format that is utilised, such as the traditional one-to-one and group arrangements. Milne and Oliver (2000) enumerated seven such formats, surveying 24 supervisees, supervisors and their managers in order to get a sense of their popularity. They reported that the one-to-one approach was endorsed by everyone they asked, followed by the use of individual supervision in a group (e.g. 30 minutes per supervisee per week, on a rotational basis, within a 90-minute group), and co-therapy. These formats can be regarded as the inner 'nest' or micro-context for supervision, moderating it in significant ways. Because of its popularity, plus the present book's emphasis on clarifying the essential elements of supervision, the one-to-one format will be given greatest emphasis. However, this is not intended to diminish the status of group-based formats in particular, which are clearly a highly valid and effective format.

A second and highly topical moderating influence on supervision concerns its goals. In the UK, the government's 'improving access to psychological therapies' (IAPT) initiative has shifted attention away from the supervisor and explicitly on to the patient. Termed 'clinical case supervision' (Richards, 2008), this minimises the traditional emphasis on caring, supportive interactions (intended to recognise and reduce therapists' burnout, through emotional support and strengthening their personal coping strategies), in order to re-prioritise problem-solving work addressing the therapist's caseload. Therefore, the goals of clinical case supervision are to try to ensure treatment fidelity, in order to maximise the welfare and safety of all clients. In this context, the convention of supervisee-led case discussion is succeeded by supervisor/service-led review of the supervisee's entire caseload. Case-based (or 'case-management') supervision is therefore 'high volume' and outcome-linked, representing a key part of the 'collaborative care' approach (an enhanced, multi-professional service system, featuring primary care-based help from mental health specialists operating through a case-manager arrangement: Katon *et al.*, 2001). This is discussed in greater depth later, for example in relation to the outcome-monitoring aspect (see Chapter 8). In summary, it is not difficult to imagine how innovations like case-based supervision, applied within flexible formats, would have a major moderating impact on both supervision and therapy.

The second main type of variable that we sought to isolate in our review of the essential, basic model of supervision was the 'mediator'. A mediator is an event occurring during supervision (the intervention or independent variable), such as Socratic questioning or the use of an instructional technique. By definition, mediators link cause (i.e. supervision) to effect (e.g. learning outcomes): they are the methods that are used in supervision.

In turn, these methods, operating under the effect of moderator variables, achieve their effect through what are called 'mechanisms' – the generative explanation for a change process, such as learning within a deterministic perspective such as CBT. A famous example in biology was Mendel's discovery of genes, the mechanism of heredity (see Bryson, 2004, for a gripping account). Classic examples of mechanisms of change in therapy are developing a fresh understanding and re-experiencing something. Therefore, a mechanism is the means through which a mediator has its effect on outcomes, typically a learning process in the case of supervision.

Moderating factors

Having established that we could code these papers in a reliable way, following a coding manual, we were able to clarify the moderators, mediators and mechanisms within these 24 carefully selected studies. As far as moderators were concerned, some 35 different moderating variables were noted by the authors of these studies. These included general organisational factors, like staff turnover and administrative support. We also found reference to aspects of the intervention itself that were thought to be influential, such as the complexity of the task and the researcher's ability to persist with it. There were also research factors and learning factors (e.g. how reactive participants were to observation; the presence of game-playing and collusion). Depending on how the authors described these moderating factors, they were given a simple grading as facilitating (a positive '+' symbol) or impeding the supervision intervention (symbolised by a negative '−' symbol). As set out in Figure 3.1, it can be seen that the different moderating variables described within our sample of 24 studies were largely facilitating. For example, administrative support was reported in 5 of these 24 papers (each positive or negative symbol within the figure represents a study).

These many and various moderating variables can be thought of as providing the kind of complex modelling of supervision that reviewers have been requesting (Watkins, 1997; Worthington, 1987). Although the causal influence of these moderators on the supervision that was studied was not manipulated (or related to an explicit effect) in these 24 studies, Figure 3.1

Systematic Review of Supervision: Summary of Author – Identified 'Moderators'

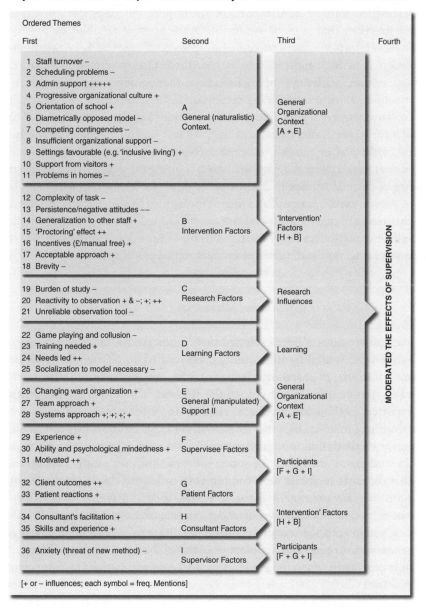

Figure 3.1 A dendrogram, depicting the 36 moderating factors identified in the 24 reviewed studies

does at least provide a contextual map for the kinds of factors that these researchers thought were important. The implication for practitioners is to try to ensure that as many as possible of the positive variables are present in their efforts to make a success of supervision. For researchers, the implication is to look more closely at how these factors actually operate on supervision. Although by definition rather general and difficult to manipulate, these moderators do appear to be significant: a mean of 2.1 moderators were identified per study, and only 2 of the 24 studies failed to identify a moderator. Consistent with the fact that these studies were educationally and/or clinically successful, 68 per cent of these identified moderators were judged as being facilitative. To bring these data to life, consider one of these 24 studies. Hundert and Hopkins (1992) noted how the nature of administrative support, and indeed the process by which it was provided, may have affected their supervision intervention. This can be negative in its influence, as illustrated by the Demchak and Browder (1990) study, where it was noted that 'staff turnover influenced this study' (p.161).

Mediators

We next scrutinised the 24 selected supervision studies to see which methods had been used by their authors. We located 26 different supervision mediators, the most frequent being 'teaching and instruction' of the supervisee (reported in 75 per cent of the studies). The next most frequently reported method was 'feedback', cited in 15 of the papers (63 per cent), which was followed by 'observing' in 42 per cent. Table 3.1 lists the 26 different methods that were cited. In total, 130 methods were used within the 24 studies, an average of 5.4 supervision methods per study. This means that different methods were combined in order to achieve the successful outcomes. For example, Miller *et al.* (2004) used 'instruction' to get supervisees up to a standard level of understanding over a two-day period, then engaged in 'collaborative problem-solving', the use of educational 'role play rehearsal and modelling', supplemented by 'feedback' (in the form of favourable comments when the supervisees made approximations to competent practice).

The list of supervision methods in Table 3.1 is perhaps more extensive than those commonly reported, but is consistent with current thinking on good practice in supervision, both in terms of the types of methods that were used and in relation to being combined together to form educational

Table 3.1 Methods of supervision in the 24 reviewed studies

	No. Studies	% Studies prevalence	Rank
1. Challenging (rethink)	3	13	15
2. Collaborating (joint working)	1	4	23
3. Confidence building (self-efficacy)	1	4	23
4. Disagreeing	1	4	23
5. Discussion (review)	5	21	10
6. Explanation (rationale provided; socialisation to model)	4	17	12.5
7. Feedback	15	63	2
8. Formulating (modelling problem)	1	4	23
9. Goal setting	9	38	4.5
10. Listening	2	8	18
11. Modelling (demonstration, live or video/ audio)	7	29	6
12. Monitoring (evaluating) client benefit/ supervisee performance	4	17	12.5
13. Observing (live or recorded)	10	42	3
14. Planning (including managing; agenda; next meeting)	6	25	7.5
15. Problem solving	2	8	18
16. Prompts (verbal and written reminders, handout, etc.)	5	21	10
17. Question and answer (information gathering; clarifying)	9	38	4.5
18. Rehearsal of skills	2	8	18
19. Reinforcement/praise/support	6	25	7.5
20. Review/reflection	5	21	12.5
21. Role-play	5	21	10
22. Self-disclosure	3	13	18
23. Self-monitoring	1	4	18
24. Summarising	4	17	14.5
25. Training (teaching skills/instruction)	18	75	1
26. Understanding checked	1	4	23

packages (Kaslow *et al.*, 2004; Bransford *et al.*, 2000). It is also worth noting that in using such packages (i.e. multiple methods of supervision), these studies are manipulating a range of ways in which the supervisee can learn from the experience (i.e. through words, actions and feelings about the experience). This reflects conventional wisdom (Bruner, 1966), as combined within the 'structured learning format' (Bouchard *et al.*, 1980).

Mechanisms

Finally, we found that the studies we analysed defined 28 different mechanisms of change in order to explain how the different methods of supervision (as listed in Table 3.1) could enable supervisees to develop competence, and apply it in their workplace. These included changes in supervisees' emotional self-awareness, their motivation and their skills. Although a daunting number of mechanisms were noted and a diverse terminology used, we were able to accommodate 23 of these to the experiential learning model (Kolb, 1984). Table 3.2 summarises these data, which indicate that the most widely used mechanism was 'experiencing' (i.e. working on the attitudes, affective awareness, and motivational dimensions within the supervisee). This emphasis on experiencing was present in half of the studies, whereas 'planning' and 'reflection' were explicit in only a minority of studies. However, this crystallisation by means of the experiential learning model is encouraging, since it provides a clear account of how supervision appears to work, one that is precise enough to enable research hypotheses to be generated, and clear enough to be practical within the moment-to-moment process of supervision practice (see Chapters 7 and 8 for illustrations).

Based on the information gleaned from this systematic review, a basic model of supervision can be sketched out (basic in the sense that it draws on the variables that are common to the reviewed studies). This is set out in Figure 3.2, which notes the different numbers of people involved at each stage, and the frequency with which different methods were employed. The figure indicates how the moderators bear down upon the mediators and mechanisms, indicating the general influence that they might have on the speed or direction of supervision. Supervisors use a wide range of popular methods, and these, according to this model, have their intended effect through the process of experiential learning. (See Milne, Aylott, Fitzpatrick *et al.*, 2008 for additional details: the table is a summary of this 2008 review paper).

Table 3.2 Mechanisms of change reported in the 24 reviewed studies

	No. studies specifying	% Studies	Rank
Conceptualising	2	8	= 5.5
Experiencing (attitude change; affective awareness; motivation/reinforcement)	12	50	1
Experimenting ('exposure'/learning by doing)	2	8	= 5.5
Planning (increased attention to goals/focusing)	4	16	4
Reflection (to raise self awareness/evaluation: positive and negative	3	12	3
Other (general 'learning'; self-monitoring)	5	20	2

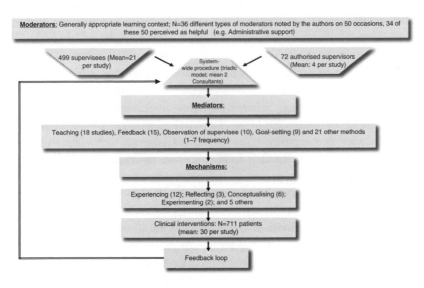

Figure 3.2 The basic model of clinical supervision

Although the basic model does have some advantages over those discussed in Chapter 2, in that it is supported by empirical evidence, it is still rather general (i.e. the parsimony is poor) and lacks the kind of elaboration needed to set out explicit predictions. There is also an absence of implied research methods and types of evidence (i.e. its assumptions are weak). On the other hand, it is compatible with many of the models summarised in Chapter 2 and it does provide an explanation as to how causal processes occur (i.e. mainly through experiential learning). Also, action implications are there (for example, try to ensure that favourable moderators are present, utilise a range of supervision methods, and facilitate experiential learning).

A Circumplex Model of Supervision

In order to bring greater precision and parsimony to the basic model above, a traditional model-building method known as the 'circumplex' was next utilised (Kiesler, 1983; see Faith & Thayer, 2001, for a more recent application). A circumplex model depicts the relationship between key variables in terms of successive, nested layers of interaction. For instance, in one of the earliest applications, a circumplex model was used to try to capture the spectrum of interpersonal behaviour (Leary, 1957). Cross-cutting axes were used to divide a circle into the main variables/dimensions (e.g. concerning the degree to which a person exerts or cedes control; is warm or cold) and their resultant segments (e.g. supervisors who are directive but nurturant, involved and accepting, could be characterised interpersonally as akin to 'guides'). More importantly, as illustrated in Figure 3.3, each of the variables (represented by boxes in this figure) within the circumplex should be thought of as capable of operating independently in relation to every other panel, like Rubik's cube. This approach recognises the dynamism and inherent complexity within the basic model, but adds a greater degree of specificity by indicating how the numerous moderators, mediators and mechanisms might interact. The moderating variables noted in Figure 3.1 are thought to concern the contextual background to supervision, such as staff turnover and administrative support This context influences how the supervisor exercises his or her skills (the outer ring of the circumplex), as in a service environment that requires the adoption of case-based supervision within group formats, a context that necessarily shapes the selection and use of the different supervision methods (such as ensuring that outcome data are included in the review of all a supervisee's cases). In turn, this engages the supervisee in a particular trajectory of experiential learning, the heart of Figure 3.3. Amongst other things, this circumplex model gives equal weight to the supervisee and the supervisor as contributors to

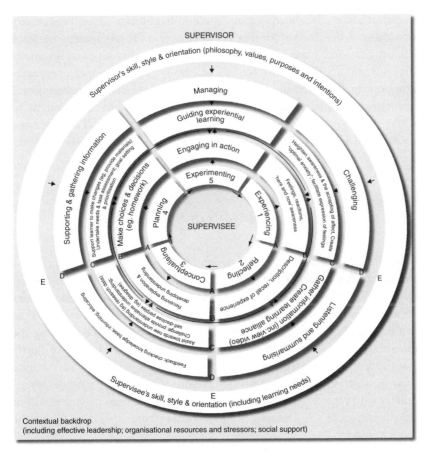

Figure 3.3 The circumplex model of evidence-based clinical supervision

the necessary experiential learning interactions, in the context of their workplace. Not depicted here but logically nested within the centre of the diagram would be the subsequent interactions between the supervisee (i.e. therapist) and the client. Similar interactions would be expected to occur at that level (e.g. there would be a moderating influence present, because of the client's characteristics, history, etc.).

The more precise, subtle and complex modelling of supervision that is shown in Figure 3.3 provides supervisors with much greater clarity than is available from the basic model (Figure 3.2) and from the essential model described within Chapter 2. For researchers, it suggests what might be important to study, allowing consequential hypotheses to be constructed. For instance, the circumplex model indicates that the relationship between 'challenging' and 'experiencing' is mediated by specific kinds of questioning, and that the mechanism for this process is heightened awareness (creating optimal anxiety and a 'here and now' engagement in supervision.) This circumplex model of EBCS was first published by Milne and Westerman (2001), when it was also given an initial evaluation. This will be discussed shortly, but for further detail on the model, the interested reader is again referred to this original paper.

A Tandem Model of Supervision

Subsequently, a more explicitly dynamic account of supervision, based firmly on the circumplex model, was developed with my colleague Ian James (Milne & James, 2005). This tandem version of supervision is a metaphorical, enhanced, and 3-D version of the graphical representation of the model as in Figure 3.3 above. However, it might be worth describing the emerging model through the lens of a metaphor, as this can help to clarify assumptions and illustrate how the model actually operates. I will also note ways in which the tandem metaphor extends the circumplex model, particularly with regard to the notion of transactions between the boxes within the circumplex model. There are numerous important assumptions within the tandem model:

- It takes two: both supervisor and supervisee need to be active contributors to supervision for it to be effective.
- Supervisor in control: The assumption in the tandem model is that, by and large, the supervisor would occupy the front seat of the tandem. This is the seat that allows the vehicle to be steered and the controls to be used appropriately (e.g. brakes and gears). This reflects the assumption that the supervisor is ultimately responsible for the direction and pace entailed in supervision. Supervisors must occupy this position with due authority, and must have the power to discharge their responsibilities. Of course, as the supervisee develops, it is only natural that they should be given more autonomy and even episodes of leadership. The model allows for this, in that literally a tandem can be cycled solo, or the roles reversed (for the purposes of a specific learning assignment).

- Developmental path: Another useful analogy that comes from the tandem metaphor is that the supervisor and supervisee are engaged in a journey. The journey is one of learning and development, for both parties. However, it is assumed that the supervisor either knows the path moderately well, or is expert in the equivalent of reading maps and finding his or her way. The metaphor of travelling seems to be highly apposite, drawing as it does on such notions as coming across unfamiliar issues and having to work jointly to find solutions. The process is also recognised as unending, and as leading to greater sophistication. Another implication of the travelling idea is that the amount of effort made by the two parties will significantly influence how much travelling occurs.

- Supervision is a wheel of activities: The front wheel of the tandem, being under the immediate control of the supervisor, is taken to represent the wheel of supervision. This is the business of establishing learning needs, negotiating supervision objectives, utilising different methods of supervision to facilitate progress down the developmental path, and evaluation. This is a direct use of the staff development literature (Goldstein, 1993), and is elaborated in Chapter 5.

- A wheel of learning: The back wheel, being closest to the supervisee's part of the tandem, is taken to represent the experiential learning cycle (Kolb, 1984). It is understood also that the back wheel provides the drive that mobilises the tandem so that it can progress down the developmental path. This reflects Kolb's emphasis on a spiral curriculum, in which different levels of engagement with reflection, conceptualisation and so forth will ultimately determine the supervisee's development.

- A frame: We take the tandem's frame to represent the notion of 'scaffolding' in supervision, the idea that learning requires proper resources and personalised learning opportunities (Vygotsky, 1978).

- Mechanisms of change: The wheels, held in place by the scaffold-like frame, need to be brought together. The tandem model addresses this through the physical means of the pedals and gears which act initially on the learning cycle (back wheel) and, through that impetus, drive the front wheel and the whole supervisory enterprise forward. By analogy, the pedals, gears, chains, and so forth are the mechanisms through which the supervisory and supervisee activity combine to produce development.

- Weathering: Again, the idea of moderating factors is accommodated to the model, quite naturally in terms of the inevitable weathering effects of the context on the tandem cyclists. We particularly recognise that the two parties bring their respective histories, styles, personalities, and so forth to the exchange. Other moderating factors are the ways that local training programmes provide the equivalent of road maps and ways of measuring progress to the cyclists.

Ten tests of the tandem

Having provided this elaboration of the assumptions and axioms under-pinning the tandem model, Milne and James (2005) then subjected it to 10 logical tests of the kind that apply to any model (and which have already been applied in this and the proceeding chapter: e.g. whether or not a model has parsimony or support, etc.). We felt that the tandem stood up to these 10 tests fairly well. For example, we thought that the tandem model was exceptionally parsimonious (it is harder to think of a leaner explication of naturalistic supervision), yet was nonetheless adequately elaborated (details regarding how the variables were organised and would be expected to interact were relatively explicit). In other respects, such as its internal con-sistency or support, we did acknowledge that the tandem model was not yet as strongly borne out by research as some other models.

However, it was an important conceptual weakness with the tandem model that led to discontinuing its use, the notion of 'transaction'. The basic and tandem models of EBCS provide a list of ingredients for effective super-vision (i.e. the variables within the models, such as the different methods of supervision), and specify how these variables interact. But this is a rather limited account of the processes that surely occur within supervision. Here I define an interaction as direct or indirect contact between one variable and another, which results in an effect on the other. To illustrate, consider how the use of informing (e.g. presenting facts) may interact with subse-quent supervisee developmental methods, like modelling and learning exercises. An example would be where a clinical formulation puzzle is high-lighted by the supervisor, who then informs the supervisee about some rel-evant research that suggests how this puzzle might be solved, then invites the supervisee to apply this material in order to generate his or her own solution. This is an example of an interaction because the different varia-bles, such as instruction, are brought together in ways that are expected to create a learning opportunity. This provides the basis for something to emerge, normally some experiential learning.

But the notion of interaction affords only a limited account of how these kinds of variables can produce learning and development. It appears to be necessary for us to understand how people learn, but not quite sufficient. For this we require at least one additional concept, and I believe that a good contender is the idea of a 'transaction'. This is defined as an interaction which results in a transformation of the material by either supervisor or supervisee. That is, interacting variables have the effect of altering one or both of them: they not only influence one another, but have the capacity to shape one another's learning and development. This idea is drawn from the transactional stress model (Lazarus & Folkman, 1984). According to this model, the different variables are understood to change one another: in general terms, stressors (triggers) are appraised (including activation of beliefs and schemas) and affect how we attempt to cope, and our coping efforts (e.g. taking problem-solving action) in turn can change the stressor, and our future capacity to problem-solve.

It is assumed that supervision, when it works well, shares this dynamic, organic quality, operating as an open system that results in development. That is, successful supervision is viewed as changing over time as a result of continuous transactional and interactive processes involving the supervisee ('reciprocal' and 'circular' causality), processes that are not at all like the linear boxes and arrows of the basic model presented earlier (and of most models in mental health), and which can exhibit subtle, unpredictable effects, like the 'sensitive dependence on initial conditions' (where seemingly trivial stimuli can initiate significant processes: Fredrickson & Losada, 2005) and produce 'emergent properties' that are not easily adduced to the specified variables (just as consciousness is difficult to relate to the brain). This is a 'probabilistic' rather than 'deterministic' world (Davies, 2004). It is akin to the familiar systems approach within mental health practice, which helpfully also identifies some of the processes that can prevent supervision from working well (e.g. homeostasis and conflict detouring: see Hayes, 1991). Such processes are regarded as better suited to understanding the 'many complexities inherent in adult learning' (Sheckley, 1993, pp.56–57).

On this logic, processes of interaction and transaction are both necessary if we are to understand how supervision achieves its outcomes, and the earlier circumplex and tandem models fail to capture this phenomenon of transaction adequately: they are surely insufficiently dynamic to truly reflect the open system that underpins human development. For this and other reasons, the more contemporary and straightforward notion of evidence-based practice has been utilised latterly, applied systematically to supervision, and duly reflecting the above ideas about how an open system operates.

An Evidence-Based Clinical Supervision (EBCS) Model

The basic, circumplex and tandem models described so far have latterly been integrated within the framework of evidence-based practice (Roth, Fonagy & Parry, 1996). As set out in Figure 3.4, the present framework simply replaces the term 'therapy' with that of supervision, otherwise being exactly as per the original version. According to this model, supervision pivots on the judgements that are made by supervisors in relation to each particular supervisory event (e.g. how best to formulate a client's presentation), judgements that draw on a range of influences (e.g. guidelines and CPD workshops). The EBCS model also shares a commitment to drawing on what experts and practitioners believe to be appropriate (i.e. consensus statements), an interest in evaluating the outcomes of supervision, and in addressing the other boxes within Figure 3.4. All of these various facets of EBCS will be covered later in this book. For instance, considerable work has gone into developing four guidelines on best practice in supervision, based on a consensus amongst colleagues in the UK (i.e. the top of Figure 3.4),

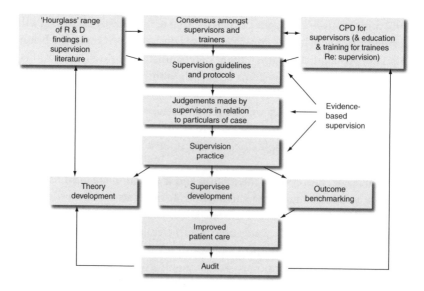

Figure 3.4 The EBCS model, based on Roth, Fonagy & Parry (1996)

and these will feature in the next three chapters. The theory-development aspect of EBCS has come from systematically reviewing the best available literature with colleagues in the UK and the USA, as already illustrated at the start of this chapter and in Chapter 1 (the definitional work). Of course, many other reviews have been conducted, and these will also be drawn on to fill out the EBCS model. In addition, a small number of intensive case studies and larger-scale, pragmatic evaluations have been undertaken. These will be considered alongside the available research on supervision, in order to contribute to the evidence-base for EBCS. Therefore, I hope to exemplify the evidence-based practice approach throughout this book, founded on the commitment to an empirical, scientific approach that is anchored in professional realities.

In summary, this current model of EBCS is my latest conceptualisation of supervision. It improves on previous models in a number of critical areas, including having greater internal consistency, precision, and by specifying how moment-to-moment supervisor and supervisee interactions can result in experiential learning within an open system. However, there are some other key challenges which need to be addressed if the EBCS model is to be considered a genuine competitor to existing models. Paramount amongst these challenges are the conventional scientific tasks of manualisation, operationalisation and evaluation. I now go on to detail how EBCS addresses these challenges, leading to a critique of the current model.

Manualisation of evidence-based clinical supervision (EBCS)

As we have seen, several of the criteria by which any model should be judged relate to setting out a model explicitly in the first instance (i.e. having appropriate focus; being duly elaborated; specifying action implications: Warr, 1980). Manualisation, which is the detailing of an intervention in a form that allows it to be replicated, is the second major challenge we face in applied science. Having constructed a working conceptualisation (the theoretical model above), we now need to show how that complex concept can be delivered. Within the mental health/social science field, the convention is to draft a document such as a manual, guide or protocol. As per Figure 3.4, the convention in evidence-based practice is to refer to this documentation as 'guidelines'. According to Parry (2000), guidelines are normally developed by professional consensus and contain a list of suggested actions and recommendations. They should be transparent and replicable, drawing on the best available evidence. Within the American Psychological Association, it is noted that the primary purpose of such guidelines is to 'assist the practitioner in the provision of high quality psychological services by providing well-supported practical guidance and education in a particular practice area' (American Psychological Association, 2005, p.976). Although not at all popular (Lucock *et al.*, 2006), and often misunderstood and misused (Parry, 2000), guidelines are nonetheless an integral part of modern healthcare. They offer the individual practitioner a summary of otherwise overwhelming amounts of knowledge, and they can also help to ensure that some core beliefs and practices exist within clinical services.

In keeping with this reasoning, and consistent with the approach used by the National Institute of Clinical Excellence (NICE), four guidelines on clinical supervision have been prepared and are noted in the relevant sections of this book. These form the core of a manual, which has been drafted to detail how novice supervisors can be trained in the EBCS approach (Milne, 2007a). Supplementing the guidelines are PowerPoint slideshows to introduce the six parts of the three-day workshop. These presentations lead into demonstrations of the methods, through naturalistic video recordings of the key aspects of supervision (e.g. goal-setting). Next are some suggestions for how the workshop leaders can engage the participants in experiential learning about the material. The sessions end with a summary and the opportunity for some discussion. This manual can be found on the Wiley website (www.wiley.com/go/milne). To my knowledge, this is the first manual of such specificity within the supervision field, as it consists of over 180 pages of detail on the approach and how to foster it through workshops for novice supervisors. The guidelines within the manual (which cover the supervisory relationship; establishing the learning contract; facilitating learning; and evaluation) were developed with the help of over 100 colleagues, and included careful evaluation and re-drafting. The manual, which was prepared with a grant from the Higher Education Academy (Psychology network), underwent piloting with 10 Doctorate in Clinical Psychology courses within the UK. This indicated that others could follow the manual successfully, and encouraged feedback so that the manual could be improved (the audit part of EBCS – see Figure 3.4). From a practical point of view, the manual makes explicit what is meant by evidence-based clinical supervision. From a research standpoint, the manual enables the approach to be implemented with fidelity, and hence evaluated properly. Of course, none of this work assumes that EBCS is superior to competing models, but rather it represents a starting point from which we can begin to examine their relative effectiveness. This is a necessary step in our efforts to improve the quality of supervision.

Operationalisation of EBCS

A clear model of supervision (the conceptualisation phase) and an explicit method with which implement it (the manualisation phase) leads to the next task in applied science, clarifying how the model should be measured. Which kind of measurement approach is appropriate, and which kinds of variables, interactions and transactions might be recorded? In relation to EBCS, the main instrument which has been developed is called 'Teachers' PETS' (Process Evaluation of Training and Supervision), although we are also developing a simpler rating of competent supervision (see Milne, 2008a, for a summary). This is an observational tool which requires samples of what the supervisor is doing (the mediators or methods that are applied), related to the reactions of the supervisee (i.e. the mechanisms). The instrument was first reported in by Milne *et al.* (2002), and the present summary draws directly from that paper. The main purpose here is to show how the EBCS model is capable of being measured through Teachers' PETS. The tandem-style logic applies, in that the front wheel, the training cycle, is set out in terms of 13 common methods used by supervisors. These are very similar to those appearing in Table 3.1 above and to accounts of CBT supervision, including 'informing' and 'guiding experiential learning' (i.e. the use of simulations, educational role-plays, behavioural rehearsal, and similar learning tasks). Related to this list of supervisor activities is the experiential learning cycle (by analogy, the back wheel of the tandem). In order to better observe this learning phase, we elaborated Kolb's (1984) four modes by distinguishing between 'experiencing' (the emotional accompaniments to action) and 'experimenting' (the behavioural aspect, such as watching a video or engaging in a role-play). The other modes from Kolb (1984) were retained, being 'reflecting', 'conceptualising', and 'planning'. In keeping with the convention in using the direct observation measurement approach, we added the category 'other' (an item included also for the supervisors, to allow the observer to record other kinds of activities, such as social chat).

Drawing on these two complementary lists, the observer (following a manual) alternately records what the supervisor is doing and then, a few seconds later, the mini impact that this appears to have on the supervisee.

This allows a profile of supervision to be constructed, and so in the Milne and James (2002) evaluation of EBCS we were able to present data on supervision to illustrate how often the supervisor (Ian James) used different methods over the period of the study. This showed that his most frequent behaviour was that of 'listening' (observed on 142 occasions, out of the 358 observed; 40 per cent). By comparison, he used 'informing/educating' on 14 per cent of occasions, 'supporting' 12 per cent of the time, followed by several lower-frequency behaviours (such as 'observing a video', 'gathering information' and 'checking theoretical knowledge': all around about 6 per cent of observed occasions. NB: these profile data are drawn from the baseline period of this 2002 study). However, Teachers' PETS can progress beyond the simple profile to provide a contingency table which expresses the relationship between these activities and the sought-after instances of experiential learning by the supervisee. In this way, it was found that, during the baseline period, by far the most common impact was on the supervisees' reflection (302 instances were observed, 84 per cent of all impacts). Very few incidents of the supervisees' 'experimenting', 'conceptualising', 'experiencing' or 'planning' were observed (there were three supervisees in this intensive case-study design, all qualified mental health practitioners undertaking a CPD Diploma course in CBT).

Therefore, it was found that the variables within the EBCS model could be set out and observed with Teachers' PETS. This could be done with good inter-rater reliability, a further criterion in applied science (see Milne & Westerman, 2001; Milne *et al.*, 2002, and Milne & James, 2002, for further details).

Implementation and evaluation of EBCS

With a clear concept of what is to be done, some clear guidance in the form of a manual on how to do it, and a measurement tool to detect the intended effects, the next stage is to evaluate an EBCS intervention. Various versions of EBCS have been applied, in keeping with the basic, circumplex and tandem models described earlier. The first published implementation and evaluation was by Milne and Westerman (2001). In that study, also an intensive, case-study design, one supervisor, Colin Westerman, was studied in relation to his three supervisees, all qualified mental health nurses. An earlier, more rudimentary version of the EBCS manual was used to guide this work, and consultancy was provided by the present author to ensure that the method was applied faithfully. Teachers' PETS was used to detect whether the intervention had any effect. This provided data that described the supervisor's profile, and the relationship this had with these supervisees' learning, for each of the three phases of the experiment (a nine-session baseline period, then nine sessions of EBCS, and then a twelve-session maintenance phase). To quote that report: 'the main findings from this study were that clinical supervision could be measured systematically, could be enhanced to a small extent and in a predicted direction through consultancy, and could result in slightly improved learning for the supervisees. Supervisee satisfaction was also very high throughout the year long study' (pp.453–454).

Learning lessons from that initial evaluation, Milne and James (2002) conducted a similar analysis, again using Teachers' PETS as the main measure, plus a supervisee satisfaction instrument. In this instance the one supervisor (Ian James) had six supervisees (supervised in three pairs). To quote again from the paper itself: 'supervision improved during the experimental phase, but most markedly during the maintenance phase. The results appear to reflect a lag effect for the intervention, which can be most readily explained in terms of a socialisation period during which both supervisor and supervisees adapted their styles of interaction' (p.55). The interventions referred to were 'general consultancy' and 'consultancy plus feedback' (feedback came from the results from Teachers' PETS, plus a summary of the supervisees' satisfaction, session upon session).

To be more explicit about the findings, during the baseline period we found that the supervisor's profile was weak in relation to the EBCS model, featuring only a limited use of the vital experiential learning methods (referred to as 'guiding experiential learning' within Teachers' PETS). By contrast, considerable use was made at this stage of the less potent verbal methods. As predicted by the EBCS model, this had the effect that most of the supervisees' time was spent in 'reflection' (84 per cent of observed occasions), whilst engaging in the essential 'experiencing' and 'experimenting' modes was only observed on 4 per cent of occasions. With consultancy and feedback during the intervention phases these figures improved, and with them the impact on the supervisees' learning became more balanced (i.e. featured all five learning modes). Thus, whilst 'reflection' decreased over time, 'experiencing' and 'experimenting' increased (from mean values of 1.8 and 0.8 during the baseline period, to 7.5 and 1.3 during the consultancy phase). These figures improved slightly more during the subsequent consultancy plus feedback and maintenance phases (e.g. 'experimenting' rose to a mean of 17.2, whilst 'experiencing' remained stable). By this stage 'reflection' had reduced from a mean of 50.3 to 35.2. Supervisee satisfaction remained stable and high throughout, indicating that we had the traditional insensitivity of reaction evaluation to an intervention.

Critical review

Whilst this tale of the development of EBCS is promising, it is only appropriate to engage in some critical reflection. It is also appropriate to apply the same criteria to the EBCS model as were applied previously to the other models (Chapter 2). In terms of the tandem model, 10 such tests were tackled fairly well by the model, when applied in a fairly unsystematic and no doubt biased way (i.e. it was undertaken by the model's proponents: Milne & James, 2005). Therefore, there is a need to strengthen the model to withstand these tests, as well as a need to develop the model in other respects, encouraging independent review. This includes attending to the logical weaknesses, such as the imprecise meaning of some of the concepts (e.g. 'experience' – see discussion below) and the unacknowledged assumptions (Machado & Silva, 2007). This kind of rigorous conceptual analysis should accompany the familiar emphasis on experimentation. These points are now discussed.

On the subject of data-collection, the EBCS model needs further support, as there are only four $N=1$ analyses, all conducted by proponents of the approach. However, these were rigorous, supportive evaluations of the EBCS model (i.e. Milne & Westerman, 2001: Milne & James, 2002; Milne, Leck, Procter *et al.*, 2008; Milne, Lombardo, Kennedy *et al.*, 2008). There has also been one large-scale evaluation, in which 22 trainers utilised at least one session from the EBCS manual (Milne, 2007a) with nearly 300 supervisors (Milne, 2008b). It follows that there is a need for neutral researchers and supervisors to be engaged in evaluations of EBCS, which might now be appropriate with large group designs.

In relation to the 'focus' criterion (Warr, 1980), American colleague Robert Reiser and I spent some time trying to differentiate EBCS from CBT supervision. I would now take the view that EBCS is entirely compatible with CBT supervision, but extends beyond it in some important respects, as set out in Table 3.3. This lists the core principles of CBT (drawn from Grant *et al.*, 2005; Lomax *et al.*, 2005), which I have translated for supervision, plus two principles from EBCS. The underlined material alongside each principle in Table 3.3 represents the additional ideas that come from the EBCS perspective, so providing the proposed augmentation. However, it is important to note

Table 3.3 General principles of CBT, showing the overlaps between evidence-based supervision (EBCS) and CBT supervision, plus ways in which EBCS might augment CBT supervision (underlined)

CBT Supervision (__augmented__)

---

1. Specified problems identified collaboratively, within a problem – solving cycle.
2. Cognitive-behavioural – affective mediation (Kolb).
3. Goal-directed (developmentally – informed / needs – led)
4. Theoretically – driven (applied psychology of learning).
5. Brief interventions (as CT, plus BT, plus psychology of learning).
6. Self-control (interpersonal discomfort; adult learner; challenge).
7. Collaborative relationship.
8. Contextualise (e.g. cultural diversity; peer support).
9. Research and development orientation (consumption – selective reviewing critical engagement; utilisation with; production/experimentation.

Source: First 7 Principles from Grant *et al.*/Lomax *et al.*, 2005: *Oxford Textbook of Psychotherapy*; additional 2 Principles from evidence-based clinical supervision (Milne, 2008a)

that this summary is hampered by limited information on the precise nature of CBT supervision (as there appears to be no manual, nor a published, psychometrically adequate, CBT-specific instrument for measuring adherence). Therefore, the summary that is provided in Table 3.3, and the comparisons that now follow, are based on what seems to be the most relevant of the available material. This consists of: two frequently cited, theoretical accounts of CBT supervision (Liese & Beck, 1997; Padesky, 1996), other CBT-specific reviews (i.e. Armstrong & Freeston, 2005; Liese & Alford, 1998; Lomax *et al.*, 2005; Perris, 1994; Pretorius, 2006; Richards & Freeston, 2007), the available research data (i.e. Bambling *et al.*, 2006; the Milne & James 2000 review of CBT research; their empirical analysis of CBT supervision: Milne & James, 2002); and on surveys of what CBT supervisors say they do (i.e. Townend *et al.*, 2002; Tyler *et al.*, 2000).

As Table 3.3 illustrates, we believe that a potential difference between the approaches is their relative emphasis on, and enactment of, the affective and behavioural parts of supervision. On the first of these distinctions, a representational or theoretical point, EBCS appears to attend more systematically to the emotional dimension of the material covered within supervision, and indeed to the supervisory interaction itself. It is probably also important to note that this emphasis is somewhat different in style (i.e. it is derived from diverse, non-CBT models within the supervision literature).

This attention includes greater affective awareness, and so may include work by the supervisor to improve the supervisee's ability to describe and identify different emotional accompaniments to the work they are describing (or to what is happening within supervision). This represents an elaboration of the 'experiencing' factor. By comparison, CBT supervision appears to privilege 'conceptualisation', achieved through conversation (e.g. sharing information and reformulating a clinical case), though I am aware that proponents of CBT argue that attention to emotions is at the 'forefront', at least in theory (e.g. Reilly, 2000). However, the limited data that are available suggest otherwise (Milne & James, 2000, 2002; Townend *et al.*, 2002). For example, in the Townend *et al.* (2002) survey of CBT practitioners in the UK, 'experiencing' is not identified as an appropriate item within their questionnaire, nor is it mentioned spontaneously by respondents or included as a recommendation. This analysis is reported more fully in Milne (2008a).

As regards implementation, EBCS explicitly encourages the supervisor to make more frequent use of educational role-plays, and various other simulations or activities, namely interactions that cause the supervisee to grasp then transact with the material (this is also stressed in some of the above accounts of CBT supervision, but observational and survey data suggest that it is not enacted as frequently as in EBCS). Returning to Townend *et al.* (2002), their survey indicated that less than 20 per cent of their 170 respondents (all qualified mental health practitioners) utilised 'experiential' methods (i.e. role-play; reviewing tapes; direct observation), leading them to conclude that adherence to a CBT approach was limited, indicating 'slippage' from the model (p.497). Similarly, the Bambling *et al.* (2006) study appeared not to require an experiential approach in the CBT supervision condition, noting instead the need for 'case discussion'. However, both EBCS and CBT would stress the value of such experiential methods, leading to supervisor feedback on the supervisees' taped clinical material, and a number of other important principles and practices (e.g. adopting Kolb's model – see below).

This greater specificity in EBCS is a third apparent distinction between it and CBT supervision, an issue that simply appears to reflect different levels of analysis, rather than mutually exclusive approaches (see Cacioppa *et al.*, 2000, for an example of this kind of multi-level comparison). Therefore, the greater detail in EBCS is not in any sense more true or accurate, but it may be a useful augmentation. This is because it can provide the foundation for the detailed manualisation of CBT supervision, and in turn for practical applications to CBT supervisor training, randomised controlled trials (in which, for example, the two complementary forms of supervision are contrasted), or to small-N studies, in which the two approaches alternate over time. This would allow one to detect, through instruments like Teachers' PETS (allied to something equivalent for CBT), the relative effectiveness of the two approaches (note that we offer SAGE as a specific measure of competence in CBT supervision in Chapter 8).

Regardless of such differentiations, a second major aspect uniting EBCS and CBT supervision that merits serious critical attention is their reliance on Kolb's (1984) account of experiential learning (see Armstrong & Freeston, 2005; Townend *et al.*, 2002). It should be borne in mind that Kolb was attempting to synthesise the ideas of some important pioneers in psychology, such as Piaget, Dewey and Lewin. It is always difficult to reproduce faithfully the work of such prolific authors, and to do so without bias. Perhaps for these reasons, four main criticisms of Kolb (1984) seem to be warranted. I will now summarise these as criticisms from the perspective of those who train supervisors, and for researchers, supervisors and supervisees. In relation to trainers, there is a lack of attention to the system in which learning occurs, and to factors such as culture and history (i.e. inattention to moderators: a de-contextualised theory). Secondly, Kolb's approach is reductionistic, and can be seen as being too narrowly psychological, and, in particular, too cognitive. This yields implausibly neat sets of stages, which have then been described as 'intoxicatingly simply' (Kayes, 2002, p.142). Another issue for trainers is that Kolb's (1984) theory, like any other general theory, lacks widespread acceptance within academic circles: indeed, there is no consensus on any one particular paradigm of adult learning.

Turning to criticisms related to the perspective of learners, Kolb places equal emphasis on all modes of learning, whereas reflection dominates in other accounts on how people learn from experience. A related criticism is that these modes may simply be different aspects of the same learning process: at one level 'reflection' may merge into 'experiencing' (for example). The Kolbian account also ignores 'higher' (e.g. metacognitive) learning, for example how the supervisee might question their own learning style; and it assumes that all learning occurs through a fairly dramatic transaction between the different modes of knowing (as opposed to simple acquisition of declarative knowledge through lectures, or rote learning for exams).

Turning to the perspective of researchers, the empirical scrutiny of Kolb's (1984) account is remarkably minimal, and the studies that do exist do not provide clear-cut affirmation (see, for example: Holman *et al.*, 1997; Reynolds, 1997). To make matters worse, Kolb (1984) makes some rather grand claims, particularly for his learning styles inventory. But the research that does exist suggests that this 'theory of life and everything' is hard to substantiate (Reynolds, 1997). Also problematic for researchers are the vagueness of the essential constructs, particularly terms like 'experience', and again the absence of reference to more measurable, conventional forms of learning, such as habituation. An incisive and damming philosophical critique of the construct validity of Kolb's work has been provided by Webb (2006), in which she questions such fundamentals as the mechanism of 'dialectic tension' between the different modes of learning, which she describes as not being a viable mechanism.

Finally, from the perspective of supervisees, the model assumes that actions are rational, linear and quantifiable. It ignores, for example, the important power relations that can arise from things like differences in gender and status, and it also ignores pre- or unconscious processes (e.g. transference: Webb, 2006). However, these are not fatal criticisms, as I attempt to show in Chapter 9.

Summary

The EBCS approach has been presented as a 'case study' of how the existing models of supervision can be challenged, and as a promising alternative or augmentation of CBT supervision (most obviously providing a logical, scientific and practical extension). It offers an unusually clear and detailed conceptualisation of formative supervision, perhaps due to the successive stages of the model's development (from a basic integration of recent research studies, through the tandem and circumplex models, then latterly adopting the evidence-based practice framework). This kind of model-building can be criticised as idle or academic, but I share the opinion that it 'represents a serious approach to science' (Watson, 1999, p.166; see also Machado & Silva, 2007), and it is hoped that the EBCS model will eventually help us to better understand how supervision operates.

Another and more unusual part of the origins of EBCS is probably the interplay between the different literatures that have contributed to the model (including the staff training, psychotherapy, human development, and adult learning literatures). But such conceptualisations are legion. What appears to better distinguish EBCS is the extent to which it has been operationalised, implemented and evaluated as part of a coherent, applied research programme. Although this has generated some promising findings, there are clearly some important caveats. Amongst these are the need to gather large-group and comparative data on EBCS (preferably through independent researchers), and to clarify still further the fundamental concepts that underpin the approach, so that they have construct validity. I pick up these issues again in Chapter 9.

4

Relating in Supervision

Introduction

 Most accounts of what matters in clinical supervision place the quality of the supervisory relationship at its very heart. Freud referred to it as the 'vehicle of success' (Freud, 1912, p.105), and its vital role is reflected in the empirical definition provided in Chapter 1. Recall that this states that supervision is based on 'the formal provision, by senior/qualified health practitioners, of an intensive, *relationship-based* education and training …'. In turn, the 'relationship-based' aspect is specified as something that is confidential and highly collaborative, being founded on a learning alliance and featuring elements such as participative decision-making and shared agenda-setting; and entailing therapeutic qualities such as empathy and warmth.

Broadly speaking, a therapeutic relationship can be defined as the 'feelings and attitudes that therapists and clients have toward one another and the manner in which these are expressed' (Norcross, 2002, p.7). In therapy, the relationship is thought to derive from various qualities and practices of the therapist (e.g. capacity to empathise), in conjunction with the characteristics and participation of the client (e.g. motivation to change). These facets of the relationship are brought together in the therapeutic work in what Norcross (2002) refers to as a 'complex reciprocal interaction … a deep synergy' (p.8). The interaction is thought to be based on the different methods that are used by the therapist, the goals that are agreed and the specific techniques that are applied. Clinical outcomes are assumed to be based on this combination of factors.

The work of the American Psychological Association (APA) Task Force, as reported by Norcross (2001), identified six variables in the therapeutic relationship that were 'demonstrably effective', as defined from the research literature. These included the therapeutic alliance, empathy, goal consensus and collaboration (ingredients primarily provided by the therapist), and ways of customising therapy on the basis of the client's behaviours or qualities (i.e. dealing with resistance and addressing functional impairments/ distress). In addition, this task force noted a number of additional relationship variables that were considered to be 'promising and probably effective'. These were positive regard, congruence/genuineness, feedback, repair of alliance ruptures, self-disclosure, management of counter-transference, and the quality of relational interpretations.

In summary, according to the task force, therapy outcomes were a product of the interaction between therapist factors and patient factors, both operating through a relationship that they likened to a diamond, in the sense that there were multiple facets. Whatever the metaphor, this basic logic has been applied since at least the work of Freud in the late 19th century; he referred to making a 'collaborator' of the client (for a summary, see Safran & Muran, 2000). Freud's prime focus was on the transference phenomenon, but apparently he also recognised the importance of friendliness, affection and the 'analytic pact'. The idea gradually developed to the point where the therapeutic alliance was widely accepted, and defined in terms of an agreement about goals, the joint tackling of the tasks that are necessary to achieve those goals (mutual engagement in the tasks), and an emotional bond that develops between therapist and client (sometimes called rapport: Bordin, 1979). Bordin took the view that the bond developed as a result of either working together on the tasks (an emergent property) and/ or on the basis of shared emotional experiences. These were thought to centre on the feelings of liking, caring and trusting that emerge from mutual engagement in a task.

As this summary of the alliance indicates, in this chapter, I will continue to draw on the different literatures that are related to supervision, particularly the fruitful psychotherapy field. As a consequence, analogies between the phenomena of therapy and those of supervision are made explicitly. In the case of relationships, this appears to be a widely accepted practice. For example, Bernard and Goodyear (2004) are amongst those who note that Bordin's (1979) reasoning on the therapeutic alliance applies equally well to supervision. Some rare empirical evidence to support this view has been provided by Patton and Kivlighan (1997), who found a significant association between the supervisees' alliance in supervision and in their subsequent therapy (though the technical skills practised in supervision were not replicated in therapy). However, there has thankfully been some relevant and recent research within the supervision field, and this will provide the main basis for the account of relationship factors in this chapter. Therefore, I will next provide a definition of the alliance in supervision, then go on to describe some of those facets of the relationship 'diamond' within supervision. Practical implications of these facets will then be specified. The next major part of the chapter will be concerned with the conditions that are necessary for these facets of the alliance to operate successfully. This will draw on those 'probably effective' relationship variables noted above, in order to consider the process of relationship rupture and repair (and similar vital processes), within the evolving supervisory relationship. The final part of this chapter examines the kinds of results that can be expected if the conditions for a gem of an alliance are satisfied. Knowing about likely results helps supervisors by clarifying the kinds of micro-outcomes that they can expect to see within successful supervision.

Defining the Supervision Alliance

Although Bordin's initial work focused on the therapeutic alliance (Bordin, 1979), he subsequently extended this work to include supervision (Bordin, 1983). Supporting my penchant for drawing on findings from therapy to inform supervision (Milne, 2007b), Bordin's extension of the concept of alliance to supervision retained the three-part approach (i.e. an agreement about the goals and tasks of supervision, cemented by an emotional bond). Shared goals refer to the specification of objectives within the supervision experience, and more broadly to ensuring that mutual expectations are clarified (Bernard & Goodyear, 2004). Whereas the specification of learning objectives for supervision is normally relatively concrete and straightforward, being recorded within a learning contract, the notion of 'expectations' is meant to cover the kinds of anticipatory beliefs that the supervisee (in particular) will have about the nature and outcomes of supervision. Therefore, Bernard and Goodyear (2004) encourage supervisors to be as clear about the expectations that each party has as they are about the more familiar learning objectives.

A complementary process definition has been generated by Efstation *et al.* (1990). They saw the alliance as: '… that sector of the overall relationship between the participants in which supervisors act purposively to influence trainees through their use of technical knowledge and skill and in which trainees act willingly to display their acquisition of that knowledge and skill ... that set of actions interactively used by supervisors and trainees to facilitate the learning of the trainee' (p.323).

Facets of the alliance

Bernard and Goodyear (2004) have provided a helpful breakdown of some of the supervisor behaviours that contribute to the learning alliance. Based on a series of correlational studies, they summarised how the supervisor can facilitate the alliance. This includes appropriate confidentiality (ethical behaviour), basing feedback and other evaluations on the agreed objectives of supervision (evaluative practices); a supervisory style that includes features such as an interpersonally sensitive and task- orientated approach (style), and moderate levels of supervisor self-disclosure (e.g. regarding personal experiences and struggles at work). Reflecting the relationship-base to supervision, another helpful element was the supervisee's perception that the supervisor had expert knowledge to offer, but that the supervisee was recognised for his or her own input (use of power).

Scaife (2001) has provided a practical elaboration of these findings, under the psychodynamic concept of developing a 'safe base' in supervision. She suggests that supervisors: demonstrate things to the supervisee, before asking them to undertake a task; share work openly with trainees (e.g. showing tapes or encouraging the supervisee to sit in on their work); always take a respectful approach to clients and colleagues, so that the supervisee sees that the supervisor is unlikely to prove unreliable; keep confidences and be consistent in relation to what they say and do; ensure that any challenges are specific and work related, providing supervisees with clear guidance on how they can regulate the supervisor's challenges; and be prepared to take responsibility where difficult issues are at stake (e.g. client safety).

These kinds of facets of the alliance can be identified within the different instruments that are used to measure clinical supervision. For example, the Manchester Clinical Supervision Scale (Winstanley, 2000) includes six items relevant to the alliance within the factor called 'support', part of the restorative function of supervision. This is meant to measure the extent to which the supervisee feels socially supported by the supervisor. Items include: 'I can unload during my clinical supervision session'; 'my supervisor

Table 4.1 The six factors in the Supervisory Relationship Questionnaire (SRQ; Palomo, 2004), together with some action implications

Components	Definitions and examples	Possible actions
A. Facilitative conditions (variance accounted for in SRQ scores)		
1. 'Safe base' (52%)	Supervisee feeling valued, respected and safe. Supervisor supportive, trustworthy and responsive	Empathise and connect emotionally (e.g. through self-disclosure); seek understanding and consensus (e.g. shared expectations); offer warmth and respond to learner's needs; avoid hostility, criticism and being judgemental.
2. 'Structure' (4.5%)	Maintaining practical boundaries, like time	Be clear about duration and purpose (including shared goals/joint agenda-setting); regular and structured supervision.
3. 'Commitment' (2.9%)	Supervisor interested in supervision and supervisee	Show interest and enthusiasm; be approachable and attentive; offer constructive feedback; address and repair alliance ruptures.
B. Goals and tasks		
4. 'Role model' (2.2%)	Supervisor perceived as skilled, knowledgeable and respectful	Draw on experience within system; provide practical support; demonstrate your approach and key skills, especially respect for patients and colleagues.
5. 'Reflective education' (1.9%)	Facilitating learning through supervisee's reflection; sensitive to supervisee's anxieties	Draw on multiple models flexibly; encourage reflection; foster theory–practice integration; promote interesting discussions of techniques; focus on the process of supervision (including acknowledging the power differential).
6. 'Formative feedback' (1.8%)	Constructive and regular, including positive and negative feedback; tailored to stage of supervisee's development	Encourage interest in feedback from the supervisee, adapting it to fit his/her understanding and level of confidence; provide feedback regularly, including positive and negative comments, made in a balanced, constructive way.

gives me support and encouragement'; and 'my supervisor is very open with me'. Similarly, the Working Alliance Inventory (adapted for supervision by Bahrick, 1990; NB: a copy is appended to the Falender & Shafranske text, 2004) was based on the Bordin model, so not surprisingly it includes the three elements of goals, agreement on tasks, and bond. The Supervisory Working Alliance Inventory (Efstation *et al.*, 1990) contains a 'rapport' factor (e.g. 'My supervisor stays in tune with me during supervision'), whilst one of the first such instruments, the Supervisory Styles Inventory (SSI; Friedlander & Ward, 1984), included an interpersonally sensitive 'counsellor' style of relating (NB: a copy of the unpublished SSI is appended to the Bernard &Goodyear text, 2004).

More recently, the Supervisory Relationship Questionnaire (SRQ; Palomo, 2004) has been developed. As summarised in Table 4.1, six coherent factors were identified within the SRQ, following analysis of the replies of 284 trainee clinical psychologists. The SRQ has 67 items and good psychometric properties, including acceptable reliability and convergent validity. As noted in Table 4.1, this analysis also supported the Bordin (1983) model, finding the essential emphasis on sharing expectations and clarifying objectives jointly, plus an emotional bond. However, the SRQ goes beyond these core elements to articulate additional facets of the supervisory alliance, including the 'safe base' stressed by Scaife (2001). The practical value of this six-fold definition of alliance is illustrated by the third column of Table 4.1, as these facets help to suggest actions that supervisors might take to promote their supervisory alliance.

Given my emphasis on drawing analogies, it is appropriate to contrast these alliance instruments with examples published in the therapy literature. A case in point is the Agnew Relationship Measure (ARM; Agnew-Davies *et al.*, 1998). The ARM was developed explicitly to obtain clients' and therapists' views of CBT and an exploratory therapy alternative. A total of 95 clients and 5 therapists completed the ARM after every session within a comparative outcome evaluation (the second Sheffield psychotherapy project). As a result, five factors were extracted: 'bond' (client feeling friendly towards the therapist; the therapist being accepting, understanding, supporting, and warm towards the client); 'partnership' (where the therapist and client agree on what to work on, and are willing to work hard to achieve these objectives); 'confidence' (where the client has confidence in the therapist, and is optimistic and finds the therapist's skills impressive); 'openness' (where the client feels free to express worries and embarrassment, does not keep things to him or herself and can express feelings and reveal things);

and 'client initiative' (where the therapist empowers the client to take the lead and enables him or her to look for solutions and to take responsibility).

It can be seen that there is considerable overlap between the Agnew Relationship Measure and this SRQ in the areas of the emotional bond (touched on within the safe base and commitments parts of the SRQ), in the efforts to work jointly towards an agreed goal ('partnership' in the ARM; 'structure and commitment' within the SRQ) and in the third main area of the traditional Bordin (1983) definition of alliance, the capacity to work jointly to specify those objectives. However, clear differences are present in relation to two distinctive facets of supervision. Unlike therapy, supervision involves an explicit, formal evaluation function (covered by factor six, formative 'feedback' within the SRQ), and an educative function (covered by the 'reflective education' factor within the SRQ). These predicted differences between the two professional activities helps to show where alliance is continuous with therapy, and where it is important to recognise a boundary to analogies.

The Process of Alliance Development

As the above instruments hint, the APA task force's analogy (Norcross, 2001), likening the relationship to a multifaceted diamond, appears somewhat inadequate. This is because the so-called facets of the alliance (such as offering a collaborative, task-focused relationship) are not fixed. Rather, they are the transient states within a dynamic process of relating, because supervisor and supervisee are 'responsive' to one another in an emerging pattern (Stiles & Shapiro, 1994). This 'open system' logic was set out in the preceding chapter.

To underscore this dynamic view, consider Table 4.1 again. Note how the definition, examples and actions are all dependent upon an unfolding process between supervisor and supervisee. For example, for the first factor to emerge ('safe base') the supervisor needs to be responsive, connecting emotionally to material brought by the supervisee (e.g. by disclosing doubts about his or her competence). Similarly, maintaining an appropriate, bounded structure to sessions and sustaining commitment and interest requires the mutual engagement of both parties. Perhaps the clearest way to underscore this point is to draw attention to situations where the alliance breaks down. Bernard and Goodyear (2004) have summarised 'how to be a lousy supervisor'. This turns the preceding advice upside-down, and extends it, by drawing out some of the lessons from research on the alliance. Lousy supervision includes not revealing your own shortcomings; not providing a sense of safety wherein doubts and fears can be discussed; placing service needs above the supervisee's educational needs; ignoring the need for emotional support from the supervisee; ignoring the supervisee's strengths and interests; and not recognising the need to share responsibility for any interpersonal conflicts that may arise. According to Falender and Shafranske (2004), one of the main ways in which the supervisory alliance may be threatened is due to supervisees having negative reactions to their clients, because the client undermines the forming of an alliance (e.g. due to having a narcissistic or anti-social personality). They take the view, consistent with the bulk of the relevant literature, that such strains within the supervisory alliance are not only common, but are, paradoxically, the basis from which the alliance can develop.

Whatever their source, disagreements and misunderstandings in supervision (or therapy) can contribute to what Falender and Shafranske (2004) refer to as alliance 'ruptures and impasses'. With Safran and Muran (2000), they note that supervision is a particularly vital opportunity for supervisees to begin to repair ruptures to their therapeutic alliances. Given that the development of competence is one of the primary objectives of the supervisee, and that an uncooperative client is an impediment to demonstrating competence, addressing therapeutic ruptures is a pivotal topic. It is one in which the bond between the supervisor and supervisee is of particular significance, as there is reason to believe that the quality of the alliance in supervision will influence the quality of the supervisee's therapy alliances (Patton & Kivlighan, 1997). It is also an environment where the supervisees can feel safe to discuss such threatening material as their perceived incompetence, and can commence the repair work. The threat may arise from something that happened (e.g. angry allegations by the client), or from the absence of alliance-related behaviours (e.g. non-compliance with an assignment). It is easy for supervisees to perceive such events as implying their incompetence. However, it appears that supervisees who report receiving empathic supervision, and feel safe in expressing themselves, regard their clinical work as more effective (Kavanagh *et al.*, 2003). The same study, based on a survey of 272 multidisciplinary supervisors and supervisees in Australia's public health service (i.e. all qualified staff), also reported highly significant correlations between perceived clinical effectiveness and gaining skills and confidence through supervision, so there is some basis for assuming that establishing a good alliance promotes competence. A further reason for optimism is that supervisees reporting a good supervision alliance show adherence to the therapy approach addressed in supervision, where this adherence was observed directly from video recordings, and rated by judges (Patton & Kivlighan, 1997).

In order to repair ruptures arising from things like a disagreement over the supervisee's competence, the procedure advocated by Safran and Muran (2000) for addressing therapy impasses can usefully be extended to supervision. According to this approach, the supervisor would explore with the supervisee the kinds of thoughts and feelings underpinning these events, modelling an open, collaborative stance. Other contributions to the repair work, in both supervision and subsequent therapy, are appropriate disclosure by the supervisor of their own experiences of ruptures, processing reactions, discussing options, building understanding, and re-engaging in a repair process with the supervisee and/or client. Helpful verbatim accounts of resolving alliance ruptures are provided by Ladany *et al.* (2005), who agree that this rupture-repair approach can be applied within supervision. Their account covers problems with counter-transference, parallel process, and other common difficulties.

It is clear from this account of the responsive, dynamic process of relating effectively to the supervisee in relation to ruptures that the supervisor requires a measure of insight (e.g. to be able to self-disclose persuasively). Within the psychodynamic and humanistic traditions this is aided by the process of personal therapy. Latterly, a process of 'self-practice, self-reflection' has been advocated in relation to CBT (Bennett-Levy & Thwaites, 2007). Based on a cognitive model of how therapists develop competence, they outline a six-stage reflective process for heightening self-awareness, improving understanding, and rehearsing possible solutions to relationship difficulties in supervision. This is 'self-practice' as some of the methods of CBT are applied reflexively to the CBT practitioner. Specifically, attention is focused on a problematic event (e.g. a relationship rupture), and imagery or role-play may be used to heighten awareness of relevant thoughts or feelings. This leads to cognitive clarification through reflection, and on to an enhanced conceptualisation of that event. The final stages are behavioural rehearsal, so as to practise how to apply the new understanding (role-plays may be used again), and to test out the strategy in therapy.

I believe that the process of addressing alliance ruptures through processes such as 'self-reflection, self-practice' can helpfully be considered in terms of a general process of assimilation, tackled by 'working through' the experience in supervision. According to the assimilation model (Stiles *et al.*, 1990), a problematic experience such as a rupture can be thought of as triggering a sequence of events. Most commonly the supervisee will initially want to 'ward off' the problematic experience, to avoid unwanted thoughts and feelings that cause discomfort. At this initial stage there may be only a vague awareness of the precise nature of the difficulty. But as the process of working through commences (as per the accounts of repair work above), the supervisee may be helped to specify and gradually clarify aspects of the unpleasant experience. As progress is made in understanding the problem, greater insight may be achieved, initiating a process of applying oneself to solving the difficulty. This phase of working through would lead to some problem resolution and closure. This sequence of events is understood to involve increasingly positive affect and gradually decreasing attention (i.e. the discomfort is replaced by a sense of understanding or mastery, and a negative cognitive preoccupation with the problematic event is replaced with an ability to focus on other things).

A related account of the process of moving from upset to mastery is the 'resolution' model in therapy (Greenburg & Malcolm, 2002). This is similar in having six steps within the process, but draws on the Gestalt approach to address how clients work through unresolved emotional experiences. In the first phase of emotional difficulty the interaction may feature blame, complaint and/or hurt. Using the 'empty chair' dialogue technique from the Gestalt approach, the supervisor may then play the role of the client, to re-enact these emotions. This may result in the expression of intense primary emotions, and the job of the therapist is to heighten awareness, to encourage differentiation, and to clarify the associated emotions. In the next phase of successful resolution these emotions are expressed more precisely, and the unmet interpersonal needs of the client are then identified and voiced. This heralds the penultimate phase in the resolution model, namely a shift in perspective: at this stage the client begins to develop a more complex and detached view of their antagonist. Finally, resolution occurs when the client is able to show increased understanding, empathy, compassion or forgiveness for the offending incident.

Textbooks on supervision contain numerous practical suggestions for enabling these processes of assimilation/resolution. For example, in CBT supervision, Liese and Beck (1997) suggest that the supervisor attend to the personal issues that the supervisee brings (e.g. passivity; avoidance), urging the supervisor to conceptualise them by raising the same kinds of questions as they would in therapy (e.g. 'What are the relevant prior experiences?'), and similarly to collaborate over problem-solving. Campbell (2006) also suggests sharing responsibility for solving problems; clarifying the factors that contribute to the problem (a variety of interesting questioning styles are suggested, including solution-focused questions); clarifying what efforts the supervisee has made to date to address the difficulty, noting anything that worked partially or for a brief time, and exploring the meaning that an event has for the supervisee (with questions such as 'What does it mean to you to be thought incompetent?' 'When this event happened how did you interpret it?). In this work it is important to focus on specifics, and to try to clarify the key details, through techniques like summarising and paraphrasing.

In this work, Campbell (2006) rightly stresses the role of the supervisee, having sub-sections concerning working with 'perfectionistic', 'defensive' or 'resistant' supervisees. This emphasis on the supervisee's contribution is echoed in Bernard and Goodyear's textbook (2004), as they dedicate a whole chapter to such topics as their attachment styles, avoidance of shame or embarrassment, anxiety, need to feel competent, and their transference towards the supervisor. Relatedly, a survey of 176 counselling supervisors and supervisees identified ways that supervisees could facilitate supervision (Vespia *et al.*, 2002). The top three were thought to be demonstrating a willingness to grow (41 per cent of respondents endorsed this item), demonstrating respect and appreciation for individual differences (29 per cent), and demonstrating an understanding of one's own personal dynamics as they relate to therapy and supervision (28 per cent). In these kinds of ways, it is important to give supervisees the opportunity to play their part in repairing the supervisory relationship. Careful, empathic discussion is appropriate, and care should be taken to engage supervisees with the appropriate support structures/authorities that exist within their system (as trainees or employees), and to abide by normal conventions of professional good practice (such as careful record-keeping). Ultimately, the supervisees should be given a realistic opportunity to make the appropriate changes, and should feel sufficiently supported within the system that they operate.

In a small analysis of the 20 different contributions that supervisees felt they made to effective supervision, collaborating closely with the supervisor constituted 40 per cent of comments (Milne & Gracie, 2001). Figure 6.1 in Chapter 6 presents the full results.

Of course supervisors and supervisees should collaborate in an effort to repair and strengthen their alliance. But what if this fails? In a novel section, Campbell (2006) recommends that the supervisor seeks consultation and guidance on how best to proceed, including approaching the director of the relevant training programme (if appropriate). If this is to no avail, it should be possible for supervisors to discontinue their rupture-repairing efforts, although it is obviously ideal for the supervisor to model the repair/assimilation/resolution process. Ultimately, all parties should be aware that the job of the supervisor is to ensure safe and effective clinical practice. If this cannot be ensured, then the supervisor is duty-bound to discontinue supervision and to alert the appropriate authorities (e.g. a licensing body or manager).

'Games' that are played in supervision

At several points in the above account there is an implicit recognition of a power dimension within alliance-building (and indeed within supervision generally, as in the supervisor's formal authority to pass or fail a trainee). Power has been defined as 'the ability to influence others' behaviours and attitudes' (Bernard & Goodyear, 2004, p.173). This power is thought to derive from a variety of sources, including the formal authority invested in the supervisor by some training institution or professional organisation, but also in relation to their expertness, attractiveness (i.e. being seen as an appealing professional model) and trustworthiness. These qualities gave the supervisor credibility and a basis for influencing the supervisee, without recourse to the more negative end of the power continuum, characterised by coercion. Again, however, it is important to keep the supervisee within our vista, since power partly emerges from the interpersonal interaction between the supervisor and supervisee. On this logic, the supervisor's authority is simply the basis on which a process of negotiation concerning status unfolds. For instance, the process can be referred to as complementary (where there is an unequal amount of power), or symmetrical (where the parties have equal status). In the former process, the negotiation is straightforward and both parties accept the relative power of the supervisor, enabling a smooth and productive interactional process. By contrast, symmetrical interactions are thought to engender tension, and to be less productive (Tracey, 2002).

Kadushin (1968) has provided an amusing account of some of the ways in which the supervisee may attempt to exert counter-control over the traditionally more powerful supervisor, couched in terms of inter-personal 'games'. The definition of games in supervision is 'an ongoing series of complementary ulterior transactions that are superficially plausible but have a concealed motivation to maximise pay-offs and minimise penalties for the initiator' (McIntosh *et al.*, 2006, p.225). According to Kadushin (1968), games that can be played by the supervisee to reduce the power disparity include 'BBC-manship', a game whereby the supervisee insists on a very high level of technical accomplishment before proceeding with an assignment. For example, the daunting requirement to produce a tape recording of his or her work may result in a series of conversations in which the anxious and avoidant supervisee plays the game of insisting that the technical quality of the recording equipment first be improved. This technical wizardry becomes the stalling tactic that ultimately avoids actually playing that tape to the more powerful supervisor. Other broad categories noted in this tradition are controlling the situation (e.g. 'heading the supervisor off at the pass'; and 'one good question deserves another'); redefining the relationship, so that the supervisor comes to treat the supervisee more like a client ('treat me, don't beat me'), or a colleague ('evaluation is not for friends'); and manipulating demand (including 'two against the agency' and 'seduction by flattery').

Such light-hearted accounts provide some welcome respite from what can be a challenging business. Although it is tempting for generally democratic professionals to abdicate their supervisory power in favour of some kind of collegial collusion, this is ultimately misguided, because of their responsibility for the welfare of the client (and for the development of competence in the supervisee). Rather, the supervisor's task is to work closely and openly with the supervisee in order to find way of devolving the power appropriately: the objective is to reduce the imbalance, within the bounds of delivering the supervisory goods (e.g. as a supervisee in initial training reaches the final clinical experience episode).

Research on power relationships in supervision include the work of Penman (1980), who created a recording system that allowed one to observe and analyse supervisory interaction in relation to the dimensions of power and involvement. This encouraged some research within the supervision field, which indicated, for example, that supervisors were more likely to reinforce high power statements when they were made by male supervisees than when these were uttered by their female counterparts (Nelson & Holloway, 1990). This demonstrated how gender affected the utilisation of power within supervision.

McIntosh *et al.* (2006) conducted a survey of supervisors of genetic counsellors, concerning their encounters with destructive game-playing (games initiated by supervisor or supervisee that interfere with the supervisee's realisation of training goals). This survey suggested that destructive games do occur in live supervision, and these were similar to the games that have been reported by other health professionals. Consistent with Kadushin's (1968) summary, which is drawn from social work, McIntosh *et al.* (2006) found that the most common supervisee-initiated game reported in their survey was 'poor me'. They also described new games, such as 'make this little change'. This is a supervisor-initiated power game in which picky feedback (e.g. relating to letter-writing) is provided to the supervisee, in order to exert authority. These games highlight the great depth, breadth and subtlety of supervisory relationships, and their decidedly interactive nature. I will return to this theme in Chapter 9, in order to provide a 'case study' in supporting a local supervisor to redress some game-playing that undermined her capacity to supervise.

Power struggles were also reported from an intensive qualitative inquiry with trainees (Nelson & Friedlander, 2001). The majority of the 13 participants reported impasses over roles, supervisors who seemed to feel threatened, and about the content of supervision. And, in the majority of cases, the supervisors were perceived by the supervisees to have denied responsibility or behaved irresponsibly. This had the effect of undermining the supervisees' trust and involvement, and contributing to their self-doubts and fears. For the majority of these trainees the struggle was never resolved, with avoidance, cynicism and distrust persisting. The authors conjectured that this ongoing conflict probably detracted from the supervisees' clinical work (mirroring the positive transfer in situations where the alliance is strong). In a similar qualitative study by Gray *et al.* (2001), the trainees were of the view that their 'counter-productive' experiences within supervision had negatively affected their clinical work. Understandably, most of them did not raise this concern in their supervision.

This parallels the ways that clients are thought to withdraw in therapy, when there is a 'rupture' (e.g. using 'story-telling', 'denial' and 'minimal responses': Safran & Muran, 2000). These authors are also of the opinion that ruptures in supervision can affect therapy, and vice versa: 'impasses in the supervisory relationship … translate into impasses in the therapeutic relationship. A therapist who is feeling judged by his supervisor is more likely to feel self-critical with his patients … (which is) … likely to translate into negative therapeutic process' (p.215). This can further accentuate criticism from the supervisor, and contribute to a vicious cycle.

Outcomes of Successful Supervisory Alliances

Although some degree of game-playing and power-struggling may well characterise most supervision, it appears rarely to disrupt it seriously. I say this based on the experience of monitoring supervision within a training programme (i.e. based on personal experience of hundreds of supervision dyads), and because the evidence consistently indicates that supervision 'works', whether judged by the participants (e.g. Kavanagh *et al.*, 2003) or more objectively evaluated (e.g. Tharenou, 2001). Therefore, I next want to consider how the alliance contributes to the general effectiveness of supervision.

The important outcomes that follow from a strong alliance in supervision were indicated over 20 years ago by Bordin (1983), who listed eight anticipated benefits, such as enhanced competence in the supervisee. To illustrate, Rabinowitz *et al.* (1986) asked 45 trainees at different stages in their training programme to rate what they regarded to be the most important processes and outcomes in their weekly supervision. The trainees put gaining competence as their most important outcome, and rated the most important process as that of 'supporting, reassuring and nurturing' by the supervisor. In stark contrast, the least important process, as judged by these supervisees, was the supervisor engaging in 'challenging, confronting and disagreeing'. Rabinowitz *et al.* (1986) found that these patterns were surprisingly consistent across the different stages of supervisee development studied, leading them to suggest that they were 'the universal elements of the supervision process' (p.298).

As this study indicates, when the facets of the alliance are present and an appropriate process occurs, then we can indeed expect to see some important outcomes within the supervisory relationship (what we might think of as the 'mini-outcomes'). According to Bernard and Goodyear (2004), there are two empirically supported examples, based on research since 1983. These are the willingness of the supervisee to disclose material to the supervisor, and the subsequent quality of the alliance (which is associated with more significant outcomes, such as improved alliances within subsequent therapy: see, e.g., Patton & Kivlighan, 1997). To underscore this dynamic pattern with a negative example, Bernard and Goodyear (2004) cited a study by Ladany *et al.* (1996), in which it was reported that 90 per cent of their respondents had omitted to disclose some negative feelings towards a supervisor, and 44 per cent had failed to disclose clinical mistakes or general observations of import (e.g. diagnoses). The main reasons cited for not disclosing were that the material was perceived as being too personal (73 per cent), too unimportant (62 per cent) or, in 50 per cent of cases, due to a poor alliance with the supervisor. Presumably a better alliance is associated with greater disclosure, an important mini-outcome in terms of allowing the supervisor access to potentially valuable information, not to mention the role it can play in enhancing the emotional bond.

The integrative approach to supervision (Norcross & Halgin, 1997) illustrates this kind of process, and the linked major outcomes: '… good supervisors are those who use appropriate teaching, goal-setting, and feedback; they tend to be seen as supportive, non-critical individuals who respect their supervisees' (p.212). They believe that relating to supervisees in this way helps them to feel understood and supported. The ideal relationship within the integrative approach is seen as collegial, empathic and collaborative, whilst acknowledging professional responsibilities and power disparities. This relationship stance is thought to facilitate the expression of insecurities, respectful disagreement and the generation of options (in relation to the ongoing clinical work). They contrast this with a more dogmatic and authoritarian style, in which supervisors fundamentally demand conformity and punish divergence.

An empirical example of the outcomes arising from the alliance is the national survey of counsellor trainees in the USA, conducted by Ladany *et al.* (1999). In an attempt to test Bordin's (1983) model, they asked 107 trainees to complete questionnaires measuring their confidence, their alliance with the supervisor (Bahrick's Working Alliance Inventory, 1990), and their satisfaction with supervision at two time points, approximately two months apart. According to Bordin (1983), a good alliance should be positively correlated with desired supervision outcomes, which in this study was assessed by the trainees' confidence and satisfaction. These researchers did find the expected association between the emotional bond aspect of the alliance and satisfaction, in that stronger bonds were positively correlated with satisfaction, while conversely trainees reporting weaker bonds reported less satisfaction. But none of the remaining correlations reached significance, leaving the authors wondering whether their methodology was the reason for their failure to verify the Bordin model, or whether the model itself was flawed.

Using different measures, more advanced trainees and only one data point, Efstation *et al.* (1990) did obtain a significant correlation between the alliance and confidence, so there is reason to suppose that the Ladany *et al.* (1999) methodology was the reason for their generally non-significant results. But Ladany *et al.* (1999) also highlighted difficulties with the model. Specifically, Bordin (1983) made the assumption that the supervisory and therapeutic alliances were equivalent, but (as noted elsewhere) there are at least two fundamental differences between them (i.e. the presence within supervision of competence evaluation and mandatory participation). Amongst their recommendations, they urged that future research includes a more appropriate, supervision-specific alliance instrument (such as the SRQ). They also wondered about the appropriateness of assessing supervisee satisfaction, since they recognise that effective supervision, involving as it does some 'struggle' (p.454), may not be experienced as satisfying. Better options, they thought, included the clinical interactions of the supervisee. This measurement point will be picked up again in Chapter 8.

Critical Review

To clinicians it must seem self-evident that the quality of the supervisory alliance is crucial to the effectiveness of supervision, as reflected in the consensus-based identification of alliance-building as a core competence for the supervisor (Falender *et al.*, 2004). Similarly, the Association of Directors of Psychology Training Clinics in the USA produced a list of key competencies in the supervisee. This included the ability to interact collaboratively and respectfully with colleagues, including specifically 'the ability to use supervision', an ability defined as working collegially and responsively with supervisors (Hatcher & Lassiter, 2007).

But it needs to be acknowledged that there is surprisingly little evidence to support this assumption. An incredibly meticulous systematic review located only two rigorous studies of the alliance, which reported only modest support for the assumption (Ellis & Ladany, 1997), consistent with the examples above. Specifically, they found some tentative support for the notion that the alliance may be related to both the supervisor's style and the supervisees' self-confidence. They concluded that the studies they located and scrutinised presented only modest evidence that the supervisory relationship was related to a few specific processes and outcomes. However, the available data did not clarify adequately what constituted the studied relationships. There were also methodological weaknesses with much of the other research that they found, including the use of new measures with only preliminary psychometric data. They called for better, unique definitions of the supervisory alliance, and it is comforting to note (from the above account of instruments like the SRQ) that some progress is now being made on that score.

In keeping with the sobering conclusions of Ellis and Ladany (1997), the reviews by Milne and James (2000) and Milne, Aylott, Fitzpatrick *et al.* (2008) found few manipulations of the supervision alliance in their sample of successful supervision interventions. That is, it appears to be possible to provide effective supervision without an explicit emphasis on the alliance. However, it seems unlikely that the alliance was irrelevant or unnecessary, as the methods that were reported in these successful studies were consistent with traditional concepts of the important ingredients and processes in the supervision alliance (e.g. collaboration; modelling; constructive feedback). Rather, this lack of emphasis might better be viewed as evidence for the accepted role of the alliance.

Conclusions

Therefore, although professional consensus is unanimous in affirming the importance of the supervisory alliance (e.g. Falender *et al.*, 2004; Hatcher & Lassiter, 2007), evidence to support the assumption is surprisingly wanting. Not only are there very few studies that directly assess variation in the alliance in relation to supervisory and clinical outcomes, but the studies that do exist tend to be methodologically weak (Ellis & Ladany, 1997). But, given the strong professional consensus supporting the importance of a strong supervisory alliance (see Padesky, 1996, for a CBT-based account), the practice implications of denying the importance of alliance, and the stronger research evidence from the parallel therapy literature (e.g. Lambert & Bergin, 1994), the position I adopt within this book is to assume that the alliance is crucial. A further reason for this position is that, in more general terms, we cannot deny that the relationship is the arena for supervision, nor the strong evidence for its importance within human development: 'relationship context strongly influences human behaviour and lifespan development' (Reis *et al.*, 2000, p.844). However, it is embarrassing that there is such a deficiency in the research sphere, and clearly significant work is indicated. It is hoped that the supervision-specific guidelines (Milne, 2007a) and instruments (such as the SRQ: Palomo, 2004) will herald better quality, affirmative research. The advent of such psychometrically enhanced, supervision-specific instruments will hopefully encourage researchers to better clarify the complex business of the alliance.

It may ease supervisors' embarrassment to know that the therapy process outcome literature has also encountered numerous difficulties in teasing out the relative contribution of the relationship to the success of therapy. Despite this, reviews of that literature indicate that the so-called common factors 'loom large as mediators of treatment outcome … we must attend to (them)' (Lambert, 2005, p.866). These common factors include a positive relationship that features reassurance and structure, the provision of corrective emotional experiences, and opportunities to regulate behaviour and master the way we think (Lambert, 1992).

5

Applying Supervision

Introduction

What are the main activities that supervisors should undertake within supervision? What goals or functions are they supposed to achieve? Which environmental factors are critical to these activities and functions? As these questions indicate, this chapter deals with what many would regard as the heart of the supervisory exercise, the facilitation of the supervisee's learning and development. In order to address these questions, I will build on the reframing of supervision that was set out in Chapter 3, particularly the augmented evidence-based clinical supervision (EBCS) model. Other relevant chapters will also be integrated, so that a coherent account of formative supervision can be developed. This creates a sound basis for the next chapter, which considers development from the supervisee's perspective.

There are a vast array of qualities and competencies attributed to the successful supervisor. In order to impose some sense of order and priority, I will next attempt to define the essential tasks and activities that confront the supervisor by drawing on the staff development literature for guidance. In order to define this supervision 'road map', and following the thinking presented in Chapter 3 (especially the 'supervision cycle'), it is proposed that these priorities are the conducting of an educational needs assessment, leading to the collaborative specification of the learning contract; the facilitation of the supervisee's learning, through the application of different educational methods; and finally the use of evaluation in order to monitor and optimally direct this development cycle. Therefore, it is proposed that supervision is basically a problem-solving cycle, one that pivots around the supervisor and supervisee, nested in the alliance and which occurs within an organisational context (the workplace environment, with the power to influence that interaction profoundly). This proposition is then tested against professional consensus (formal and informal) and the research literature. The remainder of the chapter adds detail and colour to this map, by considering important contextual considerations (including the ethical and legal dimensions; cultural competence), and then by deepening the account of the supervision cycle.

A Simple Road Map of Formative Supervision

This account of the essence of formative supervision is highly consistent with other reviews of the supervision literature, and with the staff development literature, a closely parallel body of knowledge that speaks directly to the business of formative supervision. For example, a major text in the area (Goldstein, 1993) is entitled *Training in Organisations: Needs Assessment, Development, and Evaluation*. This Goldstein book then has a chapter entitled 'A systematic approach to training' which unpacks these essential elements of the formative enterprise. Drawing on the field of instructional technology, this approach is underpinned by the principles of continuous feedback; recognition of the complex interactions that occur between different parts of the system (including interactions between learner characteristics and teaching methods); specifying the objectives of training and facilitating appropriate planning; and recognising the embeddedness of instruction within an organisational system. This can be represented within a classic model of staff development, as set out in Chapter 2 (see Figure 2.2). This account is based on the work of Goldstein (1993) and other experts within the staff development field (see Milne, 2007, for a summary of their work). As illustrated within Figure 2.2, the supervisor's initial task is to clarify the learner's status, with respect to the relevant supervisory experiences. In practice, this entails relating the learning opportunities within a supervision setting to the past experience of the supervisee, and to other important considerations (like the requirements of a professional body). Given this emphasis on the external considerations, Figure 2.2 proposes that evaluation measures are considered next, so that a clear idea is formed of the intended outcomes of supervision. Based on this initial work, the supervisor can begin to specify the content of the learning experience, conventionally recording this within a learning contract that is negotiated with the supervisee (and sometimes with other key stakeholders, such as the supervisee's line manager or a training programme). The content of this learning experience naturally implies the need to think about the methods and materials that will be required to enable the supervisee to address the content within the learning contract. Following on from this planning work, the supervisee will be assisted by the supervisor in the development of the requisite competencies. Although I've implied a 'top-down' approach thus far, I would wish to stress that I believe that effective supervision entails an appropriate balance between supervisor-led development and a more Socratic approach, one in which the supervisee is helped to acquire competence through his or her own initiative, as in an adult learning, experiential approach to supervision (Safran & Muran, 2000). Supervisees can therefore develop as a result of problem-based learning (i.e. where the supervisor encourages independent educational activity designed around the solution of a problem, normally clinical work in the mental health field). Such development activity is preceded by the designation of the supervisor, as per the definition within Chapter 1. This essential model of staff development conventionally proposes that the final task for the supervisor is to ensure that some form of evaluation is built into the supervisory system. As in other areas of professional activity, evaluation is vital if we are to determine the extent to which objectives are achieved. Evaluation data also provide the basis for properly grounded feedback, namely feedback that is suitably linked to those prior learning objectives and to any external points of reference (e.g. competency checklists generated by the supervisees' training programme). The final dimension identified within the model presented in Figure 2.2 recognises that these activities can only be understood properly within their context. This is apparent from the preceding sentences, as I have naturally chosen to give examples that imply the need to refer to the objectives that are set by the organisations that appoint supervisors, etc. In addition, there are a myriad of factors within the workplace which will play a part in influencing the way that the supervisor facilitates learning. This domain is sometimes referred to by phrases like 'situational variables', embracing such dimensions as the organisational climate, and the degree to which managers, peers and others provide support (Colquitt *et al.*, 2000). These authors also drew attention to characteristics of the learner, such as their personality, cognitive ability, and commitment to their development. In their meta-analysis, many of these factors were found to contribute to the learning outcomes that were obtained, and to the transfer of that learning to the workplace, as well as the performance of the learner on the job.

Testing the Road Map

I will detail these dimensions shortly, but first I want to address a question: is this essential account, drawn directly from the staff development literature, one that should be accepted within the supervision field? A significant test is a consensus statement on supervision produced by a group of American experts (Falender *et al.*, 2004). They defined the competencies required of supervisors, alongside thoughts on how supervisors should be trained and assessed. Based on this activity, Falender *et al.* (2004) drew up a framework that distinguished between the domains of the supervisors' relevant knowledge, skills and values, related to their social context (e.g. recognition of relevant ethical and legal issues). Do these competencies (a total of 34 across these 4 domains) agree with the essential staff development model as set out in Figure 2.2? In fact, these competencies appear to map onto this essential account fairly well. Specifically, Falender *et al.* (2004) note that (within the knowledge domain) supervisors should know about relevant models, and possess knowledge of professional/supervisee development. Presumably this would emerge from their understanding of approaches to formative supervision, which is dominated by developmental models (as summarised in Chapter 2). These are highly consistent with the outline in Figure 2.2, stressing such things as the importance of starting from the supervisees' developmental stage. Turning to the domain of skills, these authors go on to suggest that supervisors need to be competent in assessing the learning needs and developmental level of the supervisee. They also need to have relevant teaching skills, to draw on the scientific knowledge base, and to have competencies in providing 'effective formative and summative feedback' (p.778: relevant to the evaluation part of the model). Connecting to my emphasis on the setting, they also note, within their 'social context' dimension, that the competent supervisor has knowledge of the immediate system, and the kinds of expectations that exist within that system in relation to supervision. Therefore, Falender *et al.* (2004) expect the competent supervisor to be aware of the 'socio-political context within which supervision is conducted' (p.778), and to create an appropriate climate within supervision (balancing support with challenge appropriately).

In summary, there appear to be direct parallels and no disagreements between these two accounts of what is essential in formative supervision, with the Falender *et al.* (2004) one simply providing a more detailed specification.

Indeed, similarly consistent accounts of what formative supervision entails are provided in the main textbooks, such as Bernard and Goodyear (2004), and by the editor of the definitive *Handbook of Psychotherapy Supervision* (Watkins, 1997). Watkins (1997) stresses the importance of having a systematic, well-structured approach, featuring shared objectives, guided practice and constructive feedback. Within this text, Norcross and Halgin (1997) summarise some 'cardinal principles' of an integrative approach to supervision. These include customising supervision to take due account of the individual characteristics of supervisees; conducting a needs assessment; constructing explicit learning contracts; using a blend of supervision methods (such as didactic instruction, reading assignments, discussion, modelling, experiential activities, video material and case examples); assessing the supervisee's emergent therapy competencies; and evaluating the outcomes of supervision. These methods are consistent with a second consensus statement by American experts (Kaslow *et al.*, 2004). Reflecting this marked consensus, professional organisations have adopted approaches to supervision that strongly resemble Figure 2.2 and the essential account provided above (e.g. British Psychological Society (BPS), 2003).

Furthermore, this consensus on the primary tasks and activities of formative supervision is consistent with the research literature. I would like to illustrate this with two systematic reviews to which I have contributed. In the first of these (Milne & James, 2000), a systematic review was conducted of 28 studies in which CBT supervision was manipulated. These studies were carefully selected, partly on the basis of there being hard evidence that these manipulations were educationally and clinically successful. We found that these studies featured a range of methods for facilitating learning, most common amongst them being the use of feedback and discussion, followed by more experiential methods such as educational role-play and behavioural rehearsal. Less frequently utilised were live and video-based models of competent practice. Subsequently, I participated in a review of 24 studies, about half of them being within the above review (Milne, Aylott, Fitzpatrick *et al.*, 2008). We again found that these studies had utilised a wide range of methods (26 different methods in total), the most frequently used being different approaches to training and education (18 of the 24 studies used this method), feedback (16 studies), and observing/monitoring the supervisee (10 studies). On average, and consistent with the above consensus statements, each study used on average over six different methods to facilitate the supervisee's learning. A combined summary of the 'top ten' supervision methods within this literature is provided in Table 5.2.

Next, I will discuss the Falender *et al.* (2004) competencies framework in detail. The first area that I want to examine is the contextual backdrop to formative supervision. There is, of course, an almost endless list of influences within the workplace that could be included within this review. Therefore, my strategy will be to select a few critical examples, ones that appear strongly within the consensus statements and the empirical literature, and examine the evidence, advice and implications that arise from these.

Context for Facilitating Learning

Ethical supervision

The importance of ethical aspects of clinical supervision is a definite emphasis within the literature. For example, the Falender *et al.* (2004) consensus statement pertaining to the value base notes that competent supervisors should 'value ethical principles' (p.778), and additionally recognises the importance of 'ethical and legal issues' as part of the social context of supervision. There are a number of important dimensions to the ethical (i.e. proper conduct) of supervision, but these tend to revolve around three categories (Scaife, 2001). They are unethical practice (malpractice or professional misconduct), impairment (personal incapability) and incompetence (professional unsuitability). Fortunately, serious ethical difficulties appear to be rare: Falender and Shafranske (2004) reported that breaches of confidentiality and difficulties around maintaining appropriate relationship boundaries within professional practice generally were reported in 18 and 17 per cent (respectively) of incidents. Only 2 per cent of these instances occurred within supervision. However, minor examples may be far more common: Ladany (2002) surveyed supervisees in training and more than 50 per cent of them reported that they thought their supervisor had behaved unethically.

Unethical practice concerns breaching rules governing how one should work within an organisation, or conduct oneself within a profession. This subsumes inappropriate romantic and sexual relationships with supervisees (or their clients) and emotional instability (including overt anger and deception). Impairment consists of the diminished functioning of a supervisor, as in their inability to attend properly to their duties, perhaps due to stress, substance misuse or illness. Related difficulties may include poor or absent self-awareness of personal incapability, and/or an unwillingness to address any such problems. Perhaps the most straightforward category is that of incompetence, namely inadequate or absent performance of supervisory duties (e.g., making repeated, unacceptable errors).

Arising from these three areas of difficulty are some recurring, more specific ethical issues. One of these is confidentiality. As all professionals know, this is not absolute and it follows that supervisees need to inform their clients of the limits to confidentiality, including advising the client that the supervisee is in receipt of supervision. Therefore, supervisees should inform clients that the material that is discussed within therapy (or other kinds of work activity) is likely to be shared with that supervisor. It may also be disclosed to other parties too, in relation to the public interest (e.g. disclosing information about sexual abuse or terrorism). Similarly, it is important to be clear about the relative nature of confidentiality relating to material discussed within supervision, as in the degree to which information is shared with the relevant organisation or professional body. Customary advice is to make these limits explicit and to record them within the learning contract. Thankfully, normal conventions regarding professional practice apply straightforwardly to supervision. Examples are the 'parsimony principle', which dictates that a professional should disclose only the information that is necessary to address a particular issue, and the primacy of protecting clients.

A second classic area of ethical difficulty concerns accountability. In keeping with our definition of supervision (see Chapter 1), supervisors are accountable to the organisation that asks them to undertake supervision, as well as to their managers, professional body and other interested parties (i.e. there is always likely to be multiple accountability). Supervisors are accountable to these different people in relation to the performance of their duties, namely the specific responsibilities that they have agreed to undertake. In essence, these are as per Figure 2.2, such as negotiating an appropriate learning contract with the supervisee. Such accountability relationships include the right of bodies, such as the authorising organisation or employer, to hold the supervisor accountable when difficulties arise. This primarily includes responsibility for the supervisee's clinical practice, an area of particular difficulty for many supervisors (e.g. because they wish to empower and not oversee or take responsibility for the work of another professional). The 'cult of the positive' or of 'niceness' (Fleming *et al.*, 2007) makes most professionals feel decidedly awkward in exercising the authority that necessarily accompanies their accountability. But, strictly speaking, it is ethically and professionally appropriate for supervisors to make these formal relationships explicit with the supervisee, as in making it clear that ultimately the supervisor has the right to regulate the supervisee's work (e.g. to instruct a supervisee to discontinue a particular approach). In sum, supervisors who behave ethically need to exercise an appropriate level of authority (legitimate power), one that matches their level of accountability, which is managed in the conventional professional fashion. Problems can and do arise, and it is important that supervisors tackle these matters following 'due process'. This means that they should adhere closely to conventions and procedures that are set out within relevant organisations (e.g. the 'progress' regulations within a University training programme) or their professional body. In practice, this means that ethically informed supervisors know about relevant guidelines (e.g. regarding the treatment of lapses in confidentiality), and are aware of any codes or standards that may be relevant. This aids them in recognising issues that arise, and assists them in reconciling any conflicts of interest or ambiguities, working to seek an appropriate solution. This may involve gathering key information, consulting with relevant parties, and skilfully addressing issues within supervision. One helpful resource in tackling difficulties that may arise is to draw on problem-solving procedures that are relevant to ethical issues (see, for example, the five-step problem-solving cycle described by Knapp and VandeCreek, 2006). According to this procedure, the supervisor will:

1. identify or scrutinise the problem;
2. develop alternatives and hypotheses;
3. evaluate or analyse the options;
4. act or perform so as to minimise harm;
5. evaluate the actions in relation to their success in minimising harm.

   This kind of procedure can helpfully be guided by some core ethical principles. One of these is 'autonomy', which recognises that supervisees have certain rights to act freely and to exercise choice. This is perhaps most commonly recognised in the developmental progression of a supervisee through several years of pre-qualification training, during which they are gradually given greater autonomy. Secondly, there is the principle of 'beneficence', which emphasises that actions should do good, and are designed to promote human welfare. In this sense one might judge a confidentiality issue arising from the supervisee's practice in terms of the degree to which it helps or harms a particular client. Thirdly, there is the principle of 'fidelity'. This requires professionals to be faithful to any commitments or promises that they've made, and generally to act in a right or proper way (e.g. as per that earlier illustration of informing clients about how confidentiality is relative). Fourthly, there is the principle of 'justice'. This draws attention to the obligation to treat all people equally and fairly, taking account of what is due to people in the particular situation. For instance, a supervisor may judge that a trainee who is well intentioned but has yet to demonstrate competence is accorded extra help in order to progress. Lastly, there is 'non-maleficence', which is the converse of beneficence, namely striving to prevent harm to the supervisee or the people with whom he or she works. Reflecting on these principles in relation to particular ethical issues can be most helpful, and in any case does itself represent one part of ethical practice, the considered and informed reflection on issues that arise.

Legal context

If a supervisor is unethical, this may result in legal liability. This includes liability in law, liability to one's employer and liability to one's professional body. For instance, the latter may revoke the supervisor's licence or accreditation, until such time as ethical supervision can be assured. And, as touched on earlier, this may include a lack of assertiveness in preventing a supervisee from engaging in work that is beyond their competence. In order to comply with this expectation, it follows that the supervisor needs to know how competent the supervisee is (i.e. the initial needs assessment function within Figure 2.2). Similarly, it implies the need for the supervisor to actively monitor the supervisee's performance, and to give any indicated direction. In legal terms, the supervisor needs to take responsibility for the supervisee, subsuming any appropriate control over their activities (as in giving directions or instructions). Ultimately, the supervisor can be held accountable for the actions of their supervisee, and the supervisor's employer may be held vicariously responsible in law. Whilst different countries and states have somewhat different legal guidance, common liabilities are to:

1. facilitate the professional development of the supervisee;
2. inform clients in writing that therapy will be provided by a trainee, under the supervision of a suitably qualified person;

3. inform the supervisee in writing (commonly through the learning contract) about the content and methods of supervision, particularly how monitoring and evaluation will occur;
4. personally assess clients from time to time, in order to monitor treatment; and
5. document supervision (maintaining some kind of log or record, and requiring trainees to document what they are doing, both parties signing off these records).

These liabilities have arisen through the harsh examination of the legal system. For example, the facilitation of professional development has been underscored by a case brought before the courts in Delaware. Referred to as the 'Masterson verses Board of Examiners of Psychologists (1995)' case, the supervisor Masterson lost her licence because she allowed the supervisee to exploit social relationships (counselling a friend), amongst other things.

Ethical supervision is fortunately similar to ethical practice in other areas of professional life, and thankfully there are also detailed guidelines (e.g. BPS's 'Code of Ethics and Conduct', 2006), and detailed texts (e.g. Knapp & VandeCreek, 2006). In addition, as professionals, supervisors will have access to colleagues, managers and others who can reflect on difficulties with them, drawing on the above principles to engage in tackling ethical issues appropriately. These are ways in which the supervisor exercises due authority, though one hastens to add (in our cult of niceness) that these are bottom-line legal parameters: in practice, the supervisor would normally manage these issues in a low-key, sensitive and interpersonally effective fashion.

A solid value-base

The above underscores the view that one cannot function optimally as a supervisor without taking due account of the ethical and legal context. Similarly, supervisors need to be explicit about their value-base, and how this affects supervision. According to Falender *et al.* (2004), the following values are part of competent supervision:

- being respectful;
- taking responsibility (e.g. for addressing diversity in all of its forms);
- balancing support and challenge;

- empowering the supervisee;
- being committed to lifelong learning and professional growth;
- balancing clinical and training needs;
- valuing ethical principles;
- being committed to drawing on the knowledge-base (including the scientific literature on supervision);
- being committed to recognising one's own limitations.

Again, one is struck by the degree to which aspects of supervision overlap with many other aspects of professional practice. That is, one would expect professionals, well before they are sufficiently experienced to undertake supervision, to be already demonstrating many of these values (e.g. respect for their clients and a commitment to helping them change and grow). Because of this significant overlap, I will focus here on one key and potentially supervision-specific example, namely sensitivity to diversity. The other values listed above are covered elsewhere within the book (e.g. balancing support and challenging being a theme within the next chapter), or are assumed to be as per general professional practice.

Cultural competence

Cultural competence is the 'ability to engage in actions or create conditions that maximise the optimal development of the client and client systems … the acquisition of awareness, knowledge and skills needed to function effectively in a pluralistic, democratic society … and on an organisational/societal level, advocating effectively to develop new theories, practices … that are more responsive to all groups' (Sue & Torino, 2005, p.8). Implied in this definition is the ability to take different perspectives, to problem-solve flexibly and to recognise the influence of organisations or systems on our activities. It is therefore a dynamic process, carrying huge significance within our increasingly diverse societies (Whaley & Davis, 2007).

Culturally effective practice necessitates a rare degree of self-awareness and sensitivity, including the ability to respond appropriately to the individual characteristics of one's supervisees. This highlights the truth that competence in dealing with diversity entails both an awareness and a readiness on the part of the supervisor to recognise and address any issues that might arise, and to respond sensitively to any relevant characteristics of the supervisee. It is not apparent that supervisors are addressing issues fully, as indicated by a survey of cross-racial supervisee by Duan and Roehlke (2001). Their sample of 60 pairs of supervisors and supervisees provided views on cultural competence that suggested that the supervisors' perceptions of their efforts to address multi-cultural issues were exaggerated. More prominent, according to the supervisees, was the supervisors' positive attitudes to them. In reviewing a number of such studies, Bernard and Goodyear (2004, p.125) conclude that it is 'the willingness of the supervisor to open the cultural door and walk through it with the supervisee' that is of fundamental importance. Through an aware, caring and supportive approach, including self-disclosure and the provision of a 'safe space', this literature indicates that supervisors can manage cultural aspects to the satisfaction of their supervisees.

Culture is, of course, only one way in which we may differ from one another, and Hays (2001) has provided a handy summary of these characteristics in the form of the acronym ADDRESSING:

A: Age and generational influences
D: Developmental differences
D: Disabilities
R: Religion and spirituality
E: Ethnicity
S: Social economic status
S: Sexual orientation
I: Indigenous heritage
N: National origin
G: Gender

As Hays (2001) noted, each of these areas may interact with one another to create complex and unique individual characteristics. Authors tend to recommend that the uniqueness or diversity agenda is addressed openly and professionally within supervision, so that a collaborative approach can be taken to recognising how such differences influence our interactions (including those between supervisee and clients). As per ethical practice, fortunately there are a number of guidelines and standards that can assist the clinical supervisor in being culturally competent (see Whaley & Davis, 2007, for further examples). To illustrate, the American Psychological Association (2002) produced 'Guidelines on multi-cultural education, training, research, practice, and organisational change for psychologists'.

Of most relevance within the context of supervision is guideline 3. It states that, as educators, psychologists are encouraged to employ the constructs of multi-culturalism and diversity in psychological education. In support of this guideline, the document notes that cultural competence should be part of educational practice: there should be a due emphasis within teaching programmes and clinical supervision settings, one that is able to promote the student's self-awareness and cultural competence, and to help reduce processes such as stereotyping and automatic prejudicial judgements. It is noted that addressing such competencies explicitly may engender some resistance and so a challenge is identified for supervisors in creating a safe, facilitating learning environment, and to manage any emotions that may emerge (including a non-judgemental demeanour and self-disclosure). The guideline also encourages educators to increase their understanding of how the different perspectives that accompany diversity influence the knowledge-base. The aim is to 'facilitate respectful discussion ... positive modelling ... (as part of an appropriate) posture when teaching about multi cultural issues' (p.35).

Technological developments

In addition to the ethical and legal dimensions of supervision, it is worth noting some developments that build on the availability of new technology to create yet more contextual complexity. One example, already noted in Chapter 2, reflects our political context in the UK, with the advent of the case-based and outcome-orientated supervision that characterises the Improving Access to Psychological Therapies (IAPT) initiative. This 'high volume' emphasis necessarily means that the essential tasks of supervision, as listed earlier, will need to be conducted with exceptional efficiency if the goal of routinely discussing all patients on the supervisee's caseload is to be achieved. Alternatively, complementary, 'two-tier' arrangements may prove necessary, in which normative or restorative functions are handled by different supervisors/individuals (e.g. managers or therapists: Schindler & Talen, 1994; Fleming *et al.*, 2007). More worrying, it creates a pressure that may limit the extent to which the more time-consuming but educationally valuable supervision methods are utilised (e.g. listening to therapy tapes; role-play). Careful assessment of the supervisee's learning and clinical practice is therefore especially vital, to enable us to monitor the effects of case-based supervision properly.

Another development is the availability of high-technology systems that can provide the basis for novel approaches to supervision. In Chapter 2, I summarised the different formats of traditionally grounded supervision, namely the one-to-one, group supervision, and related options. These are all based on the participants being physically located in the same place at the same time. This has been supplemented by the advent of internet-based resources (e.g. electronic textbooks, manuals and guidelines: for example, see the materials that accompany this present text: www.wiley.com/go/milne), as well as email communication (e.g. relevant chat rooms to foster discussion of this web-based material), and of course web-pages with resource material (e.g. access to slideshows, video or DVD recordings: see the site that is linked to the Bernard and Goodyear (2004) text: www.ablongman.com/bernard3e). More recent, novel formats include video-conferencing technologies and real-time feedback systems. The latter entail the supervisor offering written suggestions to the supervisee, providing a real-time graph-line to provide constant performance feedback, or highlighting current clinical issues. These are displayed on a screen positioned behind the patient, but readily visible to the supervisee ('teleprompting'). For instance, Rosenberg (2006) drew on developments in cognitive science and expertise research to outline a computer-based approach in which the supervisee's therapy is taped through a one-way mirror and the supervisor can type and display, on the video monitor, real-time (concurrent) feedback whilst viewing the session. This feedback can also be provided to other supervisees who are behind the screen whilst they are watching the therapy (a variation on group supervision), and to the therapist, normally after the session. Providing feedback in a written form is an example of how the approach, called Real-Time Training, draws on cognitive science, as research in that field suggests that the simultaneous presentation of visual and aural information (i.e. the typed feedback and the words spoken in therapy) decreases cognitive load and hence fosters learning.

Wood *et al.* (2005) have described a 'tele-supervision' system that utilised similar technologies, an approach that they felt pressured to develop due to working across vast rural areas. They noted advantages of the approach, such as a diminishing hierarchical relating, improved communication, and the use of multiple instructional formats. Disadvantages can include the cost of the equipment, fears about confidentiality, and adverse effects on the quality of supervision.

Having described some fascinating aspects of the supervision context, we now focus on the core tasks of supervision, however mediated, beginning with the clarification of where to start.

Assessing Learning Needs and Establishing the Learning Contract

By definition, a learning need is something that the supervisee ought to learn for his or her own good, for the good of the relevant organisation, or for the good of society (Cogswell & Stubblefield, 1988). Crucially, this definition distinguishes a need from a 'want' or 'demand' that a supervisee might express. But this is only the start of a needs assessment process. Additionally, a need is something judged by various participants as calling for some action due to some state of want or destitution, which, if it can be met, will remedy the situation (Bebbington *et al.*, 1997). As pointed out by Goldstein (1993), the circumstances that lead to the definition of need include an analysis of what the organisation requires (specifying relevant supervision goals, clarifying the training climate and the available resources), linked to understanding details of the job and the tasks that it incorporates. As a result, an analysis can be conducted of the relevant knowledge, skills and attitudes, which provides the basis on which to define whether there is 'a state of want or destitution'. That is, an educational learning need is best understood within its context, based on the analysis that Goldstein (1993) describes, preferably (as he points out) utilising quality instruments and other methods to assess the relevant parameters. Instruments can be particularly valuable in taking the first step, which is converting the supervisee's felt needs into expressed needs (i.e. those wants or demands). These should then be related to the expressed needs of others with a stake in the process (e.g. those who purchase the training programme within which the supervisee is registered; the employers; the service users). Ideally, these perspectives are then related to a normative perspective, that is, the judgements of professionals as to what is needed (e.g. consensus statements regarding competent supervision, such as Falender *et al.*, 2004). On a local basis, it would be more common for a particular training programme to have an agreed statement of what supervision should address or, in the case of CPD supervision, a professional body or employer may have similar specifications. Finally, in an ideal world these three steps should then lead to a 'comparative' needs assessment, which is based on clarifying how the material derived through steps 1–3 relates to the standards/competencies expected by employers, and/or to any data regarding how others have specified learning objectives or demonstrated the 'fitness for practice' of any trained competencies. A recent illustration can be found in the specification of the competencies required to deliver effective CBT (Roth & Pilling, 2007). Based on these perspectives, and a negotiation process, these expressions of educational need should to be specified in terms of the learning objectives for supervision, to which we will turn shortly. As Bransford *et al.* (2000) note, 'there is a good deal of evidence that learning is enhanced when teachers pay attention to the knowledge and beliefs that learners bring to a learning task, use this knowledge as a starting point for new instruction, and monitor students' changing conceptions as instructions proceeds' (p.11). They believe that this understanding has 'a solid research base' to support it (p.14).

In summary, the purpose of an instructional needs assessment is to gain the information that is necessary to design supervision in such a way as to address the legitimate interests of all stakeholders. As Goldstein and Gilliam (1990) said, 'many programmes are doomed to failure because trainers are more interested in conducting training than in assessing needs' (p.20). Sound supervision would dictate that this stage is treated with every bit as much care and attention as the other parts of the supervision cycle. Part of this emphasis is to consider sufficient areas of the supervisee's development to be able to produce a suitably wide-ranging account of their needs. As already suggested by Goldstein and Gilliam (1990), this would normally cover the areas of knowledge, skills and relevant attitudes. Additional areas that have been suggested include the motivational level of the supervisee and their preferred learning style (Milne & Noone, 1996). An attractive way to specify educational needs is through the Learning Skills Profile approach (Boyatzis & Kolb, 1991), which adopts a spider's web figure to capture the range and depth of individual needs (measured through a 72-item Q-sort technique). There are 12 dimensions (segments) in their Profile (including relationship and goal-setting skills), each rated out of 10 (i.e. the successive rings of the web).

Negotiating the needs

As stressed by Norcross and Halgin (1997), this process of clarifying what is needed in relation to a particular supervisee may not be straightforward. In addition to areas of blindness (lack of self-awareness), they note that supervisees may have wide- ranging or quite inappropriate expectations of supervision, as in seeking personal growth or therapy, or simply declaring that they have shown up because they were assigned to a particular supervisor. As they suggest, 'supervisees come with a panoply of preconceptions and needs, many unrecognised, and it is best to examine these at the outset and to modify them as the trainee obtains experience' (p.208). They recommend tactful enquiry and the careful negotiation of legitimate needs, to be counter-balanced against the needs of the supervisor and others.

An exceptionally sensitive and thoughtful treatment of this negotiation process can be found in Safran and Muran's (2000) account of negotiating within the development of a therapeutic alliance. Indeed, they suggest that the process of negotiation lies 'at the heart of the change process ... a critical therapeutic mechanism' (p.15). They regard such negotiation in the context of therapy as more than a superficial consensus but rather referring to some fundamental dilemmas that we face, such as relating our own desires and wishes with those of another person, essentially a core struggle to identify with one's own reality at the same time as accommodating another person's reality. Essentially, there is an inevitable tension between 'the need for agency verses the need for relatedness' (p.15). Much of their book is dedicated to addressing ways in which ruptures in the relationship between therapist and client, pivoting around such negotiations, can be repaired. In CBT there is an emphasis on regular (albeit more superficial) negotiation, in the form of agenda-setting (Liese & Beck, 1997). Additionally, the emphasis is more on identifying and addressing the respective 'wants' of the respective parties, as opposed to actually negotiating a shared, needs-led agenda. However, it is clear that in the CBT model the supervisee is socialised into preparing carefully for supervision, which includes thinking of important agenda items ahead of each supervisory meeting. If a supervisee attends without any such preparation, 'they're encouraged to do so in order to use the time most productively' (p.121). For their part, the CBT supervisors are meant to prepare by reviewing what the supervisee will need, based on the study of previous supervision sessions and the customary use of the supervisee's tape-recorded work. They give the example that a tape may indicate a comparable lack of focus in the supervisee's therapy, whereby this becomes an identified learning need, to be addressed within the next supervision session.

Such general statements of good practice inevitably have boundaries. I refer to exceptional circumstances, such as where a supervisee on a training programme is required to remediate or repeat a training experience, owing to the failure to demonstrate competence during a previous opportunity. In such circumstances the balance would tip strongly away from supervisee's wants to those dictated by the training programme, typically processed through the supervisor. By contrast, an exceptionally able supervisee in the final period of initial training might be treated in a far more collegial fashion, and given considerable scope to act on their wants and preferences.

The learning contract

On the basis of the educational needs assessment process, a learning contract can be specified. The most familiar objectives within initial training concern the competencies that the supervisee should demonstrate in order to graduate, traditionally expressed in terms of knowledge, skills and attitudes (subsuming the value-base). Specifying objectives is another general area of professional practice that most supervisors will apply within their other duties, from therapy to staff training. Its application within supervision is fundamentally the same and the acronym SMARTER is a way of remembering the key criteria for the setting of sound objectives:

S: Specific
M: Measurable
A: Achievable
R: Realistic
T: Time-phased (scheduled)
E: Evaluated
R: Recorded (written down)

This acronym illustrates the bridge that should exist between the needs assessment phase and the final task in the supervision cycle, that of evaluating the extent to which objectives have been achieved. Classically, good behavioural objectives specify the 'performance' (state exactly what the learner/supervisee should be able to do); the 'conditions' under which this performance is expected to occur; and a 'criterion', being some description of what represents acceptable performance (Mager, 1984). Approximating to this degree of SMARTER objective goal-setting is extremely helpful. Amongst other things, it clarifies to the supervisee exactly what is expected of them, and indicates priorities to the supervisor, suggesting too how they need to facilitate learning. Indeed, just as needs assessment tends to be under-emphasised yet critical, so good objective-setting can contribute hugely to the success of supervision. As Goldstein (1993) has stated, 'some trainers have suggested (not without a note of sarcasm) that if the instructor communicated these objectives, the success of the programme would be assured' (p.79). There is research from schools that indicates the empowering effect of good goal-setting, as classes with this degree of clarity of purpose have been found to proceed successfully without their teacher. In the case of able and motivated supervisees, there is surely good reason to believe that properly negotiated and communicated learning objectives are sufficient to motivate and direct the supervisee towards self-directed learning. In some cases, this may be more productive than the learning that is managed in more traditional, supervisor-led ways, as in 'problem-based learning'. Indeed, in terms of the development of knowledge, it has been noted historically that 'everything that is actually known has been found out ... by some person or other, without the aid of an instructor ... there is no species of learning, therefore, which self-education may not overtake ... all discoveries have been self-taught' (Craik, 1866, p.13. Cited in Mithaug *et al.*, 2003).

Although a recognition and discussion of the educational needs assessment phase is rare in textbooks on clinical supervision, there is a clear and consistent recognition of the importance of establishing the learning contract, the way in which objectives are traditionally referred to and recorded within supervision. For example, Bernard and Goodyear (2004) and Safran and Muran (2000) noted that the establishment of the supervision contract can be seen as an educational/relational intervention in its own right. However, surveys of the use of learning contracts indicate that they are often absent. For example, Kavanagh *et al.* (2003) asked 272 qualified practitioners receiving and providing CPD supervision across Queensland about various aspects of their supervision, finding that only 44 per cent of supervisors said that there was a learning contract (supervisees put the figure even lower, at 34 per cent). However, the existence of a properly specified contract was significantly correlated with the perceived impact of supervision on practice.

As regards their content, Hawkins and Shohet (2000) describe an exhaustive, 'seven-eyed' agenda. This consists of attention to:

1. reflection on the content of therapy (to heighten awareness in the supervisee);
2. exploration of the methods used by the supervisee (what was done and how it might be developed);
3. exploration of the therapy process and relationship (studying the interaction as a whole, including the client's transference);
4. focus on the therapist's internal processes (how counter-transference, etc., affects therapy);

5. focus on the supervisory relationship (how client's dynamics affect supervision, e.g. parallel processes);
6. focus on the supervisor's counter-transference (the internal experience of the supervisor); and
7. attention to the wider context (e.g. normative matters, like policies or work standards).

According to Hawkins and Shohet (2000), good supervision involves all seven topics (which they term 'modes') within a process model of supervision entailing 'moving effectively and appropriately from one mode to another' (p.86), which requires considerable awareness and timing. CBT supervision is more circumscribed, typically being concerned with case conceptualisation, the effective application of CBT techniques, and interpersonal strategies (Liese & Beck, 1997; Townend *et al.*, 2002).

Bernard and Goodyear (2004) listed some of the headings that typically appear within contracts. These include aspects of scheduling, such as the frequency and duration of supervision sessions; the methods that the supervisor will use, including the expectations that flow for the supervisee (e.g. making recordings of routine work for discussion in supervision; assigned reading); a statement of what is to happen in the event of the supervisor being absent (back-up arrangements – contact persons; lines of authority); reference to the organisation's expectations (e.g. hours of work and dress code); the specific knowledge, skills and attitudes that make up the competencies to be demonstrated within the learning experience; communication issues (such as record-keeping and report-writing standards); and, of course, an understanding of the normal processes of review, feedback and evaluation. Other topics to consider for the learning contract include what might be termed 'professional matters', such as clarifying accountability arrangements; the legal framework; confidentiality arrangements; insurance; and ethical aspects of supervision (Falender & Shafranske, 2004; Howard, 2000). Returning to the Kavanagh *et al.* (2003) survey, respondents indicated that their most common topic was competence enhancement, as specific to each participating profession (reported by 56 per cent of supervisors). General practice skills (15 per cent) and personal issues (8 per cent) were also noted by these supervisors.

Given the widespread recognition of the importance of the learning contract, it should not be surprising to find that some approaches to clinical supervision give significant emphasis to the content and process of contracting. To illustrate, Gonsalvez *et al.* (2002) describe what they refer to as the 'objectives approach'. They argue that many current models of supervision are insufficiently specific to enable us to translate them into supervisory practice, as in failing to guide the setting of learning objectives. Therefore, the objectives approach (which coincidentally also derives from the educational and training literature) was applied to supervision. They define an objective as a 'specific statement of what trainees should be able to do as a result of a course of study' (p.69). Reiterating the convention that objectives cover knowledge, skills and attitudes, they underscore how these objectives should in turn inform the methods and resources that are applied to try to deliver them, as well as the implications they carry for evaluation. They helpfully provide some examples, as in the case of an objective concerning a CBT skill (e.g. 'trainee to demonstrate competence in identifying clients' automatic thoughts, cognitive distortions, and core beliefs'). In order to address this objective, they note that supervision needs to include individual sessions and video-taped interviews. In turn, when it comes to methods, they suggest that this particular skill can be developed through demonstrations by the supervisor, using prepared video material. The trainee is then expected to practise the competence, using audio and video-tape transcripts of therapist–client interactions. Finally, this can be evaluated, they suggest, by pre- and post-training assessment of the supervisee's competence using a test video. Although not providing any fundamentally new insights as to the importance of objectives in supervision, the Gonsalvez *et al.* (2002) paper does at least underscore the basic logic followed within this book. This is that general educational, therapeutic and other professional areas of practice can apply strongly to supervision. Similarly, they also detail how a prior phase of needs assessment is crucial. Their account also furnishes detailed examples of how this approach can work in practice, at the level of the individual supervisor (and also in relation to what they refer to as the 'macro level' of supervisor training). In order to examine their objectives approach, Gonsalvez *et al.* (2002) surveyed the supervisees ($N = 36$) and supervisors ($N = 28$) associated with a clinical psychology training programme in Australia, using an ad hoc Supervision Experience Questionnaire. Amongst their findings, they reported significant differences between the supervisors' and trainees' ratings of the importance of various objectives. Specifically, supervisors gave significantly higher ratings to objectives related to professional issues, to enhancing interpersonal skills and to raising the supervisees' self-awareness. But both groups gave similarly high ratings to the importance of developing the requisite knowledge and skills.

Other studies have uniformly provided support for the value of clear objective-setting. For example, Methot *et al.* (1996) used a blend of participative and assigned goal-setting with their supervisors, finding that this led to improved specification of outcomes for supervisees and, in turn, for their clients. Fleming *et al.* (1996) also examined the value of participative and assigned goals, finding that, in combination with other methods such as modelling and feedback, their programme increased the maintenance of competencies in supervisees. Talen and Schindler (1993) studied the learning plans of 26 psychology trainees. Their results indicated that concrete, observable and theory-based goals were perceived as the most helpful by these supervisees, and were associated with positive improvements in their learning.

As regards the value of a learning contract itself, Solomon (1992) surveyed supervisors, finding that 90 per cent regarded the learning contract as a useful tool in both teaching and evaluation, fostering negotiation and self-directed learning. These examples from the supervision literature are consistent with findings within psychology more generally. As summarised by Bransford *et al.* (2000), 'there is a good deal of evidence that learning is enhanced when teachers pay attention to the knowledge and beliefs that learners bring to a learning task, use this knowledge as a starting point for new instruction, and monitor students' changing conceptions as instruction proceeds' (p.11).

Once more, research findings are thankfully consistent with the kinds of guidance provided by professional bodies. For instance, the British Association for Behavioural and Cognitive Psychotherapies (BABCP) produced a supervision supplement on the importance of both needs assessment and goal-setting (Townend, 2004), and the same expectation that suitably negotiated and individual learning contracts are established can be found in the guidance on training clinical psychologists in the UK (British Psychological Society, 2003). A second supervision guideline has been developed to summarise this research & guidance (Milne, 2007a, accessible through www. wiley.com/go/milne). Although this section has only addressed examples from the pre-qualification field, hopefully those concerned with CPD supervision can draw out the relevant implications, as these tasks and processes are surely core to all variants of supervision. However, there are, naturally, some significant differences between supervisees when it comes to the learning objectives that result from this goal-setting process (see Temple & Bowers, 1998, for an approach to CBT supervision across diverse supervisees).

Training versus education: supervision for competence or for capability?

So far, my emphasis has been on the relatively circumscribed and uncontroversial business of developing the supervisee's competence. However,

Table 5.1 Some distinctions between two fundamental ways of facilitating learning, education and training (based on Tate, 1997)

	Education	*Training*
1 Agenda	Learner dictates it	Someone else sets it (pre-determined and imposed)
2 Objectives	Plural/divergent ('liberate the mind' to question and influence)	Raise proficiency in compliance with a standard (convergent)
3 Resources	Learners un-realised potential	External view of best practice (e.g. professions)
4 Values	Challenge and change	Conformity and compliance
5 Learners Outcomes	Wide-ranging response capability ('problem-solving')	Delimited scope and time-limited relevance
6 consequences for facilitators	Unpredictability and discomfort/personal growth and development	Predictability and control/ little stimulus to develop
7 Consequences for the Organisation	Increases its flexibility and adaptation and also the challenges it receives	Fosters conformity/loyalty but limited growth

professionals also need to develop capability if they are to be successful in grappling with complex and novel problems that naturally arise within their work. To quote Fraser and Greenhalgh (2001), 'in today's complex world, we must educate not merely for competence, but for capability (the ability to adapt to change, generate new knowledge and continuously improve performance) … education for capability must focus on process … supporting learners to construct their own learning goals … and avoid goals with rigid and prescriptive content' (p.799). To rephrase, we train supervisees in order to develop their competence, but we also need to educate them for capability. Training and education are associated with very different orientations and outcomes, as indicated in Table 5.1.

It follows that the effective supervisor will include educational goals within the learning contract and will alternate between training and educational methods in the pursuit of most or all of the objectives within the contract. An example from Fraser and Greenhalgh (2001) is that capability is likely to be enhanced through providing supervisees with unfamiliar contexts and non-linear methods (such as story-telling, and problem-based learning in small groups).

Facilitating Learning

As already recognised, we are already facilitating learning by conducting a needs assessment, collaboratively setting objectives and creating a suitable learning context. For instance, supervisees are likely to be motivated by supervisors who are willing to identify and incorporate their needs within learning contracts. At the very least, they have created excellent preconditions for the successful use of the conventional methods of supervision. These will now be discussed.

Creating change as a result of a psychological intervention like supervision is often a complex and exacting undertaking. Perhaps because of this challenge, there is an incredible range of intervention options. Some of these cohere naturally with particular theoretical models; others are developmentally based or derive from the unique models of supervision (see Chapter 2). And, as noted in that chapter, there are also pragmatic approaches which belong to no particular theoretical orientation, and are simply an extension of basic social science research, such as the outcome-orientated approach (Worthen & Lambert, 2007). Rather than attempt to list the various interventions in terms of each of these different supervision models, this chapter is organised in a more functional, integrative way, so as to clarify the main, evidence-based methods of supervision.

Have a coherent intervention plan

To begin with, supervisors are advised in many textbooks to adopt a framework or model to guide their approach, and to use a blend of supervision methods, ones that are appropriate to the learning needs (e.g. the preferred learning style) of the supervisee. To illustrate, Bernard and Goodyear (2004) encourage supervisors to base their methods on what they understand to be the supervisee's needs, interests and experience of the material to be tackled through supervision. Importantly, they also lay stress on the need to monitor how the intervention process unfolds and to look carefully at outcome data to judge whether this needs-led, personalised blend of supervision methods is producing the intended outcomes. Norcross and Halgin (1997) agree with this broad strategy, adding emphasis to the importance of having a clear guiding model, and Watkins (1997) supports the notion of having a carefully structured approach.

Utilise multiple supervision methods

Similarly, textbooks and professional consensus statements underline the necessity of using multiple, intelligently combined methods. For instance, in their consensus statement, Kaslow *et al.* (2004) recognised 'the value of modelling, role-plays, vignettes, in-vivo experiences, supervised experience, and other real-world experiences as critical instructional strategies' (p.706). One reason for combining methods of this sort is to maximise the likelihood of building on the supervisee's prior learning. In addition to underscoring the importance of having a needs-led approach and of respecting and empowering the supervisee, there is a fundamental psychological principle involved in building on prior learning. This is the view that 'all learning involves transfer from previous experiences' (Bransford *et al.*, 2000, p.68). This is part of what these authors refer to as the new science of learning, an understanding of how humans engage actively with instructional material, as goal-directed agents seeking to develop. 'Humans are viewed as goal-directed agents who actively seek information. They come to formal education with a range of prior knowledge, skills, beliefs, and concepts that significantly influence what they notice about the environment and how they organise and interpret it. This in turn affects their abilities to remember, reason, solve problems, and acquire new knowledge' (p.10).

This understanding of how humans learn is based on a combination of expert consensus and their review of the available scientific literature. It contrasts with a more passive version of how humans develop, often associated with the idea that learners come into situations like supervision as 'blank slates', just as newborn infants enter a baffling world that is a 'booming, buzzing confusion' (James, 1890). This active account of learning from experience is helpfully synthesised within Kolb (1984). Implications of this active, goal-directed, account of how people learn has massive implications, including suggestions for how clinical supervision should be pursued. Professional organisations also endorse the importance of using a blend of supervision methods, although they may give a particular emphasis to something like the need to adopt an empirical approach within supervision, namely adopting such methods on a tentative footing, studying the effects with particular individuals closely and making any necessary adjustments as the learning experience unfolds (e.g. British Psychological Society, 2003).

Consistent with these consensus statements, general reviews and professional standards, systematic reviews of carefully selected studies in the

Table 5.2 Range and popularity of the different methods identified in two systematic reviews of 52 studies of effective supervision

Supervision Method	Frequency of use (% of studies)
Feedback (including praise and constructive criticism)	42 (81)
Observation and outcome monitoring	41 (79)
Discussion (including providing a rationale; questions and answers; objective-setting; problem solving; challenging supervisees thinking)	39 (75)
Written / verbal prompts and instruction (including guidlines)	25 (48)
Encouraging autonomy (time management)	11 (21)
Formulation (including paper and pencil tasks to increase understanding)	7 (13)
Modelling skills (live/video; live supervision)	7 (13)
Behavioural rehearsal (including role play)	5 (10)
Homework assignment (e.g. guided reading)	2 (4)
Other (e.g. alliance-building work)	11 (21)
Total = 190, Mean = 3.7 methods per study	

clinical supervision field also indicate the value of utilising a blend of methods to facilitate learning. The Milne and James (2000) and Milne, Aylott, Fitzpatrick *et al.* (2008) reviews are typical in finding that a large number of methods are used within supervision manipulations, as summarised in Table 5.2. This combines the results of these two reviews to offer a summary of the top ten supervisor methods. This list is based on those methods that were used at least in two studies.

This table indicates that the above views of experts are very much in step with this highly selected group of 52 research papers, studies that were included because their supervision methods produced successful outcomes (part of the evidence-based supervision rationale of working from a seam of high-quality, interpretable studies). In essence, Table 5.2

bears out the argument that a range of methods should be used. Of the 190 methods cited within the 52 studies, an average of 3.7 methods was manipulated within each study. These include methods that are primarily behavioural (sometimes referred to as 'enactive': observation, modelling, rehearsal); methods that are more cognitive (traditionally referred to as 'symbolic': the various forms of discussion, verbal prompting, and instruction); and then methods that are fundamentally working within the visual modality ('iconic': live and video modelling; live supervision). Therefore, the methods actually tap different modes through which individuals learn.

Perhaps two specific examples will help to bring these general figures to life. The example of Fleming *et al.* (1996) is fairly typical. Their supervisors began supervision with a brief presentation of the relevant knowledge base, then used a video to show the supervisee how a skill could be preformed correctly, leading to the supervisee's rehearsal of the skill and corrective feedback. Similarly, supervisors in an analysis of training in short-term psychotherapy (Hilsenroth *et al.*, 2006) relied heavily on reviewing video-taped therapy sessions. However, in keeping with this orientation, the focus was on examining selected interactions in relation to the dynamics, including the supervisee's experiences and interventions. Alternatives were reviewed and rehearsed, with support, encouragement and praise provided to the supervisee (i.e. 'positive feedback': p.297). This approach was found to increase significantly the 15 supervisees' use of appropriate techniques (e.g. exploring wishes, fantasies and dreams), whilst there was no concurrent change in their unsupervised CBT skills.

Before leaving Table 5.2, I should stress that this is meant to provide only an approximate summary of a particularly favourable sample of the research literature. In turn, within this literature and within my attempt to capture it there was at times a lack of precision. This is because it was frequently difficult to determine, from reading these reports, exactly where one method begins and another one ends (including the different terminology that I have summarised under one heading, as indicated by the qualifying terms in brackets within column 1 of Table 5.2). Also, several of the research papers appearing in the first review were again included within the second one. This will undoubtedly have biased the summary to some extent. For these reasons, I offer this table as a rough guide, helpful mainly because it does provide greater specificity and quantification than is typically available.

Applying the methods

Of course, a general category or label like 'feedback' can subsume a diversity of educational practices. This is rarely spelt out within research papers, and indeed there is a striking lack of manuals, guidelines and other explicit statements of how these methods should be enacted (for this reason, a third EBCS guideline addresses these methods: Milne, 2007a; www.wiley.com/go/milne). Typically, therefore, one has to again turn to general professional practice for precedents and inspiration, or to the more detailed descriptions that appear in some journals and textbooks, or to the basic theory that underpins the method. To illustrate, some textbooks are far more explicit about techniques, and these are a valuable resource (e.g. Campbell, 2006; Hawkins & Shohet, 2000). There are also some manuals available (e.g. Fall & Sutton, 2004), and these tend to specify exactly how a supervision method can be applied. Detailed descriptions of how a particular method should be used are also to be found in professional journals. For instance, Ronen and Rosenbaum (1998) describe some imaginative approaches in sufficient detail to allow supervisors to follow their suggestions. These include the use of writing techniques, like drafting the chapter titles of a hypothetical book on 'the ideal therapist'. This can help to reveal the supervisee's questions and self-doubts. Similarly, metaphors within the supervisee's account can be developed to deepen understanding and clarify belief systems.

To illustrate how general theory can also provide guidance, consider the most frequently used method recorded in Table 5.2, that of feedback. Based on a review within the educational literature, Table 5.3 summarises some of the specifics that are supposed to compose feedback, in the form of an

Table 5.3 A summary of some of the main functions and methods of feedback, based on Juwah *et al.* (2004)

Facilitates (self-assessment/regulation/reflection)

Engages (prioritised/staff and students)

Energises (SMARTER objectives follow: specific; measurable; achievable; realistic; time-phased; evaluated; recorded)

Dialogues (mutual clarification)

Backs (consistent with system/support/reinforcement)

Actions (next steps clarified – for all participants)

Clarifies (standards/expectations/gaps relative to possible standard)

Knows (how to close gap/develop)

---

acronym. This can furnish the qualified practitioner with some helpful suggestions, ideas that they can apply because they require the same basic skills as per other clinical duties.

Feedback is one of the most proven of all educational methods. To illustrate, in a recent systematic review of 41 studies, Veloski *et al.* (2006), found that 74 per cent of them demonstrated a significant, positive effect. This was most pronounced when provided by an authoritative, credible source, and maintained over time.

At a more concrete level, Table 5.4 offers a breakdown of another dominant method of supervision, the use of questions with the supervisee. These appear to feature significantly in all models of supervision, though taking on suitably different forms and functions. For example, in an evaluation of brief psychodynamic psychotherapy, the supervisor who used specific questioning to adjust adherence (and who was generally more focused and active) achieved a much greater effect size than a colleague with a more general supervision style (i.e. 3.58 versus 0.46: Henry *et al.*, 1993). In CBT supervision, questions play a central role, as in gathering information pertinent to case conceptualisation, and in facilitating effective dialogue (James & Morse, 2007; James *et al.*, 2008). The list of questions in Table 5.3 will hopefully give supervisors a way to reflect on their current methods, and to consider fresh options. The table is based on Bernard and Goodyear (2004); Campbell (2006); Ennis (1985); Follette and Batten (2000); James and Morse (2007); Moseley *et al.* (2005); Rigazio-DiGilio *et al.* (1997) and Siegler (1995).

Finally, in order to ensure that the preferred methods are used as effectively as possible, the supervisor might base their selection and application on an established theory. This is valuable as it encourages the supervisor to consider what mediates their supervisee's learning. For instance, the augmented CBT supervision account, as set out in Chapter 3 (Kolb, 1984), recognises that one needs to create a certain amount of tension between different ways of understanding competence or capability. This tension can arise from the use of different methods (e.g. contrasting personal experience against textbook advice), from reflecting on experience (James *et al.*, 2004), or from challenging the supervisee's understanding (for an illustration, see James & Morse, 2007). A supervisor guided by this logic might alternate between asking the supervisee to describe something that happened, to recount some of the emotions that accompanied this event, to reflect on what possible understanding or meaning it might have within their frame of reference, and then to provide some instruction from their understanding. This might then lead to a mutually agreed way of testing

Table 5.4 An elaboration of one popular supervision method, questioning the supervisee

Function *of question (related to the experiential learning cycle)*	*Illustrative* **form** *of questions*	*Main* **focus***/purpose of this kind of question*
1. *Heighten affective awareness (experiencing)*	*Open questions* (e.g. 'what were you feeling when the client wept?') *Awareness-raising questions* (e.g. 'which negative reactions do you have to this event?')	• Recalling/describing • Information gathering • Supporting • Facilitating the alliance • Processing affect
2. *Facilitate cognitive reflection* (reflection)	*Generic questions* (e.g. 'how did that compare to the supervision you've had before?') *Exploratory Socratic questions* (e.g. 'has this kind of interaction been a feature of your clinical work?')	• Challenging (e.g. creating a tension/dialectic) • Productive/solution generating • Formal reflection (e.g. assessing /appraising) • Meaning-making (e.g. reframing; induction; interpreting) • Classifying • Hypothesising
3. *Connect to knowledge-base (conceptualization)*	*Closed question* (e.g. 'how do I know that this is the best approach?') *Critical engagement question* (e.g. 'where can we find the best evidence?')	• Summarising • Checking understanding • Informing/educating • Clarifying • Reasoning • Guiding discovery (improving grasp) • Critical thinking (e.g. analysing) • Defending viewpoint • Critiquing

Table 5.4 *(cont'd)*

Function *of question (related to the experiential learning cycle)*	Illustrative **form** *of questions*	Main **focus**/*purpose of this kind of question*
4. *Apply to ongoing work* (experimenting)	*Task-specific questions* (e.g. 'which goals are you trying to achieve?') *Miracle/imaginative questions* (e.g. 'if a miracle occurred, how would things be different?') *Transformational questions* (e.g. 'how could your understanding help to address this problem?')	• Eliciting feedback • Controlling (meta-cognition) • Monitoring • Evaluating • Extending knowledge (e.g. through analogies/deductions/ generalisations/applications) • Demonstrating • Constructing • Practising

out an understanding, one that is now significantly improved because of applying this experiential learning theory. The specifics of exactly how to do this may be left to the preferred general approaches of the supervisor.

Evaluation

The supervision cycle is concluded when the supervisor judges the extent to which these methods have contributed to meeting a learning objective, as specified in the learning contract, or agreed at the start of the supervision session. There are almost as many ways of conducting an evaluation as there are ways of facilitating learning, so we are again faced with the challenge of finding some meaningful way to capture the essence of evaluation. I will attempt this in summary form here, but urge the reader to study Chapter 8, which is devoted to the topic.

Evaluation is normally defined as a judgement of the extent to which objectives are achieved, guided as far as possible by research methods (Rossi *et al.*,

2003). That is, it is good professional practice for this judgement to be aided by relatively objective sources of information, such as direct observation (ideally based on checklists or rating scales), or by the use of questionnaires and structured interviews. Supervisors may also use what are formally referred to as 'permanent products', such as the clinical reports or letters written by supervisees. Such information helps the supervisor to form a more objective judgement of whether an objective is being achieved by the supervisee.

In supervision, it is customary to distinguish 'formative' from 'summative' evaluation, the former being concerned with corrective feedback, and the latter being focused on determining whether or not the supervisee's performance of a competence achieves some standard required for accreditation, approval or passing a course. This is why it is sometimes referred to as the 'gate-keeping' function of supervision. Backing up my observation that apparently discrete supervision methods (as listed in Table 5.2) sometimes merge into one another, note that feedback is also a form of evaluation, including as it does praise and constructive criticism. Psychologically this appears inevitable, as in order to offer praise or suggestions the supervisor must have in mind some notion of the desired performance. In practice, guided by the feedback I myself have had from many supervisors and experts over the years, it is probably most sensible to treat feedback (i.e. the formative dimension of evaluation) as a method for facilitating learning, keeping the summative or gate-keeping version as a distinct competency.

Conclusions

In summary, in this chapter I have proposed that the staff development cycle be adopted formally within supervision. I have argued that this is justified because it provides a well-founded and well-established approach to facilitating the learning of professionals and others, one that is congruent with what we know about the supervision cycle from within the supervision literature and, indeed, from basic psychological research (Bransford *et al.*, 2000). But, as this line of reasoning indicates, this is an evidence-based approach to the issue. If there is a defence for this EBCS approach to supervisory methods, it is that it may at least provide a common foundation for professionals who wish to develop expertise in more specialised approaches (for example, psychodynamic or systemic methods).

Not only is it appropriate to recognise the limited scope of the methods covered within this chapter, it is also appropriate to recognise the great difficulty one faces as an author in trying to treat a vast literature with the requisite specificity and balance. In particular, I am acutely aware of how general this chapter is in describing the supervision methods. (Again, please refer to the detailed supervision guideline on facilitating learning: Milne, 2007a; www.wiley.com/go/milne). Therefore, interpreting how they should be applied relies mainly on general clinical skills. Secondly, I would wish to give the reader every encouragement to be empirical about their efforts to try out new methods, by evaluating their work with supervisees. Chapter 8 offers a number of ways in which the reader could test out the relevance and effectiveness of some of their supervision methods, particularly the ones that have been outlined above.

6

Learning from Supervision

Introduction

Now the plot thickens: having set out the subtle and dynamic ways in which we might understand supervision (Chapter 3), I now outline how such a system is enacted. How does the supervision cycle (described in the previous chapter) draw on the supervisory alliance (outlined in Chapter 4) to produce learning? In order to make sense of this profound adaptive process, the chapter will start by setting out the basic stances to development taken by supervisors and supervisees. Of these relationship options, the emphasis will be given to the so-called 'constructivist' one, in which it is proposed that the supervisee is assisted by the supervisor to adopt an adult, active role in the construction of their own competence, an interpretation that presents the supervisee as an artful and energised collaborator. This relationship stance has been nicely captured in a review of why research findings are so often insignificant. In an article subtitled 'The perversity of humans as subjects', the editor noted that: 'Students are human and perceptive, and well aware of what is happening to them. They are also aware of the signposts of success or failure – final exams, supervisor evaluations and licensing examinations. And, by and large, they are highly motivated to succeed and highly skilled in the art of academia. So, at the end of the day, students are well-equipped to compensate for any curriculum, however novel or hide-bound' (Norman, 2001, p.2).

After clarifying the role relationship between the two parties, the next section details the ways in which the supervisee can apply these skills and motivations, in effect the 'job description' of the supervisee. This leads to a more in-depth consideration of the process whereby this list of duties actually comes together to produce learning. In particular, I examine notions of 'de-skilling' and of 'responsivity', the subtle moment-by-moment ways in which supervisor and supervisee adjust to one another, adaptively. The chapter finishes with some detailed description of the methods that appear to be primary in this adjustment process (especially the role of reflecting on experience). As a result of this in-depth consideration of how the supervisee learns from supervision, we will be moving well beyond the ineffectual 'tyranny of niceness' (Fleming *et al.*, 2007) in order to characterise an industrious, goal-directed and mutually beneficial relationship between supervisor and supervisee.

Relationship Options

The great tradition in supervision is that of the rather paternalistic master–apprentice relationship. In his historical review of psychoanalytic supervision, DeBell (1963) noted that 'from the very beginning of psychoanalysis to the present there has been a strong tendency for both the student and the teacher of psychoanalysis to rely heavily upon the apprentice system of teaching' (p.546). This is not entirely surprising, since the dominant ideologies of the time emphasised 'top-down' relationships. Take the case in point of the classic bureaucracy, a system designed to ensure that people knew their place, and that the work got done with a minimum of friction. Key characteristics of bureaucracies were the clear division of labour, where the authority and responsibilities of the parties were clearly defined, so that the different positions were organised hierarchically, with a clear chain of command. Power was granted to those with the qualifications (i.e. based on training), and competitive appointment. Strict rules, discipline and controls regarding one's duties were in place. In exchange, members of a bureaucracy were treated with kindness and justice, and remunerated fairly within a system providing stable employment (Morgan, 1997). These principles go back to the great leaders, such as Frederick the Great, and underpinned their military machines. In terms of analogy, the master–apprentice stance in supervision is akin to the potter, i.e. someone who takes raw material and fashions it to a predetermined shape.

Within supervision, the bureaucratic model for organising social behaviour has its clearest parallel in the work of Vygotsky (1978). He regarded culture (and the way it was expressed within the social environment) as crucial to development, providing the tools and models that supervisors engineered through carefully 'scaffolding' their supervisees' learning opportunities. In addition, Vygotsky believed that within this structure there was a maturational process which allowed the individual's biological potential to be expressed. Learning is critical to this maturational process, and is regarded as highly embedded within social interactions within what Vygotsky (1978) famously referred to as the 'zone of proximal development' (ZPD). This zone describes the area between what the learner brings to the situation (their baseline status) and what it is possible to learn with the help of someone like a supervisor. Such social learning becomes privately internalised and represents new knowledge or skill.

Other ways of thinking about the relationship options in supervision are behaviourism, nativism and structuralism (Strauss, 1993). Most prominent of these, at least within modern approaches to supervision, is structuralism. According to this view, we are born with reflexes and mental structures which have biological basis but which develop psychologically from experience. Development progresses from relatively weak to more sophisticated mental structures, as indicated classically by Piaget's account of different cognitive stages. These stages are reached by actively applying existing mental structures (abilities) to material (tasks). These structures, referred to as 'schema', constrain what can be understood at any one point in time, but ultimately enable supervisees to develop expertise. Structuralism is therefore intermediate between nativism and behaviourism, as regards how we relate to our environment. The emphasis is on interaction, a give-and-take relationship between the individual and the environment. A topical version of the structuralist (Piagetian) approach is constructivism. Particularly emblematic of the constructivist school is problem-solving, because it motivates learners (when it is relevant to their needs and interests), and as it draws on what they already know (Davies, 2000). Also, this problem-solving effort occurs within a context which is thought to further strengthen the learning process. This is therefore an adult learning paradigm, 'a cooperative venture in non-authoritarian, informal learning, the chief purpose of which is to discover the meaning of experience; a quest of the mind which digs down to the roots of the pre-conceptions which formulate our conduct; a technique of learning for adults which makes education co-terminus with life and hence elevates living itself to the level of adventurous experiment' (Lindeman, 1926, p.166, cited in Davies, 2000, p.15). The constructivist approach might be more familiar to some as an empowerment model (Triantafillou, 1997), entailing a shared responsibility between a supervisor and a supervisee to deal with problems within the supervisee's work, the job of the supervisor being to provide the resources and support so that the supervisee can resolve the problem successfully, with as little help as possible. This is consistent with CBT supervision (Padesky, 1996), in the sense that the supervisor should use procedures (such as guided discovery) to clarify what a supervisee already knows about a problem, then to build on these strengths, drawing out the supervisee's understanding. These are concrete illustrations of how supervisor and supervisee can collaborate within Vygotsky's zone, sometimes referred to appropriately as the 'construction zone' (Newman *et al.*, 1989). Related terms are noted by Davies (2000), ones that convey the idea that the work environment and individual learner need to be brought together skilfully by some engineer-like supervisor figure. These include cognitive apprenticeship; guided participation; reciprocal teaching; assisted performance; appropriation; and contingent learning.

The everyday analogy for this supervisee stance is that of the traveller, a journeying metaphor. Related to this, the supervisor's stance towards the supervisee is that of the mountain guide. In this sense, their relationship is one in which the supervisee needs to exert effort and take some chances, thereby contributing significantly to what is undertaken and achieved. This works best alongside a supervisor who behaves like a guide, as in exercising leadership, based on expertise (e.g. drawing on past experiences of travelling the path). By comparison, the behavioural analogy is that of the potter, like the master-apprentice stance a relationship where the supervisee feigns to know nothing, and the supervisor therefore takes complete control, shaping the supervisee to a predetermined form. In turn, the nativism stance can be represented by the gardener, one based on supervisees largely taking care of their own development, with their supervisors ensuring optimal growing conditions, to allow supervisees to develop their potential (i.e. learning opportunities; resources).

In practice, some of these more extreme stances (such as nativism) are not viable in their pure form, since the pressures of the modern workplace mean that initial or CPD supervision has to be accountable to third parties (e.g. training programmes/professional bodies/employers' requirements of supervisors). This is not to ignore the huge significance of prior learning, however, but rather to take that as an important launch-pad. That is, whilst we might not accept Plato's belief that 'there is nothing which our immortal soul does not know, prior to our birth', we might agree with philosophers that 'the advance of knowledge consists, mainly, in the modification of earlier knowledge' (Popper, 1972, pp.10–11). Hence, supervisors will tend to adopt an integrative or eclectic stance, as in conducting a learning needs assessment (to clarify 'earlier knowledge') and utilising a range of methods. Also, supervisees will naturally draw on multiple ways to develop their competence, as illustrated within the developmental model (i.e. a behavioural stance is typically preferred initially, but is then overtaken by a constructivist one). Therefore, the idea that there can be one sole and successful stance is hard to defend. More realistically, supervisors will need to be flexible, occupying different stances as necessary to enable the supervisee to progress. This can be illustrated readily within CBT supervision, where guided discovery may alternate with didactic instruction, detailed questioning, role-play and modelling (Padesky, 1996). Although stressing adult learning and problem-solving, even strong proponents like Knowles (1990) acknowledge that there is role for a range of techniques, including didactic instruction in a situation where learners have no experience of a content area, or cannot construe how material relates to their own tasks or problems. Thus, seemingly incompatible methods of facilitating the learning process may come to be seen as complementary (Davies, 2000). This is in keeping with the emphasis in this book, namely one of adopting a structured learning format, to target the supervisee's different modes of learning (as described in the preceding chapter).

Perhaps the most influential account of a broadly constructivist, experiential approach to the facilitation of learning is the integrative review provided by Kolb (1984). This has been credited with providing a helpful synthesis of these different stances, a simple but transfixing account that has been 'very influential amongst adult educators and trainers' (Tight, 1996, p.99). Because of these factors, I next turn to Kolb's account.

The Role of the Supervisee

By definition, a constructivist stance means that the supervisee is assumed to play a significant and essential role in supervision. As Driscoll (1999) has put it, 'the whole success of clinical supervision ultimately rests with the willingness and commitment of clinical supervisees to engage in it and to learn from the experience' (p.29). A number of tips are then given as to ways in which supervisees can play their part. For example, in relation to feedback from the supervisor, Driscoll (1999) suggests the following supervisee actions:

- Ask for feedback in a way that reassures the supervisor that you are unlikely to be offended.
- Listen carefully to what is being said; even if it feels uncomfortable, resist the temptation or argue, explain or disagree.
- Clarify what the supervisor is saying to you by asking questions.
- Ask for suggestions about ways of taking the issue forward.
- Ask for some time to ponder any implied actions.
- Thank the supervisor for responding openly to your request for feedback, acknowledging that it may not have been easy for the supervisor.

Similar lists of how the supervisee can enable supervision have been offered by Inskipp and Proctor (1993), Hatcher and Lassiter (2007) and Pearson (2004). Their suggestions include preparing a plan for supervision (including tentative agenda items); being aware of the dynamics that can arise (trying to anticipate ways to manage these should they occur); generally playing an active role, as in helping to negotiate the agenda once supervision commences; providing information and updates on ongoing work in a structured fashion; responding to the supervisor's efforts and initiating your own; seeking specific feedback; initiating discussions; and accepting the discomfort and anxiety that goes with some of these activities. In this context, Pearson (2004) helpfully goes on to outline some anxiety-management strategies that supervisees might wish to use (such as positive self-statements, reframing the struggle as an opportunity for growth; drawing on social support within the peer group; openly discussing the discomfort and asking the supervisors for suggestions). Carroll and Gilbert (2005) extend this emphasis by producing a virtual manual on how to engage effectively in such activities as mutual feedback, collaborative goal-setting and reflecting on experience. Inskipp and Proctor (1993) have also written a practical handbook, detailing the respective responsibilities of the supervisor and supervisee. Again, the emphasis is on the supervisee preparing and then engaging freely within supervision, so that they are open to feedback and prepared to try out new ideas in practice.

It is worth pausing to note that these tips and contributions provide detail on how the alliance ruptures (described in Chapter 4) can be repaired jointly. Even if the supervisor is understood to shoulder lead responsibility for tackling impasses, it is evident that the supervisee can sometimes provide the repair. This might arise from their personality, their motivation to make supervision a useful experience, or from the technical qualities noted above.

Additional to these individuals' perspectives on the role of the supervisee, it is important to consider consensus statements, as prepared by groups of experts. For example, a report on practicum (i.e. training placement) competencies was developed in the USA by the Association of Directors of Psychology Training Clinics (Hatcher & Lassiter, 2007). There is a comforting degree of overlap between this consensus statement and the earlier material, as both stress how the supervisee needs to be aware of local issues regarding feedback etc. This statement goes on to detail 'professional developmental competencies' such as critical thinking, reflection, and awareness of how one's own personal identity may influence what goes on in supervision. But perhaps the clearest illustration of how this consensus statement acknowledges the vital role of the supervisee is in the final section, on metacognition. It is recognised there that the training programme needs to help the supervisee to develop this particularly powerful form of reflective understanding, as it is concerned with how they know what they know, and come to discover what they don't know. Echoing the constructivist and structuralist models, this emphasis on metacognition clearly articulates how the learner can reflect, in order to draw on their available skills, and thereby solve problems. More recently, a competence statement has been generated in the UK, partly based on seeking input from experts throughout the country (Roth & Pilling, 2007). In this document, concerned with the core competencies of CBT, the main contributions made by the supervisee are thought to be:

- an ability to work collaboratively with the supervisor (e.g. clarifying respective roles; presenting an honest and open account of work undertaken; discussing work in an active and engaged manner – i.e. without become passive, avoidant, defensive or aggressive);
- capacity for self-appraisal and reflection (being open and realistic about their capabilities, and sharing this self-appraisal with the supervisors; using their feedback to develop the capacity for accurate self-appraisal);
- contributing to active learning (taking up suggestions regarding relevant reading and applying this material; taking the initiative in searching for and drawing on relevant literature);
- ability to use supervision to reflect on developing a personal and professional role (using supervision to discuss the personal impact of one's work, especially related to one's effectiveness);
- capacity to reflect on the quality of supervision (seeking advice and guidance where there is concern about the quality of supervision or where the supervisor's actions are unacceptable, breaching professional guidelines).

Where are the data?

As is often the case with a developing field, prescriptions and exhortations (as above) tend to dominate, whereas data regarding what actually happens tend to be scarce. In this context, the Ellis and Ladany (1997) review is of particular relevance, noting as it does the role that the supervisee must play in enabling the alliance to be successful. However, their conclusions about the overall significance of the alliance were muted, and no specific data on supervisee input were reported. Analyses of the supervision alliance do, however, bear out the significant role of the supervisee. The Supervisory Working Alliance Inventory (Efstation *et al.*, 1990) has a supervisee version which includes two factors, 'rapport' and 'client focus'. Relevant items include 'My supervisor encourages me to formulate my own interventions with the client ...' and 'My supervisor helps me work within a specific treatment plan ...', respectively.

There are also some data from an audit, undertaken within a training programme for Clinical Psychologists (Milne & Gracie, 2001). We took a one-year sample of the material recorded in the trainees' 'supervision record' (a standard form maintained by the trainee). Their replies to the question about how they had contributed to supervision were summarised inductively, to produce a content analysis of their input to the supervision that they had received. Figure 6.1 displays their replies, in the form of a dendrogram.

Of the possible sample of 73 trainees, 59 supervision records were available for analyses. Of these, 51 (86 per cent) had at least one entry about the supervisee's role or contribution to supervision, and a total of 239 meaning units were extracted. These were then categorised into 20 first-order themes, as set out in Figure 6.1. It can be seen that by far the most common theme was collaborating with the supervisor, which was noted on 40 per cent of occasions. This mainly took the form of actively participating in supervision, which we bracketed with sharing responsibility, discussing material, clarifying, suggesting amendments, and sitting in on the supervisor. This is highly consistent with the opinions and consensus statement above, as are the remaining first-order themes in Figure 6.1. It is heartening to see that 'prompting' is the second most frequently reported supervisee activity, backing up the idea that the supervisee co-constructs supervision.

This kind of general summary can be brought to life by personal descriptions of the experience of collaborating. For instance, Brown and Ash (2001)

Hierarchical structure of the third order theme 'role of supervisee'.
[Figure in brackets = number of mentions; there were 27 other/unclassified meaning units = 11%]

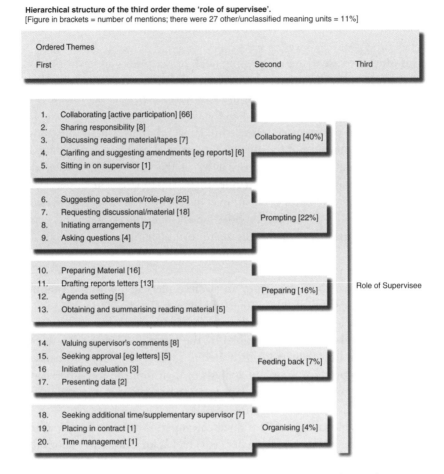

Figure 6.1 A summary of the 20 ways that supervisees reported contributing to supervision, based on an audit of one year of training

provided a 'supervisee's tale', which noted the experience of progressing from a time when supervision dragged on and was dreaded, to it becoming something that was engaging and tiring (because of the amount of effort the supervisee was ultimately investing). In a notably candid fashion, the supervisee noted how the relationship that was established played a crucial part in facilitating the expression of difficult thoughts and feelings.

A further way to enliven general pronouncements or audit data is by detailed observation of the interactions between supervisor and supervisee. James *et al.* (2004) captured their own brand of difficult thoughts and feelings by examining the phenomenology of the supervisory process. They accomplished this by means of video recordings of five consecutive weeks of CBT supervision, focusing on one index patient. Following each supervision session, both supervisor and supervisee kept independent audio-taped commentaries of the session, based of viewing the recording. The instructions to the supervisor and supervisee were: 'while watching the recording, please describe your experiences of the supervision using the Dictaphone provided. Please give specific details about your feelings, physical sensations and thoughts' (p.509). The supervisor and supervisee then met to discuss the resulting data, so as to reflect on the dynamic processes associated with their supervision. The most frequent emotion reported for the supervisee was anxiety, which was reported on 38 occasions within four supervision sessions (i.e. meetings with the supervisor falling in between the clinical work with this patient). The supervisee's transcript in relation to feeling anxious included examples such as: 'I felt put on the spot'; 'I thought: "Oh no"'; 'I was worried because…'; 'I did not feel comfortable'. The other emotions were those of feeling contained (27 occasions; included the supervisee feeling safe and pleased with herself); feeling relieved (13 occasions); feeling confused (9 occasions); feeling interested and intrigued (2 occasions); and feeling angry (2 occasions).

Finally, one can bring to life the role of the supervisee within a parallel, quantitative approach. Examples are provided in the next section, based on observing the micro- processors and outcomes of routine clinical supervision.

The Process of Learning from Supervision

The paper just discussed, by James *et al.* (2004), provides an individual, in-depth account of some of the feelings associated with the process of learning through supervision. In this section I will now provide a way of understanding this element of supervision, placing it within the tandem model (see Chapter 3). As set out in Figure 6.2, emotions of the kind recounted in the James *et al.* (2004) paper are understood to be part of the affective accompaniments to concrete action (top of the experiential learning cycle, below). Figure 6.2 is a synthesis of what I judged to be the essential points within Kolb's (1984) integrative account of Vygotsky, Piaget, Lewin and other developmental theorists. This is a complex figure, but it

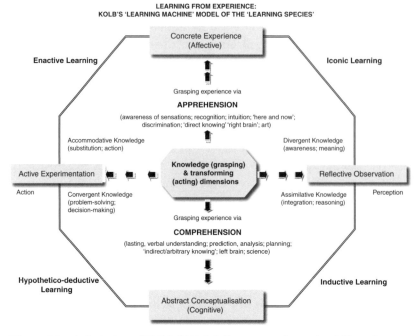

Figure 6.2 A depiction of Kolb's (1984) full account of experiential learning, showing how the cycle of four modes (AE = active experimentation; CE = concrete experience; RO = reflective observation; AC = abstract conceptualisation) relate to development

can guide our understanding of how supervisees learn from supervision. It also provides, thereby, an extremely helpful model of how to monitor one's supervision.

The complexity of Figure 6.2 also reflects the huge emphasis that these theorists placed on our capacity for learning: 'Human beings are unique among all living organisms in that their primary adaptive specialisation lies not in some particular form or skill or fit in an ecological niche, but rather in identification with the process of adaptation itself – in the process of learning' (Kolb, 1984, p.1). This Darwinian emphasis on adaptation is continued, as Kolb (1984, p.1) goes on to declare that: 'we are thus the learning species, and our survival depends on our ability to adapt not only in the reactive sense of fitting into the physical and social worlds, but in the proactive sense of creating and shaping those worlds'. He believes that we adapt to our environment like a learning machine. This involves operating within the dialectic tensions between two fundamentally different ways of knowing about our world. On the one hand, this is through grasping our experience through apprehension, versus grasping it through comprehension. These are the top and bottom boxes within Figure 6.2. As indicated there, apprehension is referred to as 'concrete experience'. It is a primarily a private, emotional way of knowing, including the awareness of sensations, and intuitive, 'right brain' awareness. This is thought to be opposed to (i.e. in tension with) the way that we understand the world cognitively, through what is termed 'abstract conceptualisation'. This latter way of grasping our experience is based on public knowledge, characterised by what is known through the scientific method, and through the supervisor's knowledge. As a result of the contrast between these two structural components (akin to the traditional contrast between knowing in one's heart or head, respectively), there is a dynamic process or 'rhythm' that moves from a rather destabilised and uncomfortable lack of knowing or incompetence (i.e. de-skilling: see next section), to a point where something is ultimately grasped. In this sense, the heart and the head find a mutually acceptable way of making sense of material, and mental balance is restored. This can therefore be thought of as the 'internal' transformation of material, a private, cognitive episode.

Diametrically opposed structures are on the horizontal part of Figure 6.2. Again, there is thought to be inevitable variation (Kolb, 1984, refers to this as a 'tension') between these modes of understanding. One of these is the relatively passive business of reflecting so as to make sense of one's experience; and the other is the act of experimentation, whereby plans are made and actions taken to test out our tentative new knowledge. This is the second fundamental outcome of experiential learning, according to Kolb (1984), which he terms 'transformation', and which we should refer to as 'external' transformation, as it is ultimately a public, behavioural episode in which knowledge is extended or extrapolated to some kind of testing out in the environment.

This account of how we learn from experience has ancient roots, as recorded in philosophy. To quote Popper (1972): 'Neither observation nor reason are authorities. Intellectual intuition and imagination are most important, but they are not reliable: they show us things very clearly, and yet they may mislead us. They are indispensable as the main sources of our theories; but most of our theories are wrong anyway. The most important function of observation and reasoning, and even of intuition and imagination, is to help us in the critical examination of those bold conjectures which are the means by which we probe into the unknown' (p.28).

In summary, the supervisee's role in this account of experiential learning is to engage actively and openly in these four different ways of knowing, in order to grasp and transform their understanding. 'Grasping' is defined (Concise Oxford English Dictionary (COED), 2004, p.621) as 'seizing and holding firmly ... taking an opportunity eagerly ... understanding and comprehending fully ... a firm grip ... a person's capacity to attain something'. Dewey (1938, p.83) gives the example of how a child grasps something: 'when a child of two ... learns not to approach a flame too closely and yet to draw near enough to a stove to get its warmth ... it is grasping and using the causal relation'. The dictionary (COED) defines transformation as: 'marked change in nature; converting or transferring material'. According to Kolb (1984, p.38): it is a 'process of continually creating and recreating knowledge, through transactions between opposed ways of knowing (including personal versus public/social)'. The function of transformation is to give personal meaning to material, and also entails applying the material to solve problems. Examples include making associations or analogies; creating metaphors; making initial inductions; understanding and applying information or a method/principle/law (e.g. constructing a framework, taxonomy or graph); an abstraction (e.g. classified, generalised and transfer). A useful guide to understanding these concepts can be found in Moseley *et al.* (2005). In this sense, then, 'Learning is the process whereby knowledge is created through the transformation of experience' (Kolb, 1984, p.38). Arguably, it is the process of trying to learn that is the most fundamental of all, what Popper (1972) called our 'groping in the dark'.

In keeping with some of the earlier accounts of the experience of being a supervisee, Kolb (1984) recognises the inherent discomfort that may arise during this process, referring to this as a dialectic between these different ways of knowing as a 'tension- and conflict-filled process' (p.30). Successfully resolving these tensions and conflicts is thought to result ultimately in either assimilation (the connection of new material to existing schema) or accommodation (where new schema are required to understand our world). Chapter 9 provides a critique and reconstruction of some problematic parts of Kolb's (1984) model, such as the appeal to a dialectic.

For now it may be relevant to step back from this complexity and realise that, as in other areas of life, some very simple elements or components can combine in ways that produce profoundly complex outcomes. Coincidently, there are only four such elements within DNA, and these substances are so mundane that they had been overlooked as possible bases for heredity for many years. But their interactive process produces amazing outcomes, as amusingly summarised by Bryson (2004): 'Genes are nothing more (or less) than instructions to make proteins. This they do with a certain dull fidelity. In this sense, they are rather like the keys of a piano, each playing a single note and nothing else, which is obviously a trifle monotonous. But combine the genes, as you would combine piano keys, and you can create chords and melodies of infinite variety. Put all these genes together and you have (to continue the metaphor) the great symphony of existence' (p.493).

De-skilling

In order to conduct my own transformations of these concepts, I want to first take a common example of where experiential learning is difficult and so may prove aversive to the supervisee (i.e. de-skilling), and then give an example of a more positive transactional process (i.e. responsivity).

De-skilling is something that most people will have experienced quite intensely. It refers to feeling confused, helpless and incompetent during a period of training. It is incorporated most clearly in the writing of developmental theorists (e.g. Friedman & Kaslow, 1986; Skovholt & Ronnestad, 1992). An example of the developmental angle on de-skilling has been provided by Stoltenberg and McNeill (1997), who assume that a supervisee's competence will fluctuate, possibly as a result of excess complexity, which shakes confidence and leads to 'confusion, despair, vacillation' (p.190). It is important for supervisors and supervisees to address these uncomfortable, seemingly paradoxical experiences, as they are widely viewed as a natural and necessary phase in human development. In this sense, it has recently been argued that there should be 'desirable difficulties' within experiences such as supervision, such as providing contextual interference or reducing feedback during learning, as this promotes long-term retention and transfer (Bjork, 2006).

Recognition of this pattern of discomfort, destabilisation and ultimate development is also part of the psychodynamic view: learning, by its very nature, is thought to challenge our current understanding and 'thus invariably involves uncertainty, some degree of frustration and disappointment. This experience is a painful one ...' (Salzberger-Wittenberg et al., 1983, p.54). Similarly, in-depth interviews with family therapy trainees (Nel, 2006) indicated that a number of these trainees had found the training experience to be 'overwhelming and de-skilling' (p.307). An integrative theoretical account of this de-skilling process has been provided by Zorga

(2002), who appealed to Piaget's notion of 'equilibration' (i.e. balance between schema). When this balance is disturbed (dis-equilibration) we feel de-skilled and material we are dealing with cannot be readily assimilated and hence appeals for a new schema, the act of accommodation within Piagetian thinking. This means that new ways of thinking about the stimulus material are developed, so that future responses are qualitatively different (e.g. occur at a higher level of processing). Successive episodes of dis-equilibration and adjustment yield the classic spiral of upward development, the process through which balance is temporarily re-established and our special talent for learning and adaptation takes place. In this sense, as pointed out by Dewey (1955), it follows that Figure 6.2 should be conceived of as a spiral rather than as a circle. According to Kolb (1984), this upward spiral is cone-like in shape, as it culminates in increased integration of the different modes of knowing, and in a progression to a more unified and sophisticated relationship to our world. Expressed differently, three developmental stages make up this conical process, initial acquisition, growing specialisation and ultimately integration (see Figure 6.2). Although these are described classically in terms of the whole lifespan (for example, 'acquisition' occurring between birth and adolescence), one can also think of these in relation to a supervisee's development of competence in one particular area over a relatively short period of time.

Although a number of authors appear to accept this account of how learning occurs, and there are experimental demonstrations (Bjork, 2006), there is surprisingly little information within the professional development literature. In one study, James *et al.* (2001) studied how qualified mental health staff attending a training programme in CBT varied in their learning trajectory over the nine-month period of this part-time course. A multidisciplinary group of 20 professionals were assessed at three time points, using the Cognitive Therapy Scale. The authors reported a mid-training dip in the competence levels of these professionals, which was attributed to a destabilising of their understanding, specifically due to systematic reflection and questioning (James *et al.*, 2006). In fact this dip was only observed for the 11 females within the study sample, and did not reach significance. Rather, it stood out because it was discrepant from the significant overall increase in competence by the end of training for the whole group. In a related study, Lovell (2002) studied the development of counsellors ($N = 67$) who were attending a Masters course. Using the Supervisee Levels Questionnaire, Lovell reported a 'discontinuous pattern' (p.235) in the students' development. He also appealed to the notion of dis-equilibration to explain how their competence fluctuated.

Although little-researched in relation to supervision, this de-skilling phenomenon is well established within the practice of CBT. For example, in CBT clinical practice it is recognised that the patient has to endure unpleasant emotions in order to better understand and cope with clinical problems. Wells (1997), for instance, describes how 'affect shifts' (changes in emotion during therapy) should be monitored, in order to access the patient's negative automatic thoughts (he even advocates using role-play, to manipulate affect therapeutically). In general, it has been noted from a review of research in CBT that minimising affect shifts can render the approach ineffective (for example, through allowing safety behaviours, such as compulsive washing rituals, to regulate anxiety: Roth & Fonagy, 1996).

One way of capturing this equilibration process is to study critical incidents within supervision. These are episodes or events that are perceived as being a catalyst for change. Furr and Carroll (2003) adopted this research approach with 84 Masters-level counselling students by means of an end-of-term questionnaire, made up of open-ended questions eliciting their experiences of 'positive or negative experiences recognised as significant' (p.485). They found that the most frequently reported critical incidents were those related to experiences within clinical supervision that affected their development as professionals, and that involved emotional obstacles and personal growth. Students also acknowledged that events beyond the training programme had also contributed significant critical events to their development (for example, personal growth arising from interpersonal involvement with partners and friends; and the private counselling that they received). Furr and Carroll (2003) concluded that critical incidents were frequent, arising from a wide range of influences, but that the dominant influence was experiential learning. 'It seemed that experiential learning activities had a greater emotional impact than did courses based on cognitive learning strategies' (p.487). In summary, although supervisees might naturally seek to minimise de-skilling experiences, it is important to reframe these as a necessary part of the undulating path of development.

The role of emotions in the learning process

Phenomena such as de-skilling are potentially problematic, as strongly aversive experiences of incompetence or discomfort may very well cause the supervisee to withdraw from experiential learning. Therefore, such emotions need to be managed carefully, which is fundamentally the job of the supervisor (because they are the formal leader), whilst it falls on the supervisee to process them constructively (as in reframing them). In terms of the EBCS approach, this means working within the supervisee's zone of affective tolerance or comfort. As noted by Bennett-Levy (2006), a state of 'inner discomfort' (p.67) can helpfully focus attention and mobilise the supervisee's adjustment, for example through reformulating the experience as potentially beneficial, or by construing it as a fascinating or perplexing business. By one means or another, the effective supervisee, aided by a containing and resourceful supervisor, will work through this challenge to engage constructively in their professional learning and adaptation. Table 6.1 illustrates how this might be done in relation to Kolb's (1984) four modes of learning from experience.

The examples in Table 6.1 represent self-regulation by the individual (Warr & Downing, 2000), involving emotional control (ways of warding off

Table 6.1   Examples of the supervisee's input to supervision

Experiential learning mode	Supervisee actions that support experiential learning
'Experiencing' (concrete experience)	Prompt the supervisor to self-disclose the emotions he/she feels during difficult/satisfying clinical work
'Reflecting' (reflective observation)	In preparation for casework supervision, draw a formulation that crystallises your current grasp of a client's difficulties. Ensure that it is clearly marked 'draft'
'Conceptualising' (abstract conceptualisation)	Ask for guided reading from your supervisor, making a point of agreeing an objective (e.g. two ideas for a re-formulation) and discussing the outcome next time
'Experimenting' (active experimentation)	Engage the supervisor in generating and appraising some options for an action plan, based on presenting a plan that flopped

excess anxiety and ensuring good concentration), motivation control (ways of staying activated when disinterested), and comprehension monitoring (procedures that allow the supervisee to assess progress towards learning goals and to modify their learning experience as necessary). This kind of self-regulation has been found to directly influence learning outcomes (Vermunt & Verloop, 1999). Sticking to the affective dimension of such self-regulation, these authors noted the following aspects:

- motivating/expecting;
- concentrating/exerting effort;
- attributing/judging oneself;
- appraising events;
- dealing with emotions.

Vermunt and Verloop (1999) provide a helpful list of coping strategies, ones that are applicable to supervisees. For instance, in relation to remaining motivated, supervisees might develop appropriate expectations about supervision and about its processes. This may include self-reinforcement for attaining sub-goals, thinking of the negative consequences of failing and generally trying to generate interest in a topic. In order to concentrate and exert due effort, they recommend focusing attention on the task-relevant aspects. When it comes to judging oneself (attributing), the authors suggest ascribing success in achieving sub-goals to internal causal factors (i.e. under the control of the supervisee). Conversely, negative experiences should be attributed to a lack of effort, or some variable that is beyond their control. When it comes to dealing with emotions, Vermunt and Verloop (1999) suggest coping with negative emotions by talking to oneself in a reassuring way and by setting realistic learning goals.

Although plausible, it appears that the relationship between these coping strategies and learning is far from straightforward (Hook & Bunce, 2001). For instance, in an empirical analysis of a training situation, Warr and Downing (2000) found an interaction between these seemingly adaptive coping strategies and learning. For example, the coping strategy of emotional control had a significant negative correlation with learning, but only for those with high levels of learning anxiety. Part of this complex relationship may also be due to the supervisor's approach. For example, consider the findings from interviews conducted with psychotherapy trainees about a counter-productive event in supervision (an experience that they perceived as hindering, unhelpful or harmful in relation to their learning and development: Gray *et al.*, 2001). A typical example was the supervisor's dismissal of the trainee's thoughts and feelings, so lacking empathy or denying a trainee's request. All of the trainees reported such events, but more interestingly they reported that this led to subsequent counter-productive interactions, such as the trainee trying hard to be agreeable, but finding the supervisor was not responding or disputed and challenged the trainee. This sequence was perceived by all 13 interviewees as weakening the supervisory alliance, to the point where most did not raise their experience of negative events with the supervisors concerned. This indicates how a vicious cycle or downward developmental spiral may arise, arguably because the supervisees did not utilise adaptive coping strategies. By contrast, they may help to engineer a virtuous cycle by working with the supervisor to try to repair such relationship ruptures (Safran & Muran, 2000). An empirical assessment of such effort has been conducted by Zorga (2002), who analysed how clinical reports were treated within supervision. There was a general feeling amongst the professionals in this study that supervision had helped them to become more confident and self-respecting, resulting in them looking to their own resources for answers, rather than relying on the supervisor. As they developed strengths and this constructive attitude to problem-solving, they were reportedly better able to recognise emergent feelings and to express these clearly and effectively. This account is akin to the Gestalt therapy process described by Greenberg and Malcolm (2002), who examined how individuals resolved 'unfinished business' (e.g. childhood mistreatment) by having them express their feelings about the issue constructively. This led to 'adopting a more self-affirming stance' (p.407).

These kinds of relationship interactions were addressed more thoroughly in Chapter 4. The main point that I am trying to make here is that the supervisee is inevitably involved in shaping the effectiveness of supervision. With appropriate coping skills, supervisees can significantly co-construct supervision.

Responsivity

The Zorga (2002) illustration points to a fascinating and vital aspect of the supervisory process, the phenomenon of responsivity. This concept, like many within this book, is borrowed from the psychotherapy literature in order in order to develop the idea of co-construction. According to the responsivity logic, both supervisor and supervisee make appropriate adjustments in their behaviour as a result of the context and the moment-to-moment changes in each other's requirements (Stiles & Shapiro, 1994). Their interaction is governed by a set of complementary roles, and results in joint participation in the supervisory process. This should be contrasted with the dominant drug metaphor concept in psychotherapy (Stiles & Shapiro, 1994), which would lead us to assume that the right 'recipe' of supervision ingredients (e.g. goal-setting and feedback) would explain the link between process and outcome. This metaphor ignores processes like responsiveness, which is thought to be made up of responsive speech acts, and which might better explain how people learn and change. Responsive speech acts include enquiring, exploring, reframing and interpreting. As these categories imply, in therapy the patient is an active contributor to this responsive process (Stiles & Shapiro, 1995). Responsivity therefore recognises the 'dance of dialogue' between the two parties (Pickering, 2006, p.734).

Methods of Learning from Supervision

Most of the competencies outlined above, from self-regulation to responsivity, are part of the general skills that supervisees bring to supervision. After all, they are part of the repertoire that initially enabled them to obtain a training place on a competitive programme (where such personal and interpersonal qualities tend to be prized), and are part of being an effective professional. Appropriately, this emphasis mirrors the rest of this book, in that I have similarly assumed the transferability of supervisors' general professional competencies in relation to supervision (see, for example, Chapter 1). If supervisors can 'hit the ground running' because of these general skills when it comes to supervision, so, presumably, can the supervisee. And to make this assumption not only enables the process of supervision, it also recognises the supervisees' learning histories, providing the baseline for defining the lower reaches of their zones of proximal development.

However, both parties should also add additional, supervision-specific, competencies. The one I wish to focus on here is reflection, probably the single most discussed goal of supervision. As illustrated in Figure 6.2, reflection is one of the four key modes of learning from experience, as described by Kolb (1984). The dictionary defines reflection in two complementary ways. These are 'deliberation' (the action of fixing one's thoughts, of giving something deep or serious consideration) and 'meta-cognition' (the faculty by which the mind has knowledge of itself and its operations; thinking about thinking). The intended functions of reflection are to enable:

- heightened awareness (for example, reflecting on the feelings accompanying supervisor feedback);
- consolidation (e.g. recognising patterns in one's therapy);
- discrimination (being aware of relationships, synthesising and connecting new information to previously learned material);
- interpretation (the analysis and reconstruction of material in a form that enables assimilation);
- extrapolation (the extension of concepts to their action implications);
- evaluation (awareness of the value judgements accompanying actions)

This summary is based on the work of Boud *et al.* (1985) and Dewey (1933). In order to achieve these outcomes, Boud *et al.* (1985) advocate allocating time and effort for reflection, including the maintenance of a reflective diary. Within supervision, the supervisee should be making efforts to recapture experiences accurately (for example, returning to salient events and recounting experiences); viewing experiences from different perspectives in order to gain distance and an orientation to how others may see an event; attending to feelings that accompany the event (as in expressing feelings); re-evaluating experiences (including associating it to prior learning); integrating experiences with other material and placing it on a conceptual map; validating the experience (through reality testing or guided imagery); and appropriation (making the new version of the experience one's own). According to Dewey (1910), reflection may occur privately, be provoked by a problem, or be triggered by something that created perplexity, hesitation, doubt, or some kind of challenge to the individual (i.e. which caused them to question their beliefs). This is viewed as sufficiently motivating to cause the individual to actively search for facts (for example, from memory or observation), to investigate and to think about the available evidence and ways that the experience may be understood. 'Demand for the solution of perplexity is the steadying and guiding factor in the entire process of reflection' (Dewey, 1910, p.11). Reflecting the above account of de-skilling, Dewey (1910) saw reflection as 'always more or less troublesome because it involves overcoming the inertia that inclines one to accept suggestions at their face value; it involves the willingness to endure a condition of mental unrest and disturbance ... (reflection) ... in short, means suspense ... which is likely to be somewhat painful (p.13). The conclusion he drew is that what is most troublesome is actually what is most essential to effective thinking.

An interesting example of facilitating reflection is to be found in the 'self-reflection and self-practice' approach within CBT. According to Laireiter and Willutzki (2003), self-reflection can be used to attend to the supervisee, focusing on relevant themes in their lives, such as their learning history and family background. This work typically occurs within group sessions lasting two hours, led by two experienced supervisors who have no other role within the training system. These leaders encourage the supervisees to analyse central cognitive–affective schemas by self-observation and through the observation of other members of the group. This is expected to enable the supervisees to define problematic patterns or themes, and to work on changing these to more adaptive alternatives. Methods used within the self-reflection process include self-observation, guided imagery, role-plays, analysis of group processes and cognitive techniques, including confrontation. Summarising the available literature, Laireiter and Willutzki (2003) acknowledged that (to their knowledge) there was no study which had examined the effects of self-practice and self-reflection (SP/SR) on the clinical effectiveness of the supervisees. However, there was some evidence that participation in the groups improved interpersonal functioning, and participants tend to perceive the group as effective in developing their empathy and ability to cope with emotional material. To illustrate, Bennett-Levy *et al.* (2003) engaged 14 cognitive therapists in a programme designed to encourage them to utilise SR-SP. One group of six engaged in a co-therapy approach with their partner, while the eight remaining therapists practised applying cognitive therapy techniques to themselves in private. Reflective diaries maintained by both groups indicated that there were improvements in their ability to communicate about CBT, and enhanced attention to the therapeutic relationship. They also felt better able to reflect on their practice, and were more inclined to use self-reflection spontaneously following the group. Subsequently, Bennett-Levy (2006) has constructed an information-processing model to account for how therapists develop competence, placing reflection at its heart.

Outcomes of Learning from Experience

Based on successfully negotiating the challenging processes of supervision, including drawing on the above methods, which kinds of outcomes should a supervisee anticipate? What are the milestones along our supervision map? How can a supervisee tell whether their 'probing of the unknown' is progressing satisfactorily, particularly as the journey is undulating? Table 6.2 attempts a reply by collating the views of a number of authors who have written about the effects of experiential learning, namely Bloom *et al.* (1956), Krathwohl *et al.* (1964); Boud *et al.* (1985); Kolb (1984); and Klein *et al.* (1986).

According to Table 6.2, supervisees can infer that they are making progress when engaged in the experiencing mode of learning from experience if they find (for example) that they are more aware of their current emotions (e.g. they are better able to list and articulate their feeling states). Similarly, the reflecting supervisees who are able to integrate this experience with existing material will have grounds for believing that they are progressing. Milestones whilst conceptualising include accessing new material, or comprehending existing material better. Lastly, productive engagement with the 'experimenting' mode is indicated by creating plans, etc. In keeping with the travelling metaphor, these milestones can be placed in order, corresponding to how readily they can be achieved. Bloom's taxonomies are a classic example of this approach (1956, 1964). To illustrate, the Experiencing Scale (Klein *et al.*, 1986) recognises the early stages as simply entailing talking about events with an emotional tone, whereas at 'higher stages' these are explored and result in heightened awareness and meaning-making. This kind of engagement has been found to predict beneficial change in therapy (Castonguay *et al.*, 1996), and is one of the recognised 'change processes' in therapy (e.g. based on the opportunity for catharsis/ventilation; affective experiencing; assimilation of problematic experiences: Grencavage & Norcross, 1990; Lambert & Bergin, 1994). It is also accepted as an 'essential' part of productive supervision, though CBT approaches to supervision seem to place somewhat less emphasis on processing experiencing within supervision than many other approaches (Follette & Batten, 2000; Reilly, 2000).

Conclusions

Until recently, the contribution made by the supervisee to effective clinical supervision was surprisingly neglected. To illustrate, we counted the number of references to the supervisee's contribution within the definitive *Handbook*

Table 6.2 Trainees' milestones in learning from experience

If I experience, I will...
- be more aware of my current emotions/sensations;
- recognise/define my own feelings;
- develop my intuition;
- have had a 'here and now' moment;
- be more aware of the emotional or sensory accompaniments to my activity;
- recognise my own attitudes or motivation better (e.g. concerns; barriers; uplifts).
- discriminate amongst the emotions/sensations I experience at work.
- better regulate or manage my emotions (positive or negative ones).
- recognise patterns that arise in my work;
- interpret my emotions/patterns;
- draw out the action implications of my patterns/emotions;
- evaluate how I feel;
- process some of my affect/sensations.

If I reflect I will...
- integrate my material with other material (e.g. prior learning experiences);
- assimilate things into a personal, reasoned understanding;
- ground my experience (etc.) in my own understanding, (particularly through personal images; metaphors; etc.).
- tell my story, recalling and summarising recent events;
- prioritise things (e.g. work objectives);
- clarify things (e.g. a formulation);
- reconcile conflicting pressures/beliefs;
- develop and define my own belief system or personal 'stance'.

If I conceptualise, I will...
- access new material (e.g. compare what I know with supervisor's grasp of a topic);
- comprehend something better (improve my grasp of a knowledge-base);
- integrate new material with my own understanding (including theories, data, literature, drawing on knowledge-base);
- analyse material (e.g. try to figure out what maintains a clinical problem);
- synthesise new material with my old ideas (e.g. from reflection);
- evaluate my comprehension (e.g. reviewing work/idea critically, to define my strengths and weaknesses);
- explore ideas;
- develop a new understanding (e.g. re-formulation).

If I experiment, I will...
- action plan;
- make predictions;

(cont'd)

Table 6.2 (*cont'd*)

- set myself a goal;
- agree a 'homework' assignment;
- decide/summarise what I want to do next.
- want to test things out;
- address a puzzle/concern/worry (e.g. rehearse a new skill in order to see what happens, gain competence, or to get feedback);
- engage in role-play; learning exercises; assign myself a task (like conducting an 'experiment').

---

of Psychotherapy Supervision (Watkins, 1997) and estimated that only about 9 of its 613 pages (1.5 per cent) were concerned with supervisee's input (Milne & Gracie, 2001). This is a perverse state of affairs for a relationship-based enterprise such as supervision, as every health practitioner knows that, whether in therapy or supervision, the process and outcomes will be influenced greatly by the other person. Without question, 'it takes two'. Indeed, in one of the chapters in Watkins' handbook, Dewald (1997) stated that: 'The nature of the patient and his or her aptitude and capacities to use the analytical procedure effectively have a major impact on the entire supervisory situation. A naturally good patient can make a poor student look competent, and a difficult or un-analysable case can make a good student seem to have major difficulties' (p.33).

In this context, I feel justified in having given a whole chapter to the supervisee's role within supervision. However, I should also acknowledge that the whole book could readily be devoted to the subject, as there are many fascinating and important ways in which the supervisee contributes to the profoundly important business of supervision, surely as many and varied as there are in relation to the supervisor (see, for example, Carroll & Gilbert, 2005).

Within the above discussion I have covered the basic stances or role-relationships that the supervisee and supervisor may take to the enterprise, concluding that the traveller–guide relationship (i.e. the constructivist/ structuralist combination) is generally most appropriate, though there will surely be times when other stances are at least fleetingly appropriate. I then considered the role of the supervisee within this stance, recognising again how this could not be understood in isolation. The next section looked at the micro-processes of interacting effectively, including the notions of de-skilling and of responsivity, critical processes underpinning perhaps the most commonly acknowledged supervisee duty, reflection. These '3Rs' of successful supervisee-hood (roles, responsivity and reflection) are intended to deepen our appreciation of the complex contribution made by the supervisee, but are recognised as being only a sample. Arguably, they are themselves only milestones on the journey towards competence in the profound process of 'probing the unknown'.

7

Supporting Supervision

Introduction

Within professional circles the emphasis on clinical supervision is resounding, but attention to how supervisors themselves might best be supported and developed is muted. That is, whilst there are specified standards and general messages of encouragement, there appears to be no established framework, and a notable lack of practical support. Thus, within the UK's National Health Service there is recognition that staff should to be 'trained, organised and managed properly ...' (Department of Health, 1998, pp.46–47), that they need to be 'supported' (Department of Health, 1998, p.36) and that an infrastructure is required to enable them to be 'skilled', drawing on 'multiple knowledge and learning sources, technical and other resources' (Department of Health, 2001, p.ix). However, it appears that no practical assistance is available (e.g. guidelines or toolkits). To re-quote Watkins (1997), 'something does not compute' (p.604). This recognition that supervisors require a variety of supports to enable them to do their work effectively is also echoed by practitioners working within the health and social services. For example, Stallard *et al.* (2007) noted that, in order to extend the availability of CBT, their survey indicated 'an urgent need to develop a training and supervisory infrastructure' (p.504) for therapists. In social work, a survey by Harmse (2001) concluded that the participants did not receive support in their work, but that systems like peer support groups and a supportive work culture could be effective. In clinical psychology, only 17 of 127 respondents to a UK survey (i.e. 18 per cent) were satisfied with their supervision arrangements (Gabbay *et al.*, 1999).

As these quotes indicate, many of these policy and practice statements are directed at how supervision itself can be delivered effectively, rather than addressing the question of how supervisors themselves can be supported and developed. However, reference to creating an appropriate infrastructure does imply that this will be tackled systematically, and there are some clues within the above policy statements as to how this might be achieved. In the absence of explicit guidance, I will again draw on the evidence-based clinical supervision (EBCS) model for inspiration (see Chapter 3). This appears promising, as it suggests several elements towards an infrastructure, including CPD, consensus-building work, and evaluation. But first I want to check whether the EBCS model is sufficient, and will do this by contrasting it with some alternatives. Note that this chapter does not address the support that is provided within supervision itself, the so-called 'restorative' function, as this overlaps strongly with the alliance material(addressed primarily in Chapter 4), and also it is assumed to be a core (transferable) professional competence. For example, it includes the 'common factors' of providing structure to sessions, facilitating catharsis and offering the 'core conditions' (i.e. warmth, respect, empathy, acceptance and genuineness: Lambert & Bergin, 1994).

One alternative to the EBCS way of thinking about a suitable infrastructure to support supervisors is to draw on the organisational development (OD) literature. An example of a promising system has been detailed by West and Farr (1989). In its favour, this model was developed from an analysis of how health visitors worked within the UK's National Health Service. According to their system, a number of factors should appear within a suitable infrastructure (examples from supervision added):

- factors that are intrinsic to the job (e.g. availability of the necessary supervision resources);
- group factors (e.g. specific support and cohesiveness amongst supervisors);
- relationships at work (e.g. effective leadership and good feedback);
- organisational factors (opportunities for the development of individual supervisors; agreement about the goals of supervision).

These broad system factors are related to individual characteristics within the West and Farr (1989) model, including the supervisor's confidence, motivation and skill. Based on the interaction between these organisational and individual factors, we should be able to predict the degree to which organisational development (OD) occurs (that is, whether implementation results in innovation, defined as constructive, novel ways of undertaking our work, such as introducing new support systems for supervisors). Leaving aside differences in terminology, this model is entirely consistent with the EBCS one, with the exception that the evidence-based practice model (Roth, Fonagy & Parry, 1996) and the original EBCS model (Milne & Westerman, 2001) did not specify a leadership function or these 'individual characteristics' (though the latter equate somewhat to the EBCS panels of 'judgements made by supervisors' and 'supervision practice': i.e. panels 1 and 2 in Figure 7.1 below). Leadership has therefore been added to this figure, as part of the 'context' for a suitable infrastructure, while individual characteristics are discussed shortly, as an elaboration of 'practice'. Context merits recognition as an additional general factor, not least as it was noted within a consensus statement on supervision (Falender *et al.*, 2004). These American experts concurred that context could be thought of in terms of both proximal aspects (e.g. the workplace as a setting for supervision, including management), and distal aspects (e.g. accrediting bodies and the legal system). I'm relieved to note that 'context' was an explicit backdrop to the original EBCS model (see Figure 2 in the paper by Milne & Westerman, 2001), but the examples of the context that were noted then were 'physical environment; social milieu, etc' (p.448).

Another promising way to design an infrastructure, one that overlaps explicitly with supervision, is the framework of 'practice improvement methods' summarised by Cape and Barkham (2002). This includes staff training, clinical guidelines, audit, collecting outcome data, and bench-marking of these data. In short, these practice improvement methods are directly comparable to the EBCS model, and can be thought of as the kinds of processes that would facilitate OD. It is reassuring to note how these two approaches agree so strongly with the EBCS model. This overlap increases my confidence that, in adding other examples of context to Figure 7.1 (i.e. effective leadership and proximal/distal system factors) and to the original EBCS model, we have designed a promising, integrative infrastructure for supervisor support and development.

One last test of this emerging, integrative model is the rare discussion of a suitable infrastructure within the supervision texts. In their final three chapters, Hawkins and Shohet (2000) discuss the organisational context in which the supervisor operates. They stress the importance of individual supervisors contributing to a learning culture by, for instance, undertaking an 'appreciative enquiry' into the current strengths of supervision within the workplace. This may result in their enhancing the local policy and practice, for example through dealing with resistance to change, and by promoting experimentation. Like Cape and Barkham (2002), they note that a key policy is to train and support supervisors, linked to a system of audit and iterative infrastructure development. But a difference is that Hawkins and Shohet (2000) urge supervisors themselves to shoulder responsibility for developing their own support systems. This is again consistent with the EBCS model, but places more onus on the individual supervisor. To reflect this, the directional arrows in Figure 3.4 have been replaced by bi-directional links in Figure 7.1, to indicate that any one panel can influence any other.

Therefore, a further implied addition to the EBCS model is to specify how the individual supervisor might influence their supervision system. In effect, this means that the panel labelled 'supervision' (panel 2 in Figure 7.1) should be expanded, to add ways that supervisors adapt to their organisational context. An obvious contender for this elaboration is the long-established transactional stress model (Lazarus & Folkman, 1984), which allows us to think psychologically about the supervisor's options. Coping is defined in terms of a broad range of thoughts, feelings and behaviours that individuals utilise (consciously or otherwise) in response to stressful events (i.e. things that they appraise as threatening or requiring a response). This is viewed as part of a process of transacting with people and events, in order to achieve as much mastery as possible (e.g. stress reduction; developing one's own support system; confidence enhancement). Classic forms of coping adaptively include logical analysis, positive appraisal, and seeking support. But coping can also be maladaptive, as in cognitive avoidance, seeking alternative rewards and emotional discharge (for an example, see the Coping Responses Inventory; Moos, 1993).

In summary, in the absence of an explicit infrastructure that clarifies how supervisors should be supported and developed, I have compared and contrasted the original (2001) EBCS model against a range of alternatives. These are essentially similar, suggesting that simply integrating the novel details from these alternatives will yield a suitable framework. Specifically, the current, integrative EBCS infrastructure (see Figure 7.1) incorporates new examples of the context (e.g. the importance of effective leadership), and elaborates the 'supervision practice' panel, so that individual characteristics are duly recognised (including supervisors' personal coping strategies). This infrastructure is consistent with relevant review articles (e.g. Cleary & Freeman, 2006; Kavanagh *et al.*, 2002). In the remainder of this chapter, this infrastructure is used to identify the different theoretical options for supervisor support and development, as summarised by the

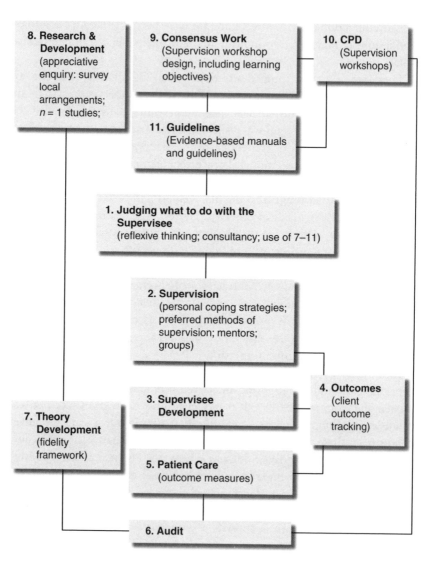

12. Context
effective leadership and proximal workplace factors (including local policies and practices; stress) distal system factors (e.g. course accreditation/professional registration); social support;

8. Research & Development (appreciative enquiry: survey local arrangements; $n = 1$ studies;

9. Consensus Work (Supervision workshop design, including learning objectives)

10. CPD (Supervision workshops)

11. Guidelines (Evidence-based manuals and guidelines)

1. Judging what to do with the Supervisee (reflexive thinking; consultancy; use of 7–11)

2. Supervision (personal coping strategies; preferred methods of supervision; mentors; groups)

7. Theory Development (fidelity framework)

3. Supervisee Development

4. Outcomes (client outcome tracking)

5. Patient Care (outcome measures)

6. Audit

Figure 7.1 Supervision of supervision: the EBCS support framework

bold headings in each of the 11 panels (boxes) in Figure 7.1. As you will notice, these headings are linked to some specific practical examples, showing how the EBCS model can be applied to the task of supporting and developing supervisors. The lower part and left-hand side of the figure note the research and development activities (panels 3–8), to be discussed primarily in the next chapter. However, I will first discuss some simple but useful ways that supervisors have engaged in research here, as they are perhaps best considered as professional coping strategies. Also, I will assume that Chapter 6 addresses panel 3, 'supervisee development'. Therefore, the remainder of this chapter deals with the panels that are not covered elsewhere in this book.

I will next describe these practical examples, starting at the heart of the model, with the moment-to-moment demands that tend to be placed on supervisors, and the critical role of their personal coping strategies. Note that these strategies naturally address other panels, providing dynamism to the infrastructure model that is not apparent from Figure 7.1.

Personal Coping Strategies for Supervisors

Recognise the inherently stressful nature of supervision

The definition of coping presented immediately above notes the inseparable link to stressors, which are regarded as part of the context (panel 12; e.g. ineffective leadership), and part of the 'judgements made by supervisors in relation to the particulars of the case' (panel 1; i.e. what the supervisee brings to supervision). Part of coping effectively is recognising that supervision is an intrinsically stressful activity. Within the transactional stress model, this recognition is termed 'appraisal', and includes judging whether an event requires a reaction, then, if it does, judging whether one is able to respond effectively. Key parameters of stressors are their predictability and controllability, though several other factors are important, such as whether the stressor is a result of something you did, or rather was something done to you. For example, a supervisee who has a rather fixed and non-threatening way of using supervision, and who responds readily to your guidance, will tend to be appraised as presenting few stressors. However, supervision is typically dominated by a more stressful profile of events, which I will now describe.

As indicated by the notion of the 'seven-eyed supervisor' (Hawkins & Shohet, 2000), supervisors need to attend to complex information, on several concurrent channels. They not only have to deal with their supervisees' therapy, but also how this is being presented in supervision, and other related topics. It is stressful in other respects, because the supervisor is charged with integrating formative, normative and restorative functions. As Holloway and Wolleat (1994) put it, '… because the goal of supervision is to connect science and practice, supervision is among the most complex of all activities associated with the practice of psychology' (p.30). Indeed, it is arguably the most complex of all the so-called 'complex interventions'.

Another stressor is the growing requirements of supervisees. As they become better trained and more knowledgeable about what it is reasonable to expect from supervisors, they are likely to put increasing pressure on supervisors for more opportunities and relevant experiences. Schindler and Talen (1994) underscored this trend, recounting how 'trainees were more articulate in identifying their developmental training needs, better equipped to define the goals of supervision, and more informed about the styles or strategies of supervision that would help them meet their goals (e.g. video tape, co-therapy, live supervision). In essence, now that they know more, they want more' (p.304). They also noted that supervisors were facing more complex demands within the workplace, becoming responsible for administrative supervision and the monitoring of complex ethical, legal and policy issues. Furthermore, theories of both clinical practice and supervision have been developing, placing supervisors under pressure to understand and apply new clinical ideas, as well as to undertake accreditation as a supervisor (Greenspan *et al.*, 1991). Other pressures intrinsic to supervision that were listed by Bernard and Goodyear (2004) include the following:

- Additional responsibilities: Alongside a reduction in direct client contact (with the attendant reduced ability to directly influence quality of care), supervisors also have to accept responsibility for their supervisees' cases.
- Parallel processes: It is not unusual for supervisors to experience some of the complex and uncomfortable emotions that are encountered by their supervisees in therapy. This means that the supervisors need to deal with clinical practicalities, whilst also attending to process phenomena.
- Maintaining control: There is often a complex dynamic around the exercise of power within supervision, and it is not uncommon for struggles

to occur between the supervisor and the supervisee (e.g. striking a balance between behaving as a colleague, and exercising some form of control over the supervisee).

- Needs-led supervision: Whilst it is of course highly desirable to tailor supervision to the individual characteristics of the supervisee (including aspects of race, culture, gender, sexual orientation and religion), this represents a considerable burden on the supervisor's coping strategies.
- Interpersonal effectiveness: In addition to these various pressures on the supervisor's ability to function, the not-uncommon phenomenon of sexual attraction between supervisor and supervisee may add further spice to the interpersonal recipe.

At a more general level of the system, there appears to be an unrelenting increase in positive social, economic and professional practice developments. On the negative side, re-engineering, downsizing, job and budget cuts, and reductions in technological and other resources have also been related to supervision (Bhanthumnavin, 2000). To illustrate, Deery (2004) noted how midwives had been given new powers and greater influence, while at the same time being asked to increase the number of people they see, to improve the care that they provide to clients, to reach out and help previously under-served groups in deprived areas, and to introduce new antenatal screening programmes. As a result, 'the climate of continual change often brought about by various policy directives has become a potential health hazard for midwives, leading to stress-related disease' (p.162). In their effort to cope, Deery (2004) reported that midwives worked longer hours, but still experienced emotional exhaustion. This is substantiated by a survey of multi-disciplinary staff within mental health services: Kavanagh *et al.* (2003) found that 55 per cent of their supervisors had issues concerning a high clinical workload, a quarter of them felt there were insufficient guidelines to support their supervision, and a fifth of these respondents felt there was lack of support from their line manager. Similarly, the supervisees in this sample thought that the amount of clinical work that they had to undertake was an issue (41 per cent of respondents cited this as a difficulty). Cleary and Freeman (2006) also noted additional 'realities' affecting supervision, such as inadequate facilities (lack of distraction-free, quiet rooms) and token committees.

Such stressors are a formally recognised part of supervision. For example, the Department of Health in the UK noted that the workforce needs the opportunity to learn and develop within a system that provides support.

In the absence of these factors there can be 'a downward spiral that manifests itself ... in poor morale in the workforce, an increase in complaints, and dissatisfaction for everybody' (Department of Health, 2007, p.3). In this stressful context, supervisors require effective personal coping strategies. In the above, I have tried to suggest that the first of these is accurate appraisal, namely recognising that supervision inevitably comes with some complex stressors. This appraisal is a preferable way of coping, as it is grounded in reality and should minimise the alternative appraisal, in which difficulties are attributed to oneself as a supervisor. I will now describe three broad types of adaptive coping that build on this appraisal process. Adaptive (effective) coping has repeatedly been found to be approach-based, that is, concerned with tackling stressors, rather than avoiding them. In addition, I will be utilise the distinction between behaviours, thoughts and feeling reactions, three established parameters of coping. Specifically, I will outline how supervisor training can strengthen supervision skills; summarise ways of developing supervision-linked thinking; and note how groups (and other arrangements) allow supervisors to process the emotionally loaded aspects of their work.

Developing skills as a supervisor

By far the most popular approach to supporting and developing supervisors is to provide them with relevant training, the 'continuing professional development' part of the infrastructure (CPD: see Figure 7.1, panel 10). However, such CPD may not reach everyone: a survey of CBT practitioners indicated that only 108 of 170 respondents in the UK (i.e. 64 per cent) had received some form of training in supervision (Townend *et al.*, 2002). Also, there appears to be a huge gulf between the complex, stressful role of the supervisor and the kind of training that is usually provided within health-care systems. In this vein, Watkins (1997) concludes the *Handbook of Psychotherapy Supervision* in exasperation, noting that: 'Something does not compute. We would never dream of turning untrained therapists loose on needy patients, so why would we turn untrained supervisors loose on those untrained therapists who help those needy patients?' (p.604). He is of the view that supervisor training should be given the same degree of importance as initial training. Surveys of practitioners tend to support this negative view, and it is widely thought that '... most psychologists have never received formal training and supervision in supervision' (Falender & Shafranske,

2004, p.19). They go on to add that '... many, if not most, supervisors practise without the benefit of education, training or supervision ... It is likely ... that supervisors' behaviours are based on implicit models of supervision, culled from their experiences as a supervisee, from their identification with past supervisors, or from skills derived from psychotherapy or teaching' (Falender & Shafranske, 2004, p.7). This appears to have been the case for years, regardless of theoretical orientation (Perris, 1994).

In response to this unacceptable situation, these authors and others have produced a consensus statement regarding competent supervision (Falender *et al.*, 2004). Similarly, professional organisations are increasingly requiring that supervisors receive proper training in order to practise within initial training programmes. For example, the British Psychological Society (2007, p.65) states that training programmes in clinical psychology 'must organise regular supervision workshops to train supervisors in methods of supervision'. Similarly, all of the other nine NHS professions within a review of supervision arrangements conducted a decade ago (Milne, 1998) expected their supervisors to attend some form of training in supervision, with workshops lasting between one and five days. However, at that stage none of these 10 professional bodies required supervisors to be trained in supervision, with the onus placed instead on the relevant professional training programmes, which were expected to offer this training in order to be accredited by their professional bodies. Alongside the workshops provided by local programmes of initial professional training, independent, university-accredited courses in clinical supervision began to emerge, such that Wheeler (2004) was able to note that training courses for supervisors were becoming common, ranging from brief one-day workshops to two-year, part-time Masters courses. She surveyed 10 expert supervisors in the field of counselling and psychotherapy and concluded that supervisor training should vary from a minimum of 45 hours of theory and 45 hours of practice to a maximum of 200 hours in total. These experts were optimistic about the effectiveness of this supervisor training, particularly where this took account of organisational factors that impinge on effective supervision. In the same book, Fleming (2004) recounts the history of supervisor training within clinical psychology. Fleming surveyed the Doctoral training programmes in the UK and Ireland in 2001, obtaining an 87 per cent response rate. All respondents reported providing training for supervisors, averaging 4.6 training events per annum. However, most of these workshops were only of one day's duration, and there was little attention to evaluating the effectiveness of the workshops or of seeking any form of accreditation.

On the other hand, there was significant consensus on the content of these workshops, the great majority emphasising the need to cover learning processes, different theoretical models, and the vexatious issue of failing those trainees who are not making satisfactory progress. Fleming (2004) concluded that the situation regarding supervisor training was improving, as it was being provided on 'an increasingly systematic basis within an enactive framework. There is a good uptake of training by supervisors generally' (p.91). In a second survey (involving 95 qualified psychotherapists of various orientations), training was perceived as the third most influential factor in their development (Lucock *et al.*, 2006). A mapping exercise conducted by Docchar in 2007 suggested that there were by then 85 supervisor training courses in the UK, split equally between university and independent-sector providers, and ranging from Diploma to Masters programmes (though about a third of these were not accredited at all). These courses also varied significantly (e.g. in cost, supervision methods addressed, delivery, etc.). Against this apparent progress, it should, however, be recognised that supervisor training courses are rarely accredited by professional organisations, that regulation of individual professionals may only require them to 'recognise the role and value of clinical supervision' and that there is no scheme, within the largest UK organisation, to regulate supervisors (Health Professions Council, 2007, p.39). Some professional groups do, however, accredit supervisors (e.g. British Association for Counselling and Psychotherapy (BABCP)).

Therefore, while these burgeoning supervisor training courses may mollify Watkins' angst (1997), the system is still informal, in the sense that courses and professionals are still free from any form of accreditation or approval. I next turn to accounts of supervisor training within the research literature. Does that also cause angst? A number of traditional (i.e. narrative) reviews have sided with Watkins (1997), recounting numerous shortcomings in the training of supervisors (e.g. Cape & Barkham, 2002; Falender *et al.*, 2004; Kaslow *et al.*, 2004; Kilminster & Jolly, 2000; Russell & Petrie, 1994; Spence *et al.*, 2001 and Zorga, 2002). Their recommendations for rectifying supervisor training are set out within Table 7.1. It can be seen that this includes addressing the supervisory relationship, utilising certain training formats, as well as suggesting how these workshops might best be evaluated.

Although these authors were sceptical about the current status of published accounts of supervisor training (in keeping with Watkins, 1997), their narrative approach to reviewing this literature has its own shortcomings (i.e. being highly subjective in style, it can be inaccurate and misleading).

As outlined earlier in this book, a systematic approach often yields a rather different picture. Therefore, Table 7.1 includes a summary of a systematic review of an equivalent sample of 10 of the best available analyses of supervisor training (see the right-hand column of Table 7.1). This suggests that some published summaries of supervisor training fully satisfy the standards set by the narrative reviewers. Indeed, there were a number of sophisticated developments within this sample, ones that actually went beyond those envisaged by the narrative reviewers. Examples included the provision of empirically based rationales for the supervisor training approaches employed, and the use of competency-based formats that were well-grounded in modern approaches to training. The 10 studies within Table 7.1 are: Fleming *et al.* (1996); Harkness (1997); Methot *et al.* (1996); Milne and James (2002); Milne and Westerman (2001); Milne *et al.* (2003); Reid *et al.* (2003, 2005); Reichelt *et al.* (2003); and Shore *et al.* (1995).

Given their relevance to the present focus on developing supervisors, it is important to list these skills:

- negotiating learning goals;
- understanding the components of feedback;
- objectively monitoring supervisee performance;
- asking key questions;
- providing constructive feedback;
- supporting and positively acknowledging supervisor participation;
- empathy;
- collaboration.

Illustrative examples of supervisor training

Barrow and Domingo (1997) provided training in supervision to 15 moderately experienced supervisors, allocating 43 students to receive supervision either within control or experimental groups. None of the supervisors had received any formal training in supervision, despite having practised for an average of 6.4 years (within the field of speech and language therapy). The experimental group of supervisors received a 10-hour course, spread over 8 weeks. During this time the control group of supervisors received no training. Analysis of the effectiveness of this supervisor training course was based on the Individual Supervisory Conference Rating Scale. This 18-item observation instrument covers: the supervisee asking questions and the

Table 7.1 Standards for the training of supervisors, as represented in narrative reviews and found in a systematic review (frequency, out of 10)

Training parameters	Narrative review: current practice	Narrative review: future guidelines	Systematic review findings
Context	Emphasis on personality of supervisor	Establish and maintain a respectful and facilitating learning environment (including mentoring)	Educational pyramid of up to five levels (researchers–consultants–supervisors–supervisees–patients), utilised as part of a pragmatic, organisational development initiative (6); empirical studies involving the last three in above pyramid (2); training evaluations (2)
Foundation of training	Rare to base training on learning needs; rarely empirically or theoretically based	Needs-led training and learning contracts; addresses research and theory systematically (assigned reading, lectures/discussion, etc.)	Empirically and theoretically based rationale provided (i.e. applied behaviour analysis; organisational development; organisational behaviour management; CBT; interactional social work; experiential learning model; behaviourally based outcome management) (10)
Topics	Models of supervision; relationship dynamics; methods; evaluation; legal and ethical issues	Knowledge (models, ethics, development, etc); Skills (teaching; feedback; scientific thinking, etc); Attitudes (respect; empowerment, etc.)	Knowledge: negotiating goals; components of feedback; objective monitoring of supervisee performance; asking key questions (8); dignity of patient (1) Skills: 1–26 competencies addressed (e.g. providing constructive feedback)(10) Attitudes: supporting and positively acknowledging supervisor participation (5); empathy (1); collaboration (2)

Format	Brief seminars or workshops	Formal training programmes, lasting a semester or more. To include didactic and experiential course work	Brief workshops (workshops 3.5 hours–5 days) (4); training through a series of CPD workshops and seminars over a two-year period, and/or weekly consultancy during research period (5); unspecified duration or format) (1)
Methods of training	Lectures, written guidelines/manuals and skills-training workshops	Experiential work in supervision with modelling, observation and consultancy/feedback. Didactic work; discussion reflection, developmental sequence to progressively treat more complex skills. Joint problem solving. Direct observation of supervision; impact on learning and patient care (cost–benefit analysis)	Competency-based formats, featuring written material (guidelines/checklist/assignment), and experiential, adult-learning, skills-training workshops; or 1:1 consultancy (including shared problem-solving, live and video-based modelling of appropriate and inappropriate behaviours; reflection; feedback; on-the-job practice; discussion) (9) Not specified (1)
Evaluation			By self-report (satisfaction with training) (6); direct observation of supervision (7); ratings of supervision skills, outcomes and relationship quality (9, including empathy, e.g. assessed by supervisees); learning (3); generalisation to therapy (4); and impact on patient care (5)

supervisor making suggestions; discussing ways to improve therapy techniques; and preparatory behaviours (e.g. the supervisor stating the objectives of the meeting). The predicted change in supervisors becoming more facilitating in their style was obtained: significant differences were found between the two groups, which resulted in supervisees' feeling better able to express their learning needs, related to the supervisor becoming a more active listener and enabler of the supervisee as an active participant (e.g. the supervisor making more use of the supervisee's ideas in discussion, and responding to statements, questions or problems presented by the supervisee). Similarly, directive behaviours decreased (including discussing weaknesses in the supervisees' clinical behaviour, and making value judgements about the supervisee).

In a second controlled evaluation of supervisor training, McMahon and Simons (2004) studied the effects of supervisor training on 16 practising counsellors. They received a four-day workshop, involving didactic and experiential methods (including the use of tape recordings, learning exercises based on case discussion, role-plays, and practising supervision techniques). These methods were used to address seven supervision competencies (e.g. developing the supervision contract, the use of case presentations and dealing with processes within supervision). They developed the Clinical Supervision Questionnaire to evaluate the success of the workshop, including items on confidence, understanding theories, and practical skills. Whilst the experimental group obtained a significantly higher score on this questionnaire following training (and maintained this at a follow-up assessment six months later), no significant changes were reported for the control group.

The third and final example is more focused, describing the development of teaching skills in supervisors. Busari *et al.* (2006) allocated supervisors of medical students to either an experimental group ($N = 14$) or a control group ($N = 13$). A two-day workshop was provided to the experimental group, covering six topics: effective teaching, self-knowledge in teaching ability, feedback skills, assessing prior knowledge, trouble shooting, and time management. The teaching ability of the supervisors was assessed by the students using a teaching effectiveness instrument, covering 15 different skills (e.g. 'Establishes a good learning environment'; 'Gives clear explanations/reasons for opinions, advice, actions, etc.'). There was also a supervisee satisfaction questionnaire. Once more, the experimental group alone yielded significantly improved results, as judged by their supervisees. But this was only obtained for the teaching skills assessment: satisfaction ratings for the two groups were not significantly different (the status of satisfaction as a measure of supervision is addressed in the next chapter).

These examples illustrate some key, recurring guidelines for supervisor development, such as incorporating didactic and experiential work, covering developmentally appropriate material, which is organised systematically (Russell & Petrie, 1994; Falender *et al.*, 2004). Significant additional material is available in the five chapters about supervisor training in the *Handbook of Psychotherapy Supervision* (Watkins, 1997) and in the other major textbooks.

Effectiveness of supervisor training

These three examples of supervisor training provide clear evidence for its effectiveness, but reviews of the evidence are guarded. For example, in medical education, Kilminster and Jolly (2000) acknowledged that training for supervisors was valuable and necessary, but they noted that training programmes are often not empirically or theoretically grounded. They concluded that: 'there is some evidence that training can have a positive effect on supervisors' (p.835). Spence *et al.* (2001) reviewed the evidence in occupational therapy, social work, speech pathology and clinical psychology. Reviewing the handful of supervisor training studies that they were able to locate, these authors concluded that 'although there is some tentative evidence to suggest the training supervisors can produce a change in supervisor practices and supervisee subjective ratings of the benefits of training, it remains to be demonstrated conclusively that such training achieves long-term impact on supervisee clinical practice and client outcomes' (p.149).

Thinking Effectively About Supervision

Clearly a number of very helpful ways of thinking about one's personal functioning as a supervisor are treated within supervisor training workshops, manuals and guidelines. Also, local training programmes and national professional associations will produce handbooks, guidance documents, and even online advice. However, to emphasise the importance of how we think about our role, two further ways of developing our thinking are discussed. The first of these is the practice of 'reflexivity', used here to refer to the application of supervisory principles and practices to the supervisor.

This is a meta-cognitive skill, with huge potential for enabling us to understand supervision better and to cope more adaptively as a result. The second example that I will discuss is the use of consultancy as a means to support supervisors' thinking (e.g. logical analysis and positive appraisal). As far as the infrastructure model is concerned, this relates to the business of 'judging what to do with the supervisee' (panel 1 in Figure 7.1), although of course many other sources of inspiration are likely to occur to the supervisor. Therefore, this is reflected in having 'use of panels 7–11' in the figure too (e.g. judging what to do based on an evidence-based guideline, or on something one learnt at a workshop).

The reflexive supervisor

One of my favourite cartoons, used when I lead workshops for supervisors, nicely captures the idea of reflexivity. Drawn from *Punch* magazine, it depicts someone arriving home to read a note which says 'Gone to philosophy class, your dinner does not exist'. Just as in philosophy, the supervision literature is replete with ideas that can be applied to our coping strategies as supervisors. After all, within this chapter alone we have described a number of ideas with potential to support and guide supervisors. A case in point is parallel process, a phenomenon that will also occur between a supervisor and a consultant. To illustrate, Frankel and Piercy (1990) described the effects of live supervision within family therapy. Their results showed a strong relationship between effective supervisory support and subsequent use of support by the supervisees. The more likely the supervisor was to provide this support, the more likely the supervisee was to support their clients. Conversely, low supervisor support was associated with poor supervisee support for the clients. Although they studied other relevant behaviours, such as the supervisor's use of teaching, it was the supportive behaviours that seemed to have the most powerful predictive power. The authors believed that this echoed the general finding from the psychotherapy literature that relationship skills have a primary function.

Self-supervision

Sometimes referred to as the self-management or self-regulation approach, self-supervision has been defined as 'a systematic process in which a professional works independently, directing his or her own professional development … in the context of counselling … It involves assessing and modifying … ineffective patterns and improving clinical skills' (Dennin & Ellis, 2003). These authors used a small-n design to evaluate self-supervision in four novice trainees, finding no effect on the main outcome of improved empathy. However, the authors were more sanguine about its value in the hands of competent counsellors, concluding that, once staff are trained to use self-supervision, 'it shows promise as a means by which they can maintain or enhance counselling skills and competence' (p.81). Presumably, self-supervision could be applied by supervisors to themselves.

In CBT, the example of 'self-practice, self-reflection' also illustrates a reflexive approach. Bennett-Levy and Thwaites (2007) described it as the use of CBT techniques on the CBT practitioners, especially effective in relation to interpersonal skills, which are tackled within supervision and self-supervision. The self-practice method is based either on homework (a workbook of structured assignments) or through 'co-therapy' (i.e. four to six sessions of providing CBT to one another). Self-reflection is viewed as addressing otherwise tacit, automated interpersonal processes. It involves focusing on the personal self within a safe, non-judgemental supervisory environment. Six stages of the reflective process are proposed: focusing attention on an interpersonal problem (e.g. therapist avoiding emotionally laden material); heightened awareness of the relevant thoughts, feelings and behaviours (e.g. through a reverse role-play, in which the therapist played the client, and the supervisor the therapist); clarifying this experience (reflecting on how hurtful it felt to have a therapist avoid the client's feelings); conceptualising the problem more objectively (formulating why this pattern occurred); developing new skills (practising within role-plays); and finally testing out the new skills in therapy (apply in the next clinical session). Bennett-Levy and Thwaites (2007) report some evidence that these approaches can facilitate therapists' development.

Consultancy for supervisors

Research on supervision frequently involves a consultant who supports and guides the supervisors within the study. For example, in the review I conducted with Ian James (Milne & James, 2000) we scrutinised 28 studies, which included 28 consultants who participated in nine of these studies. The consultants were reported to observe the supervisors (four studies), to provide active assistance (two) to provide feedback (three), and to hold meetings and discuss progress with the supervisors (five studies). Very little information was provided about the consultants themselves, or of how they applied these methods.

The better described and more routine example is the use of consultation breaks within live supervision. According to this procedure, the supervisor will interrupt therapy so as to guide the supervisee (e.g. by making a phone call, or by co-working within therapy). Numerous variations on the phone-in are described in a review by Goodyear and Nelson (1997). They also cite an in-depth study by Heppner *et al.* (1994), which helps to characterise phone-ins and other forms of live supervision relevant to consultancy. They found six dimensions underpinning their study of supervisors. Of these, the most relevant to consultancy was the use of methods to direct, deepen, offer cognitive clarification and provide emotional encouragement. However, as this example illustrates, the term consultancy is often used interchangeably with that of supervision, confusing matters. For present purposes, consultancy is understood to differ from supervision in terms of the role relationship and the treatment of responsibility. That is, the consultant is an adviser to the supervisor, having no formal authority over the supervisor. Therefore, consultancy is an opportunity for the supervisor to seek guidance and support from a suitably qualified peer. Also, for present purposes, I will restrict my discussion of consultancy to those activities that are intended to promote the cognitive functioning of the supervisor. Table 7.2 summarises some examples of this work, based on the functions of supervision cited in Figure 2.1 (Chapter 2). These examples are meant to be illustrative rather than exhaustive, and I imagine most readers will be able to think of additional ways in which supervisors are able to think more effectively through the process of reflecting on their work with a suitably senior colleague. The methods cited within Table 7.2 are drawn from a major textbook on consultation (Kilburg & Diedrich, 2007), supplemented by material from my own experience.

To take an example from Table 7.2, self-awareness is widely recognised as an important professional skill, particularly so within the complex business of supervision (e.g. consider its implication in transference and parallel process phenomena). Self-awareness depends on a combination of meta-cognitive skills, such as the ability to self-monitor. Not only will these skills foster more effective supervision, they also help us to understand incompetence (Kruger & Dunning, 1999). One of the examples of imperfect self-assessments cited by these authors is the tendency for most people to view

Table 7.2 Cognitive functions of consultancy for supervisors, with illustrative methods (page numbers refer to sources in Kilburg & Diedrich, 2007)

Cognitive functions	Methods used by consultants
Heightening self-awareness	• Expressive writing (p.312) • 360° feedback (gaining views of a wide range of significant others on the supervisor) • Assessment centres/techniques (e.g. in-basket task and prioritization of work) (p.6)
Improving self-care	• 'Ventilation' – encouraging emotional expression to reduce tension (p.312) • 'Deep interpersonal communication' (e.g. acknowledging concerns conflicts and the 'loneliness of leadership' (p.314)
Greater self-confidence	• Affirmation of strengths to promote avidities understanding (e.g. of conflicts in team: p.300) • Rational–emotive therapy to foster personal growth (p.7) (e.g. 'should be perfect')
Science-informed practice	• Discussing personally relevant research • Considering local applications of research (e.g. use of instruments) • Guiding supervisors research activity
Educational	• Hearing about the organisational system by providing technical information • Opportunities to experiment and practise in a safe, respectful, confidential environment ('gentle but honest': p.264)
Critical understanding	• Questioning contentional accounts (intensive analysis of critical event/ situation) • Examining different types of data; different explanations • Synthesising a fresh formulation • Evaluating the strengths and weaknesses of this formulation
Decision-making	• Emphasising cooperation and identification with others (including

(cont'd)

Table 7.2   (*cont'd*)

Cognitive functions	Methods used by consultants
	empathy and compassion and their link to helping others: p.294)
	• Seeking 'win–win' solutions
	• Encouraging tolerance
Problem-solving	• Clarifying problems (aiming for operational definitions perceptions)
	• Generating options (e.g. modify; substitute; rearrange; combine; copy: p.306)
	• Appraising options
	• Judging results
	• Drawing out implications for future practice (e.g. by facilitating reflection)
Supporting self-monitoring	• Facilitating reflection on key events
	• Considering sources of information (e.g. 'helpful aspects of supervision questionnaire')
	• Interpreting results and informal information

themselves as 'above average', resulting in what can be a serious overestimate of one's performance. The literature on expertise bears out the relationship between meta-cognitive skills and proficiency, in that novices are much poorer at judging their own performance than experts. Kruger and Dunning (1999) evaluated what they referred to as a dual burden: the observation that the unaware individual is poor at self-monitoring (burden one), hence making unfortunate choices which their incompetence robs them of realising (burden two). They are 'unskilled and unaware of it' (p.1121). In one of their studies, they examined this double burden in terms of a logical reasoning task. Forty-five psychology undergraduates completed a 20-item logical reasoning test, then they compared their ability with that of their peers, as well as estimating their own score. The authors found that the less able participants overestimated their ability to reason relative to their peers, placing themselves in the 66th percentile (i.e. significantly higher than the actual mean of 50). In a sub-analysis, Kruger and Dunning (1999) were able to attribute this gross mis-calibration to those participants with the least reasoning ability: it was the participants from the bottom quartile ($N = 11$) whose estimates of their reasoning differed most from their actual performance. Even though these individuals averaged scores that placed them at the 12th percentile, they believed that their reasoning ability placed them at the 68th percentile. Not surprisingly, their estimates as to how many items they answered correctly were significantly below the actual score. The authors were able to show that a short training programme, which taught unskilled participants how to test the accuracy of logical syllogisms, improved their ability to monitor their success (and to become significantly more self-aware than their untrained peers). Interestingly, it wasn't just the relatively incompetent individuals who miscalibrated, showing this lack of self-awareness. The work of Kruger and Dunning (1999) also indicated that the relatively expert students underestimated their ability, which the authors attributed to these participants believing that, because they had done well, their peers must have done likewise. Once these better-performing participants were given information to the contrary, they raised their self-appraisals to a more accurate point. There are thus burdens on both the relatively incompetent and the relatively competent. They conclude by suggesting that one of the key explanations for these burdens is the failure of individuals to act on corrective feedback.

A number of other ways in which the supervisors' cognitive functioning can be enhanced are defined within Table 7.2. For each of these, some ideas are listed in terms of methods that might be used in consultancy to achieve these goals. However, it should be realised that these are simply illustrative examples, as opposed to evidence-based interventions (and indeed this literature tends to be pitched at the level of anecdotes and case study material). Therefore, supervisors would be wise to engage in consultation rather cautiously. In conclusion, I suggest that we treat these ways of strengthening supervisors' thinking as relevant to the panel of the infrastructure model that focuses on 'judging what to do with the supervisee' (see Figure 7.1, panel 1).

Enabling Supervisors to Process the Emotional Accompaniments to Their Work

In this part of the discussion of coping strategies I wish to continue the emphasis on how others can play a crucial role in supporting supervisors.

A suitable context for supervision will include opportunities for social support, mentoring and 'peer consultation' groups.

The role of staff relationships is an example of a 'social milieu' factor within this infrastructure. What kinds of social processes does an effective infrastructure require? According to Bennett-Levy and Thwaites (2007), they include 'a sense of safeness, non-judgemental acceptance, affirmation, empathy, care, warmth and encouragement to explore ...' (p.264). They add important considerations, like providing a rationale for the supportive approach that is adopted, and providing appropriate models. They quote Ladany *et al.* (2005), whose suggestion concerning supervision is to 'do unto others as you would have them do unto others' (p.215). That is, there is a good case for treating the support of the supervisor as per the support provided to the supervisee, on the assumption that this will cascade down to the client. This is often termed the 'restorative' component of supervision, including the provision of a 'safe-base', appropriate structure, and commitment (Palomo, 2004). Palomo (2004) defined the safe-base in terms of making the supervisee feel valued, respected and secure. The implication is that the leader (e.g. a consultant) who supports the supervisor should be trustworthy, empathic and responsive, able to maintain practical boundaries, interested in the supervisor and enthusiastic about supervision itself. Table 4.1 in Chapter 4 spells out these qualities more fully.

Mentoring

Mentoring has been defined as 'a personal and reciprocal relationship in which a more experienced (person) acts as a guide, role model, teacher, and sponsor of a less experienced (person). A mentor provides the protégé with knowledge, advice, counsel, challenge and support in the protégé's pursuit of becoming a full member of a particular profession' (Johnson, 2007, p.20). Clearly, as discussed at length in Chapter 1 in relation to the definition of clinical supervision, mentoring overlaps with supervision both in its forms and in its functions. According to Johnson (2007), the mentor functions actually complement supervision, emphasising an enduring personal relationship and emotional support. Extrapolating from Johnson's (2007) account of 'transformational leadership', mentoring for supervisors would include: a partnership stance with their mentors, so that the mentor could shepherd them safely through vulnerable transitions and other stressors;

showing concern for the supervisor's welfare and development; and attempting to offer wisdom, empathy and compassion.

Additional ideas for mentoring that can be defined by extrapolating from discussions of effective supervision include the work of Safran and Muran (2000). For instance, in their discussion of self-exploration, they describe the importance of helping the supervisor to attend to their own moment-by-moment experiences, and trusting these as a basis for intervening. They believe that addressing self- exploration requires an explicit discussion about the role this can play in training, contributing to the careful establishment of a working alliance around agreed objectives. They also emphasise the need to acknowledge that this process may not feel comfortable to some supervisors, but encourage them to enter into a trial period. Concerns that may be felt by supervisors about feeling safe enough to explore feelings, conflicts and other work issues are acknowledged, and they are given permission to keep selected observations private. Self-monitoring comfort during self-exploration is a further consideration, and the mentor is encouraged to respect needs and experiences so as not to push supervisors too far. Respectful attitudes and responsiveness to the ongoing work are critical, as are trustworthy mentors.

Groups for supervisors

I am relieved to note that Bernard and Goodyear (2004) share my penchant for extrapolation, themselves noting that many of the techniques and formats involved in the supervision of supervision can reasonably be transferred from supervision itself. In this sense, they believe that the group is the most frequently used method for supporting supervisors, serving didactic and supportive functions.

A popular version of group work is so-called 'peer supervision'. Note that this is technically an oxymoron, in that supervision is by definition hierarchical and hence cannot be provided within a peer relationship (see Chapter 1). This relaxed use of the term 'supervision' does not seem to have dented its popularity, although Bernard and Goodyear (2004) note that it actually sits somewhere between consultation and supervision proper, and may be better labelled 'peer consultation', because these groups also tend to be voluntary, and they rarely involve the explicit exercise of differential power (e.g. evaluation or feedback: Campbell, 2006). Perhaps this is why Bernard and Goodyear (2004) were able to cite evidence for the popularity of peer supervision from a survey. This suggested that 24 per cent of psychologists in private practice had belonged to a peer supervision group, and a further 61 per cent expressed a desire to belong to such a group. Groups tend to be formed amongst colleagues with some sense of compatibility, including similarities in their activities and methods, not to mention individuals who know and respect one another. Although by definition leaderless, peer supervision groups tend to require some structure, and so a convention is for the Chair to rotate. The normal content is case presentations and discussion. According to Bernard and Goodyear (2004) and Campbell (2006), the popularity of peer supervision groups is due to a number of perceived benefits:

- provides insight into novel approaches;
- allows reflection to occur, aiding problem-solving;
- suitable throughout the career-span;
- offers peer review;
- provides a source of continuing professional development;
- offers reassurance, validation and other products of effective groups, reducing the likelihood of burnout;
- combats loneliness and isolation;
- more collegial and less affected by evaluation or other power issues.

However, this cosy relationship can bring its disadvantages, as noted by Proctor and Inskipp (2001). They conjectured that supervisors in such groups can become rather too relaxed, failing to accept challenges or take risks. The lack of leadership may also compromise the sense of safety, promoting destructive group processes. There may then be a pressure on those present to exercise facilitation skills in lieu of a formal leader, in a context where senior members exercise poor group 'manners'. Not surprisingly, the focus of the group may then become contentious, or hard to maintain. Campbell (2006) offers some tips to make them 'more meaningful' (p.260), such as adding some mutual feedback through utilising rating scales occasionally, or by inviting someone of suitable experience and stature to offer feedback. Other tips that she offers are to establish a group purpose, to agree expectations, and to appoint an observer to monitor the group process and keep it productive.

A supervision-of-supervision group that appears to address eight recurring issues productively has been described in the USA by Ellis and Douce (2001). These issues include the anxieties experienced by supervisors, group cohesion and intervention choices. Remarkably similar issues were found in a UK survey, also of counsellors (Wheeler & King, 2000). In the Ellis and Douce groups, five to eight supervisors meet for two hours weekly to work through these issues, and each week a different supervisor presents a supervision case. This is supposed to start with the supervisor explaining what they want from the group, then includes review and discussion of taped segments of the selected session. The group also allocates 30–60 minutes to consider pressing concerns of the others present. A 'trainer' provides supervision to the supervisors, using established methods (e.g. role-plays; role reversals; discussion; interpersonal process recall: IPR). IPR (Kagan & Kagan, 1997) is an effective yet relatively non-threatening way to present taped material, as the supervisor is given the power to select which sections to replay, and the group's reactions are meant to be inquiring (about underlying thoughts and feelings present during the segment) and generally facilitating and supportive. Although the methods used in the groups encountered by the respondents in the Wheeler and King (2000) survey were not specified, they did find them very helpful in their own supervisory work (accorded a mean rating of 80 per cent).

Context: the example of receiving and reciprocating social support

The value of these various ways of helping supervisors to process the emotional accompaniments to their work is inextricably linked to a basic human process, 'social support'. This is one of the examples of the 'context' for supervision noted in the infrastructure model (i.e. Figure 7.1, panel 12). Social support is traditionally defined as the provision of informal interpersonal help with emotional issues (Cowen, 1982). It subsumes the provision of emotional, informational and practical assistance, as well as general positive social interaction or companionship. As a result of these forms of support some vital functions are served. These include a sense of attachment, in the sense of feeling close to others (thereby allowing nurturance and unconditional assistance to be provided); social integration or belongingness; social validation (the recognition of one's identity and competence); and guidance (the availability of advice and information). In short, it is hard to overestimate the importance of social support, as, apart from its direct use, it can be seen as critical aspect of other interventions. Some go as far as to assert that it is the basis of human life, as well as its context (Reis *et al.*, 2000).

Therefore, activities like peer supervision, mentoring and consultancy can all be understood as formal devices for promoting one or more of the functions of social support. This general observation is borne out by the available research within supervision. For example, Barrow and Domingo (1997) noted, from their study of supervisor training, that those supervisors who were more supportive and exhibited more facilitating of interpersonal conditions created more change in the supervisee. Their programme explicitly included research on the role of interpersonal relationships, and so they encouraged the recognition of a supportive atmosphere. The opposite also seems to be true: Deery (2004) explored the need for support amongst midwives, recognising that significant negative emotion was generated but was difficult to regulate, resulting in them expending energy needlessly. She noted that maladaptive coping strategies were employed by the midwives in response to the emotions (such as 'pseudo cohesion' and 'resistance to change'). Deery (2004) concluded that more effective methods of support were needed, such as supervision. Indeed, supervision does appear to ameliorate the kinds of stress reported by healthcare staff. In one study, burnout (i.e. emotional exhaustion, depersonalisation and low levels of personal accomplishment) were reported by a sample of 189 community mental health nurses (Edwards *et al.*, 2006). But those staff receiving effective supervision (measured by higher scores on the Manchester Clinical Supervision Scale: Winstanley, 2001) reported lower levels of burnout. Similarly, Greenspan *et al.* (1991) surveyed 198 social workers, finding a significant association between supervision that was perceived as supportive and effectiveness (e.g. a better focus on the clinical work). These findings are consistent with studies of problematic supervisory relationships, where support from peers comes through as a major coping strategy (Nelson & Friedlander, 2001).

Consensus amongst supervisors

A variant of social support that can furnish informational, emotional and practical help is the professional consensus. This may serve as a substitute for an adequate evidence-base, or interpret it in acceptable, practical ways. The individual supervisor can draw on such considered views of experts, representing a source of guidance and collegiality. An example of the use of consensus-building in the absence of adequate research knowledge is the derivation of a training programme for supervision workshops (Green, 2004).

The Delphi technique is one of a group of consensus-building methods (Jones & Hunter, 1995), and Green used it to enable a panel of 50 experts to define a supervisor training curriculum through the completion of a succession of increasingly refined questionnaires, together with feedback on how their individual replies compared to those of the other experts. The technique succeeded in building consensus, and a number of possible topics were rank ordered by the group (which included those 'clinical tutors' who trained supervisors, supervisors themselves, and the directors of the training programmes of which they were all part). The most popular topics were 'considering when and how to fail a placement', which received a mean rating of 6.8, out of a possible 7. Closely behind were the topics of addressing the legal responsibilities of the supervisor, ensuring that the client receives appropriate care, and knowing how to negotiate a placement contract (all rated above 6.5). Least supported were 'requiring supervisors to provide recordings of their supervision' and other topics carrying high threat.

An illustration of a consensus that is based on an adequate knowledge-base is the definition of supervision competencies (Falender *et al.*, 2004). This consensus was achieved by forming workgroups from amongst the experts attending a conference, and having them engage in three days of discussion. The participants drew on their knowledge of the literature to agree a list of competencies, as well as how they should be trained and assessed. Their competencies framework included knowledge, skills and values, such as 'knowledge of ethics and legal issues specific to supervision', 'relationship skills – ability to build supervisory alliance', and the values of respect and empowerment. They considered that supervisor training should include didactic coursework and experiential methods (e.g. 'observation of supervision, with critical feedback'). This should be assessed in a variety of ways, including evidence from this direct observation, supervisee feedback, and the assessment of the outcomes of supervision (including supervisees' learning and their clinical results with clients).

Guidelines

Of course, one thing that can emerge from consensus work is a guideline. Although manuals and guidelines are amongst the least popular of the influences on the practice of healthcare staff (Lucock *et al.*, 2006), they nonetheless have the potential to support the coping repertoires of supervisors. This is reflected in the ratings given to professional guidelines by this sample of 96 qualified therapists, as (on average) they rated professional guidelines at 3.9 on a 6-point scale, equating to 'slightly helpful'. By contrast, supervision obtained a mean rating of 4.8. Treatment manuals were less well regarded, except in the case of those practitioners who came from a CBT background (they rated treatment manuals at 4 on the rating scale). Whilst manuals have become essential within psychotherapy efficacy studies (Nathan *et al.*, 2000), these modest ratings probably reflect numerous objections that many practitioners have to manuals. Amongst these objections is the view that manuals do not deal with the specific idiosyncrasies of specific patients; that they give little or no scope for clinical judgement; that there is inflexibility in the scheduling of the different elements within the manual; and that fundamentally therapy is more of an art than a science. On the other hand, manuals provide explicit information that can help supervisors to know what the main options are, and they do seem to contribute to improved outcomes (Neufeldt, 1994). However, manuals for supervisor training and development are extremely thin on the ground, Neufeldt's (1994) being one of the first. It was designed to foster 26 discrete supervisory skills, drawn from Bernard's discrimination model, plus ideas regarding reflective practice. The manual defines these skills and offers step-by-step procedures (including a transcript to provide illustrations). It was designed to support weekly supervision seminars, which utilised role-plays and reflections on the participating supervisors' video-presented material. Examples of these skills are: 'Assist trainee to conceptualise case'; and 'Present a developmental challenge'.

More recently, Fall and Sutton (2004) have designed a workshop to accompany Bernard and Goodyear's textbook (2004). This provides learning exercises, examples, case studies and illustrative transcripts to enable the supervisor to develop. There are also self-assessment questionnaires and checklists. However, this is primarily intended to be used by a workshop facilitator and is therefore of limited value to the individual supervisor. The most sophisticated manual is the one developed by Baltimore and Crutchfield (2003), who provided an interactive, CD-Rom-based training programme. This covers 16 modules, from definitions and models, to ethical and legal issues. The manual contains learning objectives, reflective exercises, experiential activities, and references, whilst the CD has video and audio clips. Henggeler *et al.* (2002) also described the use of a supervisory protocol to support their supervisor training efforts in multi-systemic therapy. This was linked to annual workshops for supervisors, and to measures of the supervisor's adherence to the therapy.

Like Bernard and Goodyear (2004), there is a manual accompanying the present text, which can be accessed at the website: www.wiley.com/go/milne. This includes four guidelines on clinical supervision and DVD clips of naturalistic supervision. All items reflect the EBCS model.

Patient Care, Outcome Benchmarking, and Audit

According to the infrastructure model (Figure 7.1, panels 3–6), the supervisor's attempts to influence the supervisee's development should be monitored through a range of performance indicators. These logically start with the supervision (e.g. whether it is delivered according to some standard or achieves a benchmark profile/score), linked to an evaluation of whether the supervisee is learning the kinds of competencies outlined in Falender *et al.*'s (2004) consensus statement. If these are shown to be present, then one can also look for stepwise results, in terms of the supervisee's provision of clinical care (e.g. as assessed by adherence to local audit standards), and by the clinical outcomes (e.g. improved health). One appealing and coherent way to think about these linked indicators is the 'fidelity framework' (Borelli *et al.*, 2005). This will be addressed in the next chapter, as this is where I treat the main evaluation issues. However, there are some aspects of performance monitoring that are best addressed here, because they represent coping strategies that supervisors might utilise.

Three arguments for measuring one's supervision have been noted by Campbell (2006). The first is that it can help to set limits on the personal and other resources that are invested in supervision. Secondly, it can help one to feel more effective and useful. Another is to address one's natural inquisitiveness. A method that satisfies at least two of these needs is 'systematic client tracking' (Worthen & Lambert, 2007). Their example is with adult out-patients, and entails weekly completion of a standard symptom/wellbeing questionnaire. Scores from the individual supervisee's clients can then be compared against normative data from hundreds of other clients, allowing judgements to be formed about whether the client is progressing as well as would be expected. Real-time feedback is provided against this national clinical outcome benchmark, which indicates whether clients are progressing satisfactorily or where there is a risk of a negative outcome. A written feedback message is provided, suggesting evidence-based ways of rectifying problems (e.g. client drop-out from therapy might be addressed by reviewing progress collaboratively and by considering the client's readiness to change). Four clinical trials of this feedback system have indicated that it could improve therapy significantly (overall effect size of 0.34). As the authors note, this kind of routine clinical evaluation could enable supervisors to more rapidly identify problems and potential solutions. A related approach, termed Continuous Quality Improvement, has been applied to the supervision of nursing teams within residential care (Hyrkas & Lehti, 2003).

Another example is to audit one's supervision, which can also be aided by using published instruments and by comparing one's profile with that of others. To illustrate, Edwards *et al.* (2006) surveyed 260 community mental health nurses in Wales with the Manchester Clinical Supervision Scale (MCSS; Winstanley, 2000). The MCSS contains seven sub-scales (e.g. 'trust/rapport'; 'support/advice' and 'improving care/skills'), providing the basis for a supervision profile. In the Edwards *et al.* (2006) sample, these three factors were equal to or better than the normative data published with the MCSS. An individual supervisor could use the MCSS in a similar way, by asking supervisees to complete it in relation to his/her supervision, then comparing the resultant profile with these norms.

A further topical example concerns case-based supervision, in which the focus is upon the supervisees' clinical effectiveness with their caseload, guided through routine clinical outcome monitoring (Richards, 2008). This is relevant here as one can regard the monitoring data as feedback on the supervision, as well as on the therapy that the supervisee is providing to these patients. However, this feedback on the supervision is mediated by the independent functioning of both the supervisee and the patient, so is two steps removed and hence potentially insensitive to the quality of the supervision. Therefore, it has to be treated with caution, but logically there is still some potential value in it, particularly where stepwise links can be demonstrated or reasonably assumed (e.g. the treatment goals of all three parties are agreed and communicated regularly, so that clinical goal-attainment could serve as a common thread). A further issue that this case-based approach implies is that the organisational context of supervision needs to include effective leadership (e.g. managers who can secure the technical resources to build and maintain the feedback system), and an innovation culture (e.g. creative planning and addressing resistance collectively). These kinds of factors have been identified as necessary for the implementation of outcome-monitoring systems (Lyons *et al.*, 1997), and are well illustrated in the introduction of the clinical instruments HoNOS and CORE in the UK (Milne *et al.*, 2001; Barkham *et al.*, 1998). In short, to paraphrase Machiavelli, innovations like routine outcome monitoring are devilishly difficult to achieve.

Conclusions

This chapter has considered the widely recognised but little-addressed need for the supervision of supervisors (Hawkins & Shohet, 2000; Proctor, 2000). While there is an explicit and widely accepted way of thinking about the framework within which the supervisee operates (i.e. Vygotsky's scaffold around the ZPD), there is nothing comparable regarding the supervisor. Although formal governmental policy recognises that there needs to be an infrastructure of this kind, including effective leadership from managers, there appears to be no suitable framework available. Therefore, in this chapter I have extended the EBCS model by integrating some fundamental ingredients for successful supervisor support and development from neighbouring literatures, such as organisational development. This revised model is set out in Figure 7.1, using the self-same panels and variables as the original EBCS model (see Chapter 3), but with these extensions noted and some practical examples of supervisor support and development listed.

A major part of the extended model is the incorporation of the transactional stress model, in order to place the individual supervisor at the centre of the model, as well as to make more systematic sense of how we might support supervisors. In particular, we recognised the unrelentingly stressful nature of modern healthcare systems, and the intrinsically stressful business of supervision. It is not surprising, then, that many surveys of health practitioners indicate that significant numbers are complaining of burnout. But this model does not accept that such stressors necessarily lead to burnout or other forms of distress. In theory, such stressors might equally well be transformed into a sense of job satisfaction and even mastery, through adaptive coping. This means that it is important to attend at least as much to the ways that we cope with these stressors, in a 'restorative' system that helps supervisors to feel that they are supported, accepted, nurtured, acknowledged and validated. Formal arrangements, like peer supervision groups and mentoring, have been found to be helpful. In addition, I noted how informal processes were vital to wellbeing (i.e. social support). Supervisors also require a normative system of support, and I have presented some arrangements that can help them to come to terms with the demands that their host organisations place on them (e.g. through peer and individual consultation). Lastly, support arrangements could be construed in terms of the formative function, as in facilitating the supervisor's functioning through such means as structured reflection and training (Winstanley, 2000; Lambert & Bergin, 1994).

Using the transactional stress model also helps us to formulate how a supervisor can enter a vicious cycle as a result of an unfortunate combination of excessive work demands, maladaptive coping (including faulty appraisals of the stressors that are experienced), and absent social support. In this kind of cycle, supervisors will readily perceive themselves as failing, and risk spiralling downwards to professional burnout. By contrast, effective coping strategies that are well supported within a healthy organisation are likely to lead to the supervisor feeling positive about the role, to enhanced effectiveness and to higher levels of job satisfaction. The major study of therapist development by Orlinsky and Ronnestad (2005) justifies and elaborates this kind of coping analysis.

Although we can be reasonably confident about this kind of relationship between the coping cycle variables, it has to be acknowledged that the literature that I have been able to harness within this chapter lacks the degree of scientific rigour and replication that has been found within the literature used in previous chapters. That is, the material in this chapter is primarily of a case study and anecdotal variety, rich in qualitative detail but not yet convincing. I suspect that the absence of a strong literature in this area is not due to inferior searching on my part, but rather reflects the limited attention accorded to the much-needed infrastructure within the scientific literature. It is appropriate, then, for supervisors (and others) to treat this material with particular caution, seeking opportunities to evaluate the relevant ideas. Some suggestions for evaluating one's work were noted above, and the next chapter suggests more formal ways of improving what we know about supporting and developing supervisors. In conclusion, the supervision of supervisors is the most deficient area in the whole enterprise of clinical supervision.

8

Developing Supervision

Introduction

Evaluation is 'the use of social research methods to systematically investigate the effectiveness of social intervention programmes in ways that are adapted to their political and organisational environments, and are designed to inform social action to improve social conditions' (Rossi *et al.*, 2003, p.16). Put more concretely, evaluation entails a judgement about the extent to which supervision objectives are achieved, an assessment that is used to develop supervision. It is an integral, indispensable part of all systematic models of clinical supervision, perhaps most prominent in CBT supervision, as indicated in Chapters 1 and 3. Indeed, evaluation is fundamental to any basic problem-solving process, as reflected in its increasingly emphasised role in modern healthcare. The following factors have been thought important in the rise of evaluation (Knapp, 1997):

- the purchasers' requirement to assure themselves that they are getting the best value for their money;
- sharply increased healthcare costs (e.g. new, expensive medication);
- the emergence of a business culture in the UK, following on from the establishment of managed care in the USA;
- new treatments that imply the need for fresh, comparative evaluations, including new treatment environments and new interventions, not to mention new providers of health services;
- greater fiscal stringency;
- the evidence-based practice era, in which healthcare resources are allocated on the basis of compelling evidence.

As noted by Fonagy *et al.* (2002), the consequence of these growing public demands on health service providers has been to create an environment in which health professionals now shoulder much greater accountability for their services, to clients and to those who purchase the services. We can think about these various pressures as part of the context for supervision, as set out in Figure 3.3 (Chapter 3), and moderating upwards the emphasis on evaluation.

Reflecting its central role, Bernard and Goodyear (2004) have referred to it as the 'nucleus' of supervision (p.19). It appears reliably in all textbook definitions of supervision, such as the Falender and Shafranske (2004) one. They wrote that: 'supervision ... involves observation, evaluation, feedback, the facilitation of supervisee self-assessment ... and mutual problem-solving' (p.3). This is similar to the definition provided in Chapter 1, underlining the link between formative evaluation (corrective feedback) and the summative function of evaluation, in which a judgement is made about fitness for practice or award ('gate-keeping'). Whilst these are the two dominant purposes of evaluation, as many as 10 such functions or objectives of evaluation have been articulated within the supervision and closely related literature (e.g. the evaluation of professional services akin to supervision). Table 8.1 lists these 10 objectives, in the context of a stepwise, comprehensive approach to evaluation.

Prior Reviews

Reviews of the evaluation of clinical supervision date back over 30 years (Hansen *et al.*, 1976) and tend to concur on the exceptional methodological sophistication required to evaluate supervision effectively. For example, Lambert (1980) summarised the instruments available at that time, concluding that the most reliable ones focused on the supervisee's behaviour, but that outcome data should be collected from multiple sources, including the clinical effectiveness of supervision, and the interaction between the supervisee and the client. But Holloway (1984) questioned the restriction of measurement to such areas; particularly as intervening outcomes were not assessed, resulting in rather global and imprecise evaluations. Additionally, she noted that there were multiple functions of supervision, as well as the different roles that the supervisor and supervisee may occupy. She concluded that 'these aforementioned assumptions have led to a narrow and restrictive body of research that no longer reflects current models of supervision' (p.172). Another crucial criticism made by Holloway (1984) was the lack of attention to the interpersonal interaction between the parties, which she assumed would have a reciprocal influence. Therefore, she argued for an expanded view of the relevant outcomes in supervision, advocating more precise measurement that was specific to supervision. Similarly, Holloway and Neufeldt (1995) argued for considering the effectiveness of supervision in terms of a number of levels in the educational pyramid, and the linkages between these factors. Specifically, they saw outcome evaluation as embracing the following:

- the supervisee's acquisition of attitudes, beliefs and skills relevant to treatment;
- the supervisee's performance in therapy related to supervision;
- the interactional processes in therapy, as related to processes in supervision;
- client changes related to supervision.

More recently, Wampold and Holloway (1997) reiterated the importance of examining supervision in terms of a social interaction, highlighting the need to examine contingent patterns of activities (as in a sequential analysis of supervision interactions). They advocated a stepwise approach to evaluation, but noted that some of these steps have proved very difficult to demonstrate. As a result, they suggested that it may well be best to focus on more 'micro' connections between supervision and the consecutive outcomes, focusing on mediators in the causal process, rather than trying to show causal relations between supervision and more distal elements, such as clinical outcomes. In essence, they conclude that researchers need to simplify the phenomena of supervision to make research realistic and feasible. This gels with reviews of the psychotherapy outcome literature, in that different levels of analysis, treated collectively and seen as responsive to one another (Norcross, 2002), including micro analysis of content, impact and outcome, are advocated as ways of resolving traditional problems in the evaluation of psychotherapy (Shapiro, 1995).

Based on these prior reviews, Table 8.2 lists a variety of examples that suggest how this kind of stepwise, in-depth, micro-analysis of process and outcome might be undertaken. It needs to be stressed, however, that these are purely intended to illustrate some of the options, and are not intended to represent some kind of systematic overview of the possibilities. To structure this summary I draw on the six dimensions along which evaluations can conducted (i.e. its SCOPPE: Milne, 2007c). This is described below. Later in this chapter I summarise a more systematic option, the fidelity framework.

In summary, although there is unanimity concerning the pivotal role of evaluation (and concerning the complexity of evaluating supervision), these reviewers differ in how they propose that evaluation should be conducted. Also, within the general literature on supervision there is considerable dissent when it comes to selecting from amongst these 10 functions of evaluation. Within the evidence-based clinical supervision (EBCS) model (see Chapter 3, Figure 3.4), there are three panels devoted explicitly to evaluation, those of 'outcome benchmarking', 'supervisee development' (covering feedback and gate-keeping), and 'audit'. These panels suggest that evaluation should focus on the learning and comparative clinical outcomes of supervision, relative to local or professional standards that may be in place for supervision (such as the amount of time that is allocated to each professional per month). Although this EBCS model offers a rational and feasible approach to evaluation, it underemphasises some of these 10 functions of evaluation (e.g. economy and efficiency). According to Rossi *et al.* (2003), and many authors before them (e.g. Donabedian, 1988), it is also essential to know about the 'structure' or resources that are allocated to supervision. In this sense the minimum meaningful evaluation needs to provide some information on structure, process (i.e. the supervision) and outcome, as only by linking the resource investment (sometimes labelled 'effort') to the nature of the intervention can we logically interpret the kinds of outcomes that supervision achieves. If we apply this logic to the EBCS model, the most obvious deficiency is the lack of attention to this resource element, which might be treated under the heading of audit. Outcome benchmarking can be thought to refer to the clinical outcomes achieved by supervisees, and the learning outcomes that are facilitated through supervision could be addressed within the supervisee development panel. However, this represents an inelegant and incomplete solution, so I will shortly suggest how the notion of intervention fidelity can be applied to supervision.

Whilst this brings some order and logic to evaluation, it should be acknowledged that it is still somewhat limited in scope. For example, it does not address one of the general drivers of evaluation mentioned above, the need to obtain the best possible treatment for the lowest possible cost. Therefore, 'efficiency', including cost–benefit and cost-effectiveness evaluation, is one of three additional basic dimensions of evaluation that should

Table 8.1 An integrative summary of a stepwise approach to evaluating supervision comprehensively

Steps	Objectives	Evaluation questions and criteria
1. Designing supervision	a. *Conceptualisation*: justifies and specifies the model, guiding supervision. b. *Implementation planning*	Addresses the questions: *What is the right way to supervise? Which resources are required?* Frequency, duration and content of supervision (accessibility); supervisors' and supervisees' 'credentials' (selection); supervision model and guidelines that are relevant to the need (involve service users)
2. Training supervisors	c. *Implementation integrity*	*Is the right supervision being done?* Describing and standardising supervisor training (manual); assessing competence acquisition and auditing maintenance, in terms of adherence to model.
3. Delivering supervision	d. *Faithful implementation* (performance monitoring)	*Has supervision been done right?* Assessing and enhancing the supervision contents, processes (alliance), procedures (method fidelity) and proficiency (skilful adjustments – e.g. 'dosage'/ timing).
4. Receiving supervision	e. *Supervisee development*	*Did supervision lead to the right learning?* Effectiveness evaluation (plus acceptability/participation/reactions/etc.). General development promoted.
5. Transferring supervision	f. *Outcome benchmarking* g. *Generalisation* h. *Formulating*	*Did supervision produce results/did it work?* Clinical outcome evaluation, based on transfer of learning, related to performance standards/norms/barriers and boosters in workplace (e.g. patients' characteristics; social support).
6. Developing supervision	i. *Create feedback loops* j. *Economy and efficiency* (continuous quality improvement)	*Are we getting good value? Have we got our system right? Is there a better way?* 'Cost–benefit' analysis (including 'summative' decisions about 'blacklisting'/ accrediting supervisors and 'gate keeping'/ promoting supervisees: reduce 'wastage' and retain/develop talent); dismantling and coordinating/ streamlining supervision; enhancing (e.g. outcome monitoring and supportive feedback); improving environmental factors (e.g. leadership/equipment) or any of 1–5 above (e.g. supervisee socialisation/induction).

ideally be considered, the other two being 'procedures' and 'content'. Together they are thought to afford appropriate SCOPPE to evaluation (Milne, 2007c). Although logically coherent and practically useful, these six dimensions of evaluation can contribute to a sense of complexity and unwieldiness, not helped by the hundreds of instruments that are available, the varied methods one adopts in applying these instruments (e.g. self-report and direct observation), the different participants deemed to be significant, the various research designs that may be justified, and the different functions of evaluation. This potentially overwhelming range of options is reminiscent of the chaos identified within the psychotherapy literature by Froyd et al. (1999). They reviewed outcome measurement within psychotherapy and found, from their review of 21 journals, that 1430 different outcomes measures were reported within the 334 research papers; 851 of these measures (60 per cent) were used in only one paper and, of these, 278 (33 per cent) had no reliability or validity data. They concluded that this merited attention, otherwise 'psychological therapy outcome measurement will remain in a state of disarray, if not chaos, with individual practitioners or separate mental health entities selecting outcome measures without thought for communication across clinicians, treatments sites, or problem domains' (p.15). I fear that a similar review of research within clinical supervision would indicate a more chaotic situation, even without considering the other five possible dimensions along which evaluation might vary, and the fact that, by considering supervision, we are adding a further tier to any evaluation. This is potentially fatal to the evaluation endeavour, as supervision is itself a multidimensional intervention (Heppner *et al.*, 1994).

Therefore, in order to offer a concise and coherent approach to evaluation, one that is feasible yet still sufficiently systematic (i.e. addresses the above points), this chapter adopts the fidelity framework (Borelli *et al.*, 2005). As set out in Table 8.1, I have expanded and significantly elaborated their five-step approach by drawing on a range of relevant literature, including the foregoing material about health service systems generally, as well as discrete analyses of clinical supervision. In addition to the work of Kirkpatrick (1967) and the others noted in relation to outcome evaluation (i.e. Steps 4 and 5 in Table 8.1), this expanded framework drew on material from: Wheeler and Richards (2007); Milne (2007, 2008); Bruce and Paxton (2002); Oakley *et al.* (2006); Watkins (1997); Godfrey *et al.* (2007); Harmon *et al.* (2007); Beutler (2001); and Wilkes and Bligh (1999). This extended framework is consistent with accounts of evaluation in supervision texts, but significantly extends them in what I believe to be a novel and empowering fashion.

Table 8.2 Novel approaches to the evaluation of supervisions, illustrated using the SCOPPE dimensions

Evaluation dimension	Illustrative study
1. **Structures** (resource analysis)	a) *Participants*: 40 supervisors, selected based on a supervision competence rating (and 'paid by being given free training in supervision'), all qualified and experienced mental health practitioners. b) *Training*: Two 1-day supervision workshops for 127 therapists, also selected based on therapeutic competence, also repaid with free training; 6 trainers, who rated all therapists' and supervisors' competence; 127 adult clients, with anxiety or depression given 8 hours of therapy (1 per supervision approach – i.e. a 'skill' or a 'process' focus); manuals supported the training and guided evaluation. Seven 16-hour workshops provided to the therapists. c) *Materials*: All therapists and supervisors provided with packs, including manuals, measures, audio tapes and a procedural booklet. Example from Bambling *et al.* (2006)
2. **Contents** (material covered, including types of supervision utterances)	Qualitative description of the interactional sequences between supervisor and supervisee, in order to illustrate the event-based paradigm (e.g. exploration of feelings about clients, or about the supervisee's progress in training). From Ladany *et al.* (2005)
3. **Outcomes** (judging the success of supervision)	Microgenetic analysis of the path, rate, breadth (generalisation), variability (individual differences), and sources of change. From Siegler (1995)
4. **Procedures** (organisation; systems)	State-wide training of 386 supervisors following established policy and principles (e.g. State's policy of person-centred care; use of adult learning principles), in 26 competencies (e.g. 'error correction' and 'problem-solving') within a 4-day curriculum designed to address supervisors' learning needs with evidence-based material. From Reid *et al.* (2003)
5. **Processes** (provision of supervision with fidelity and interpersonal effectiveness)	Rating scale to assess the supervisor's adherence to the CBT supervision model, operationalised through 16 items (e.g. 'relationship core conditions' and 4 further facets of interpersonal effectiveness), and explicitly related to the supervisee's responses. From: James *et al.* (2005)

(cont'd)

Table 8.2   *(cont'd)*

Evaluation dimension	Illustrative study
6. Efficiencies (optimising benefit and minimising waste – e.g. through dismantling supervision packages or via distance or e-learning)	Identification of 'critical incidents' (major turning points in developing as a therapist in supervision), including relationship, emotional awareness and autonomy episodes, incidents that might make supervisor training more efficient. From Ellis (1991)

Chapter Aims

Illustrating its coherence, the three EBCS panels will be assimilated to this fidelity framework, which will represent the heart of this chapter. In addition to detailing the framework with reference to clinical supervision research, I also aim to give further attention to the crucial issue of implementation: as noted in the previous chapter, the applied psychology literatures (especially the psychotherapy literature) suggest that significant attention needs to be given to the implementation of measurement, if it is to fulfil its purpose. In support of enhancing the utility of evaluation, I will encourage the reader to consider the use of straightforward instruments and evaluation designs, alongside thoughtful approaches to the inclusion of stakeholders in the evaluation process.

Evaluation within individual, routine supervision has been addressed within Chapter 5, and is summarised in one of the EBCS guidelines (available on the website: www.wiley.com/go/milne). The present chapter focuses on the evaluation of supervision within discovery, effectiveness or implementation research (e.g. the evaluation of the supervision provided by multiple supervisors within a clinical service).

The Fidelity Framework

According to Borelli *et al.* (2005), there are five related aspects of a systematic evaluation, which represent successive steps in evaluating an intervention like supervision.

Intervention design

The first aspect of fidelity concerns specifying and justifying a model for the intervention, alongside providing information on its structure (including how long the intervention takes; how frequently it should be applied; what its content or constituent parts are; the qualifications or background of supervisors or others involved in the intervention; and any other resources that are required). In essence, then, step 1 of the fidelity framework is to offer a conceptualisation of the supervision intervention and to specify its implementation. Working towards these objectives allows us to address two fundamental research questions, namely 'what is the right thing to do?' and 'which resources are required to do it'? Another important aspect of an intervention 'design' is the credentials of the supervisors and supervisees: on what basis are they allowed to participate in supervision? Table 8.1 sets out these facets of the design, alongside the subsequent five steps.

Training supervisors

The second step in the fidelity framework is to train supervisors in ways that ensure that the right thing is being done. This entails carefully describing and attempting to standardise the way that supervisors are trained, most conventionally achieved through the development and application of a training manual. Evaluation of this step should also include demonstrating that competence has been acquired and can be maintained in a form that is faithful to the model in step 1. As noted in the previous chapter, although there are many published studies of supervisor training, there appear to be few recent examples where this training has been based on a manual and very few where a clear conceptual framework has been justified and specified as the basis for any such manual (Milne *et al.*, 2007a).

Delivering supervision

Having designed and delivered a programme for training supervisors, the next step in the fidelity framework is to evaluate whether the supervision has actually been conducted correctly. This addresses the objective of faithful implementation, usually through the monitoring of how supervision is performed. It would typically concern an evaluation of what is covered within supervision (content evaluation), the processes or procedures that are followed, and the skill with which they are administered. As set out in Table 8.1, this step subsumes a number of exacting and vital analyses. Specifically, the different models of supervision will each have their own distinctive contents, processes and procedures, although all will require that supervisors are appropriately skilful, including the use of the right amount of the relevant ingredients, applied in a timely fashion. An example of the contents of supervision is the material covered in Chapter 5 about EBCS and the use of questions (see Table 5.4). These questions are faithful to a CBT model of supervision, and so an evaluation that demonstrated their presence would help to show that it is being performed with fidelity. By contrast, a psychodynamic approach might use rather different questions, timing their use differently, and expecting them to serve rather different functions (e.g. insight, rather than information-gathering).

An audit example

This is an appropriate step in the fidelity framework to discuss one of the three panels in the EBCS model that refer to evaluation explicitly. Audit could apply at the level of the individual supervisor, or to the health service system. At the individual level, the faithful delivery of supervision can be measured through direct observation. My own involvement in this regard has been to study tape recordings of supervision, and to code the content in terms of some well-established elements of supervision, such as setting an agenda collaboratively, and providing corrective feedback. These elements were contained within an instrument called Teachers' PETS (Milne *et al.*, 2002), which was described in Chapter 3. Instruments of this kind are required if we are to treat supervision seriously. That is, supervision as a professional competence should be something that we can observe reliably, so that training can be provided and evaluations arranged, contributing to feedback and further supervisor development. Instruments of this kind can also help to audit the performance of a team of supervisors.

However, Teachers' PETS was primarily designed as a research tool, necessitating many hours of training for the observers in order to achieve this level of reliability in their intensive, momentary time sampling of supervisor and supervisee behaviours. Also, it gave little attention to the so-called 'common factors' that have shown themselves to be a powerful influence on the therapeutic relationship and on outcomes. Since the approach taken to supervision in this book is closely based on what we know about therapy (see Milne, 2006, for a reasoned analogy), this appeared to be an important omission. Thirdly, we required a system that could serve the same functions as Teachers' PETS (e.g. profiling, auditing and furnishing corrective feedback), but which could offer a competence assessment, be completed by raters requiring fewer hours of training, more quickly, all anchored in a competence approach. For these reasons a new instrument, SAGE, was created (Supervision: Adherence & Guidance Evaluation; Milne & Reiser, 2007). With SAGE we moved from intensive time-sampling to a seven-point competence rating scale, which ranges from 'incompetent' to 'expert', based on the popular Dreyfus definitions (1989). The difference was that, following the lead provided by Blackburn *et al.* (2001) in developing the revised Cognitive Therapy Scale, we added more extreme ratings (i.e. a lower level of 'incompetent' performance; and a seventh rating point to capture expert functioning under difficult/adverse circumstances).

A fourth reason to modify Teachers' PETS was to reflect the growing evidence-base regarding the methods that were effective in supervision. A series of systematic reviews of the more rigorous studies of effective clinical supervision indicated a need to alter the emphasis of the original Teachers' PETS items. For example, in developing an empirical definition of clinical supervision (Milne, 2007a; see Chapter 5, Table 5.2), it appeared that the primary methods used in effective supervision were 'feedback', 'observing and outcome monitoring', and 'discussion'. Also, a related systematic review indicated the importance of the experiential learning cycle (Milne, Aylott, Fitzpatrick *et al.*, 2008). A further important influence from the literature was professional consensus, as indicated in Kaslow *et al.* (2004), and the major texts on clinical supervision (e.g. Bernard & Goodyear, 2004; Falender & Shafranske, 2004), which collated more recent empirical and theoretical developments. As summarised in Chapter 2 (see Figure 2.1), this indicated the need to give weight to those 'common factors' (i.e. the core conditions, such as empathy and congruence), and to slightly restructure and restate the supervisory interventions so that different levels of analysis were set out within SAGE. Another part of the professional consensus that underscored these common factors and shaped SAGE was an unpublished instrument called STARS-CBT, developed by colleagues in the north-east of England in order to try to operationalise supervision within a CBT model (James *et al.*, 2005). I will return to the discussion of SAGE in the final chapter.

Receiving supervision

Having designed a system for training supervisors and ensured that it is being delivered faithfully, the next step in the fidelity framework is to evaluate whether or not this results in the 'right' initial impacts on the supervisee. Logically, if the prior steps are implemented correctly, then we would expect to see clear evidence that the supervision is being received and is having the intended effect. This corresponds to the mini-outcomes illustrated by the Teachers' PETS instrument. It is the first fidelity step that involves outcome evaluation and asks: is supervision resulting in the right (mini) outcomes? Outcomes refer to improvements that are targeted through an intervention, and they have traditionally been regarded as the paramount measure of various forms of healthcare. As far as the National Health Service in the UK is concerned, activities such as staff development and clinical supervision are regarded as instrumental and pragmatic ways to foster changes designed ultimately to improve patients' health outcomes (National Health Service, 1998). The most popular approach to measuring outcomes in relation to staff development is the Kirkpatrick taxonomy (1967). This consists of four levels of outcome, ranging from simple reactions (i.e. supervisees' satisfaction with their supervision) to impacts on a service system (including health outcomes for the service users). This taxonomy has latterly been augmented by Kraiger *et al.* (1993), Alliger *et al.* (1997) and Belfield *et al.* (2001). As a result, changes in knowledge, skills and attitudes as a result of learning have been added; and a fifth level of outcome evaluation inserted, namely a new initial step of 'participation or completion'. There are therefore a wide range of options for evaluating the receipt of supervision.

Supervisee satisfaction

As per Kirkpatrick's (1967) taxonomy, the first step in outcome evaluation is to assess the reactions of the learner, typically couched in terms of their satisfaction with an intervention like supervision. To this day, satisfaction appears to be the most widely accepted and widely utilised of evaluations, at least under routine training/supervision conditions (i.e. outwith formal research programmes). This is because satisfaction is seen as a precondition for participation in supervision, as well as reflecting the importance of capturing the supervisee's perceptions, usually attempted through qualitative means. A case in point is the events paradigm (Ladany *et al.*, 2005), in which the supervisee is asked to identify something that occurred within supervision that was helpful. This is described in the supervisee's own language, linked to a simple quantitative rating of helpfulness. For example, see The Helpful Aspects of Supervision Questionnaire (HASQ; reproduced in Appendix B, Milne, 2008, p.245).

However, whether it measures satisfaction, affective reactions, enjoyment, usefulness, or the acceptability of an approach (Hook & Bunce, 2001), the relation between reactions and outcomes is far from straightforward. For example, Alliger *et al.* (1997) found the correlation between affective reactions (including the degree to which a training session was enjoyed) and immediate learning to approximate to zero. Interpreting these findings, Hook and Bunce (2001) suggested that there are no theoretical or empirical reasons to expect variables such as the pleasure or enjoyment of learning to be associated significantly with things like knowledge gain. However, in their study of 57 telesales staff receiving training in relation to a new computer system, they obtained findings that clearly indicated an important role for affective reactions on the training outcomes. Interestingly, their sub-analysis indicated that the more empathy the trainers provided, the less the group learnt. They speculated that the inconsistent pattern of relations between reactions and learning may be explained by the relative amount of challenge provided: insufficient challenge and excess empathy may produce limited outcomes. This is consistent with the EBCS model, which posits that a moderate degree of de-stabilisation is necessary for competence enhancement (see Chapter 3, for example). This may not be appreciated by the supervisee, at least in the short term, resulting in lower satisfaction ratings when the supervisor is actually doing a great job, at least judged by other criteria or by observers (e.g. if assessed in terms of learning, by the supervisor). Conversely, there is good reason to believe that a non-threatening, relaxed approach leads to higher satisfaction, as a review of some old studies in education have found that students who learnt the most rated their instructors least favourably (e.g. Parker & Thomas, 1980). This kind of relationship between challenge and satisfaction helps us to understand the more recent finding that relaxed ('degraded', i.e. largely conversational) CBT supervision was associated with high satisfaction (Townend *et al.*, 2002).

Bambling *et al.* (2006) also noted a complex relationship, this time in relation to client satisfaction and treatment outcome. They speculated that the lack of a clear relationship might have been an artefact of allegiance or expectancy effects. A further possibility has been suggested by Harkness

(1987), whose correlational study of social work supervision in a mental health centre indicated that the supervisees' satisfaction with supervision was negatively correlated with the clients' depression, but positively correlated with client satisfaction and goal attainment. This indicated to Harkness (1987) that the supervisees based their satisfaction ratings on the degree to which supervision helps to promote clinical benefits (i.e. it is actually a proxy measure of outcome).

In conclusion, there are theoretical and practical reasons for treating the measurement of satisfaction with considerable caution, as it appears quite possible that 'effective supervision is not always the most satisfying supervision (i.e. the struggle inherent in learning may not always be experienced as the most satisfying)' (Ladany *et al.*, 1999, p.454). These authors therefore recommend that researchers also include other outcomes of supervision, and also do not rely solely on trainee self-report.

For instance, less popular but arguably more searching additions are evaluations of outcome, based on methods such as quizzes or performance tests (such as simulations). Table 8.3 provides a breakdown of these different kinds of outcome measures, reflecting the augmented Kirkpatrick (1967) taxonomy. This summary notes the frequency with which the different types of evaluation were conducted within the sample of supervision studies included in the series of systematic reviews of the literature that underpin this book (e.g. see Milne, 2007).

Table 8.3 shows that measures of the supervisees' reactions to supervision were infrequent (14 per cent of these studies), whereas measures of learning (cognitive and behavioural) were applied in 29 per cent of studies. Similarly, evaluations of the transfer of learning to the workplace were reported in nearly half of the included studies, most commonly in terms of the transfer of supervision to therapy (48 per cent of studies). Note that these percentages reflect the proportion of instances out of the overall total for all 24 studies, which amounted to a sum of 89 different forms of outcome measurement. That is, on average 3.7 different kinds of outcomes were evaluated for each of the 24 studies in these recent reviews. These data suggest that evaluations have been conducted thoroughly, at least in this sample of studies. Therefore, consistent with the preceding material, in these 24 programmes satisfaction is little emphasised, whereas learning and transfer represent around half of all assessments made.

The third and final evaluation panel within the EBCS model is outcome benchmarking. This goes beyond the material just discussed to relate learning and its transfer to some kind of external standard or norm. That is, did the

Table 8.3 Profile of evaluation approaches, from a systematic review of 24 studies of clinical supervision

1. Evaluation methods and their relative frequency		
a) Archival data	1	(1.4%)
b) Interviews	2	(2.9%)
c) Ratings	9	(12.9%)
d) Observation	33	(47.1%)
e) Questionnaires	24	(34.3%)
f) Other (focus group)	1	(1.4%)
Totals:	70	(100%)
Mean percent measures per study =		2.9%
2. Supervisee outcomes		
A Cognitive learning		
Knowledge (declarative – e.g. quiz)	2	(2.2%)
Knowledge (procedural)	0	(0)
Knowledge (strategic)	0	(0)
B Behavioural learning		
Learning skills	19	(21.3%)
Adherence	5	(5.6%)
Automaticity	0	(0)
Generalisation:		
Time	11	(12.4%)
Persons	24	(27%)
Settings	7	(7.9%)
Behaviours	1	(1.1%)
C Attitude change		
Attitude change	0	(0)
Motivation change	0	(0)
Reactions/acceptability	12	(13.5%)
D Other		
Quality of care	1	
Interpersonal skills	2	
Implementation	2	(9%)
Personality	2	
Use of drugs	1	
Total number of supervisee outcomes:	89	(100%)
Mean number:	3.71 outcomes per study	
3. Clinical outcomes		
Symptoms/distress (e.g. mood)	3	(25%)
Functioning	5	(41.6%)
		(cont'd)

Table 8.3   (*cont'd*)

Risk reduction	0	(0)
Quality of life	2	(16.7%)
Service satisfaction	2	(16.7%)
Totals:	12	(100%)
Mean number:	0.5 per study	

supervision produce the expected results, assessed in terms of some established outcome? In research terms, this is like a replication study in which one attempts to reproduce findings, normally within a routine service situation. However, studies of the relative effectiveness of clinical supervision are scarce (e.g. see Bambling *et al.*, 2006, described shortly). Table 8.1 also suggests that this step in the fidelity framework involves formulating the factors that contribute to the transfer of supervision. This has been studied more frequently, in terms of factors such as staff stress, leadership, and general organisational 'barriers and boosters'. As seen in the previous chapter, it also includes the degree to which supervisors feel supported.

Transferring supervision

Perhaps the most common example that approximates to outcome bench-marking is the evaluation of the clinical outcomes obtained with clients. The use of this criterion has often been argued to be the acid test of the effectiveness of supervision (e.g. Ellis & Ladany, 1997; Stein & Lambert, 1995). According to the fidelity framework, this is termed 'transferring' supervision (see Table 8.1, row 5). Table 8.3 provides a breakdown of the evaluation methods used within the Milne (2007) review that assess such transfer. This illustrates that 42 per cent of these studies utilised some measure of clinical outcome, most commonly measures of clinical functioning (such as self-injurious behaviour). Measures of distress (such as low mood) were measured in a quarter of the studies, whereas clients' quality of life or satisfaction with the service that they received was measured in 17 per cent of instances (in both cases). Such assessments create the possibility for comparing different models of supervision in terms of their relative clinical outcomes (see, for example, Bambling *et al.*, 2006, summarised below). It also allows auditing to occur in terms of achieving a benchmark standard.

Freitas (2002) reviewed two decades of research into whether clinical supervision improves clinical outcomes for clients, focusing on 10 studies conducted between 1981 and 1997. Freitas (2002) reiterated the oft-mentioned concerns about the limited rigour of these outcome evaluations (as per Ellis & Ladany, 1997; Ellis *et al.*, 1996), recognising how this rigour was compromised by the complexity of studying the full educational pyramid. However, he felt that many of the methodological weaknesses in this small sample of studies could be remedied relatively easily in subsequent, replication research (e.g. by providing psychometric data on the instruments used). Overall, these 10 studies indicate highly diverse approaches to outcome measurement, tapping variables such as the theoretical congruence of the supervisor and supervisee, the timing of feedback, and the relationship between the therapists' competence and the clients' ego level. Not surprisingly, clear conclusions were very hard to draw, although those studies that did approximate to a straightforward measurement of the relationship between supervision and clinical outcomes produced affirmative data, indicating the value of supervision.

Example of outcome evaluation, in terms of clinical symptom change
Bambling *et al.* (2006) conducted a randomised controlled trial in which 127 depressed clients were allocated randomly to therapists who were either receiving supervision or who were unsupervised, and who provided eight sessions of a problem-solving therapy. The Beck Depression Inventory (BDI; Beck *et al.*, 1987) was utilised as the symptom measure. There were two conditions of the supervised therapy, one focusing on processes (i.e. psychodynamic) and the other on skills (i.e. CBT). In the process supervision condition, the discussion of patients focused on helping the supervisees to understand the interpersonal dynamics occurring within therapy (e.g. implicit feedback from the client, resistance, or the flow of exchanges). In the skill focus condition, attention was given to specific therapist behaviours, and advice and guidance was provided on optimal ways of treating the patients. Eight sessions of supervision were provided, one before treatment commenced, the remainder taking place after each of the first seven therapy sessions. A total of 60 patients were treated by therapists in the unsupervised condition, with 33 therapists in the skill-focused supervision group, and 34 in the process-focused supervision group. Supervisors were qualified mental health practitioners with at least two years of experience in providing supervision. They received a one-day workshop to try to ensure their competence within the different approaches, which were both manualised.

The results indicated that the BDI scores for the full sample of patients reduced significantly by the end of the eight-session treatment period. Supervision had a significant main effect on the average BDI score, which indicated that therapists receiving supervision obtained the best clinical outcomes. However, no difference was obtained between the process and skill approaches to supervision. Measures of client satisfaction with therapy and rates of client completion also favoured the two supervision conditions significantly. The mean BDI scores for clients seen by the supervised therapists corresponded to remitted depression by the end of the study, and indicated that in 44 of the 65 clients depression was no longer clinically evident. Bambling *et al.* (2006) concluded that the study provided initial evidence that supervision can enhance treatment outcome.

Outcome-orientated supervision

One promising extension of outcome/transfer evaluation is a system whereby client outcomes can be monitored on a routine basis, and then feedback provided regularly to the supervisor and supervisee. For example, Worthen and Lambert (2007) have outlined a system for tracking the client's response to treatment longitudinally, and comparing the data against norms for treatment response. When there is a discrepancy between the results from the local provision of therapy and the outcomes achieved within the normative sample, then a system is in place to alert therapists and their supervisors to this relatively poor progress. This includes providing therapists with a problem-solving decision tree, together with recommendations for possible interventions to boost progress. An earlier variation on this approach is to define limits to the variation in outcome data statistically (statistical process control), which is fed back to staff and supervisors in graphical form (thereby indicating whether the outcomes are 'in control', i.e. are as expected, or are 'out of control', i.e. requiring attention). These data, which were derived from weekly staff and patient satisfaction questionnaires, were tabled and discussed at monthly meetings, resulting in significantly higher patient satisfaction (Hyrkas & Lehti, 2003).

Within the UK's Improving Access to Psychological Therapies (IAPT) initiative, an even more sophisticated 'patient case management information system' has been developed (PC-MIS; York University, 2007). This provides real-time information on structure (therapist/patient contacts; demographic data), process (nature of contact activity), and outcome (clinical functioning). In addition, PC-MIS has multiple other potential uses, including prompting therapists about next steps (e.g. assertive follow-up of a patient), and allowing them to prompt their supervisor for help at any stage, or access the supervision notes from the last session. In turn, the supervisors can readily access all of these data, enabling outcome monitoring in relation to their own supervisees, and in relation to the whole service (outcome benchmarking). This allows one supervisor to readily monitor dozens of cases (in treatment or on a waiting list, partly aided by graphically presented data), as well as multiple supervisees' clinical effectiveness.

Developing supervision

Finally, the augmented fidelity framework implies the need to have a system of monitoring the supervision arrangements so that feedback is available, and so that decisions can be made that promote the economy and efficiency of the system. This addresses questions such as whether we are getting good value for the resource that is invested in supervision; whether we have we got our system right; or whether there is a better way? Traditionally, this would subsume cost–benefit and other economic analyses, which might feed into summative decision-making (e.g. a judgement that a given form of supervision provides minimal benefits at excessive costs, and so should be replaced by a better alternative). In routine practice it might involve decisions about discontinuing the use of low-fidelity supervisors, and setting up systems of accreditation and monitoring so that appropriately trained and effective supervisors are engaged properly and duly rewarded for their high-fidelity work. Other related activities that are identified in Table 8.1 include reducing the loss of good supervisors (whilst identifying and developing talented supervisors); dismantling supervision, and the methods used to train supervisors, so as to better identify the most effective ingredients; and creating feedback loops that allow us to monitor and support supervisors (e.g. to help identify and remediate environmental factors that may help or hinder supervision).

Implementation

It is tempting to assume the well-intentioned, enthusiastic and faithful implementation of new technologies, whether they are fantastic developments arising from the space age or straightforward toolkits (collections of instruments) with which to evaluate supervision. However, implementation is actually one of the most exacting and unsatisfactory areas within health service development. Interventions such as organisational development, organisational change and service innovation testify to how surprisingly difficult it tends to be to get clinicians to implement changes to their practice, including routine outcome measurement. This has been observed repeatedly, regardless of the specifics of the situation, going back through a long history of organisational change efforts (see, for example, Georgiades & Phillimore, 1975). Since their early account of doomed efforts at facilitating change in organisations (i.e. the 'hero-innovator' approach), there have been a number of specific examples where attempts to introduce outcome measurement have floundered (Marks, 1998). Such authors have noted obstacles in the use of outcome measurement, including the extra administrative burden, poor funding, the need for training, the insensitivity of the available tools, their limited value (in terms of informing the delivery of care), the reliance on temporary research workers, and clashes with other crude systems of outcome measurement within healthcare systems. As summarised by Lyons *et al.* (1997), 'without a careful implementation strategy, any effort at outcomes measurement ... is unlikely to succeed' (p.129). Their idea of a careful implementation strategy was an eight-stage approach:

- needs assessment: clarifying what the system needs and what the staff can manage within the available resource;
- planning: agreeing what is to be measured, when, why and by whom;
- working the organisation: identifying and addressing any barriers or resistance, while working to boost or increase motivation to implement outcome measurement;
- pre-testing instruments and procedures: fine-tuning the measures and methods before commencing, including piloting and feedback;
- training and initiation: providing on-site training and support to all those involved in outcome measurement;
- maintenance and management: agreeing targets for each participating supervisor and ensuring that a data collection system is in place, so that quick feedback is provided to supervisors in a timely, credible and relevant form;
- analysis and interpretation: additionally, general feedback should be presented regularly to those involved, and efforts made to maximise understanding of the results; and

- re-engineering: lessons learnt should be identified and set out within some kind of report, so that implied actions can be specified and agreed (e.g. workshops for supervisors on the topic of outcome measurement). This phase is discussed below.

This procedure of Lyons *et al.* (1997) is echoed in other similar reviews of outcome measurement (e.g. Barkham *et al.*, 1998). The essential message is that outcome measurement cannot normally be introduced and maintained without significant system-wide effort, allied to intelligent selection of instruments so that they provide maximum yield to users, probably encouraged by key champions within the organisational system who will motivate and address obstacles (Corrigan & McCracken, 1997). It also appears to be the case that there needs to be an efficient and supportive information system (Marks, 1998). An illustration of applying the eight-stage approach to the implementation of a nationally disseminated clinical outcome measure can be found in Milne *et al.* (2001).

Fortunately, most supervisors will spend at least part of their supervision time working in conjunction with local training programmes, which provide systems that support the implementation of outcome measures (and other forms of evaluation). For example, most initial training programmes will have instruments with which to measure the supervisees' reactions to their supervision, as well as ways of monitoring their involvement and participation. Additionally, it is not uncommon for more searching forms of evaluation to be applied, such as the clinical competence checklists that are used within the Newcastle University Clinical Psychology Doctorate programme (reproduced in Appendix A of Milne, 2008, pp.235–243). This allows steps 4, 5 and 6 of the augmented fidelity framework to be addressed (see Table 8.1). Supervisees' learning can be monitored in terms of their gradual demonstration of competence over the three-year programme. This is assessed by the supervisor and verified by the clinical tutor, a representative of the training programme who visits the training placements routinely, to ensure that supervision is occurring faithfully and to enable the required evaluation work to occur (all features of the competence model). The accumulated checklists create the basis for feedback through this supervision system (as illustrated by Figure 6.1, in Chapter 6, which summarised how the trainees felt they contributed to supervision over a one-year period). A detailed account of this evaluation, and a copy of this checklist, can be found in Milne (2008, Appendix A).

As this illustration shows, another big advantage that supervisors have in relation to outcome measurement is that they have what should be a close collaborator, namely their supervisee. Although most supervisees will understandably wish to minimise evaluation, there are certain approaches as well as certain circumstances in which their motivation may be sufficient to allow a joint approach to unfold. For instance, use of the Helpful Aspects of Supervision Questionnaire (HASQ; Appendix B in Milne, 2008) allows the supervisee to shape their supervisor's behaviour in a gentle, helpful way, and therefore may be mutually beneficial. Similarly, both parties may be keen to ensure that some kind of clinical outcome measurement occurs on a regular basis. Training programmes may cement this collaboration, through assignments that require the student/supervisee to furnish both kinds of data.

Further aids to those who are interested in implementing some form of evaluation system are the toolkits that have helpfully been appended to textbooks on clinical supervision. For example, the 'supervisor's toolbox' in Bernard and Goodyear (2004) includes a simple, eight-point Supervision Satisfaction Questionnaire, a more detailed, 29-item breakdown of the supervisee's perceptions of their supervision (e.g. 'I was not comfortable using the technique recommended by my supervisor'); and even a measure dedicated to assessing the evaluation processes within supervision itself. This latter instrument, called 'Evaluation Process Within Supervision Inventory' (Lehrman-Waterman & Ladany, 2001) includes items such as: 'The objectives that my supervisor and I created were specific'; and 'My supervisor balanced his or her feedback between positive and negative statements'. Falender and Shafranske (2004) also appended a toolkit, which includes the 'Supervision Outcomes Survey' (Worthen & Isakson, 2000). This has 20 items, and is designed to assess the supervisee's perception of the learning outcomes achieved through supervision. Items are rated on a seven-point scale and include: 'Supervision helps me improve my ability to conceptualise my cases' and 'My supervisor's feedback encourages me to keep trying to improve'. There is also a scale for measuring the supervisee's competence, called the 'Therapist Evaluation Checklist' (Hall-Marley, 2000). The supervisee's proficiency is rated in terms of competence, either being a 'strength', being 'commensurate with the level of training' or 'needing improvement'. Items include the contribution made to team-working and general therapy skills. Within the latter category are assessment skills, such as establishing an alliance and demonstrating objectivity; within the intervention category are skills in developing a working alliance and in addressing interpersonal issues.

Evaluation Designs

Another way of making the introduction and maintenance of evaluation more likely is to adopt relatively straightforward research designs. Again, these have been summarised in research textbooks, particularly those concerned with quasi-experimental designs (see in particular Shadish *et al.*, 2000). These texts helpfully set out the core requirements, when utilising the kinds of instruments just described, that allow one to draw inferences about the effectiveness of supervision. A particularly appealing design to consider is the 'small n' or $n = 1$ methodology (Hayes *et al.*, 1999), as this allows the supervisor to evaluate key parts of the augmented fidelity framework with relatively minimal effort, whilst gaining maximum ability to interpret findings. Thus, instead of the considerable work entailed in recruiting many participants to experimental groups and then trying to match them with control participants, the small-n study can be conducted rigorously with just one supervisee. This is achieved through making the supervisee his or her own control, and by using a number of different experimental conditions in a sequential, systematic manner. The classic example is the multiple baseline design, in which a baseline condition is followed by some kind of intervention, which is followed by a maintenance or a reversal phase. To be concrete, this might involve supervision as usual, which is measured in terms of the supervisee's experiential learning (e.g. with Teachers' PETS: Milne *et al.*, 2002), alongside a suitable measure of supervisee satisfaction. In the experimental (intervention) phase a specific form of supervision is introduced, ideally based on a manual, while the same form of measurement continues. It might be predicted that this will result in a greater receipt of supervision, as measured through the supervisee's enhanced learning (i.e. step 4 in Table 8.1). Teachers' PETS could also be used to clarify whether supervision is being delivered faithfully (step 3 in Table 8.1). The third and final phase in this design allows one to infer that the new approach to supervision is responsible for any obtained outcomes. The reversal design entails reverting to the baseline (supervision as usual) condition. If the learning outcomes revert to the initial baseline level, following a clear, significant and stepwise increase during the intervention phase, then it is reasonable to infer that the manipulation was the reason for the improved learning (Kazdin, 1998).

There are many variations on this theme, but, sticking with the option of looking at only one supervisee's development, one can also consider the design in which there is a multiple baseline across different supervisee behaviours. This would identify three or more competencies that the supervisee should develop over time, and each of these is tackled in turn, in such a way that, ideally, a stepwise pattern of the intended changes occurs.

The $n = 1$ design is an example of a broader class of designs called 'microgenetic' (Siegler, 2002). These furnish a feasible yet fascinating approach to the study of learning and development. For instance, Siegler (1995) studied how five-year-old schoolchildren acquired number conservation.

Concluding Evaluations Successfully

Part of the challenge in evaluation is ensuring that the results make a difference. The best designs, instruments and implementation strategies are arguably of little merit if the resulting information gathers dust on some office shelf. Reflecting the need to adopt a more systematic approach, initiatives such as the 'stakeholder-collaborative' model (Ayers, 1987) and the more detailed sequencing of problem-solving activities and relational tasks explicated helpfully by Bouwen and Taillieu (2004) indicate how intelligent approaches to ensuring effective evaluation might be pursued. Such participatory, collaborative or even empowerment approaches to evaluation make good psychological sense (in terms of engaging key parties in the evaluation process), and probably lead to the best outcomes (Rossi *et al.*, 2003). In essence, like a foreign movie, a good evaluation has an appropriate 'FINI': the F stands for the feedback of results stage (in which stakeholders' attention is gained and the relevance and clarity of the information is assessed); the I stands for the inspecting of these results, in the sense that stakeholders, collaborators and others are able to verify, check and ideally illuminate the data; N represents negotiating (which includes agreeing what the results indicate – the sense or meaning of the data); and finally, 'I' stands for implementing the results, that is, drawing out the action implications (including repeating evaluations in due course: based on Rossi *et al.*, 2003).

Chapter Conclusions

In this chapter I have attempted to clarify a coherent, novel and useful framework for evaluating clinical supervision. In contrast to the divergence that exists within the field, I have put forward an integrative, extended fidelity framework which draws on accepted principles for service evaluation, and on specific examples pertinent to supervision. In addition to being well founded, the fidelity framework will hopefully impress as having clear and logical steps towards a comprehensive evaluation. Being made up of some discrete, potentially straightforward steps, I believe that the framework is also empowering, in the sense that it enables supervisors (and others) to engage readily with the evaluation agenda. As set out in Table 8.1, this framework proposes that the comprehensive evaluation of supervision entails undertaking all six steps within this approach. I have argued that the minimum interpretable evaluation would require information on the structure, process and outcomes of supervision, following Donabedian (1988). This is because we require to know not only whether something works (the outcome criterion), but also what activities occurred (i.e. the processes, contents and procedures) to produce this outcome. Finally, it is of little value to know that certain processes yield certain outcomes if we know nothing about the input or resource (structures, effort) on which this was based (e.g. impressive outcomes may be prohibitively expensive). We therefore need to know what resources were invested, including the supervisors and supervisees involved, the amount of time and energy that they gave to the enterprise, and any other equipment or resources entailed. Together, the structure–process–outcome analysis provides a coherent, meaningful evaluation of supervision. However, a comprehensive evaluation provides us with additional information, which may be highly informative. For example, as in step 2 of Table 8.1, it allows us to audit whether or not supervisors are adhering properly to a training manual, and whether or not it is having the intended effect on the supervisee. In relation to all the fidelity steps, I have urged that self-report instruments, especially when used to assess the supervisee's satisfaction with supervision, are treated with caution, requiring the addition of more objective instruments to afford a balanced evaluation.

Also, I have suggested that there is a further challenging aspect to evaluation, namely the business of implementation. As with other kinds of service development, the introduction and maintenance of a system of evaluation is no trivial matter. Respecting this challenge, an eight-stage process was summarised, and some key factors identified (such as the importance of using instruments that are 'owned' by their users, and that have high clinical yield: Cape & Barkham, 2002). The concluding phase of this process is to try to ensure that findings contribute to informed change, and this was therefore treated as a further section above, with an emphasis on closely collaborating with the stakeholders in an evaluation.

Although the chapter has covered a significant amount of material, including in passing some attention to the kinds of evaluation designs that one might consider (such as the small-n approach that was outlined), it is important to acknowledge that there are many other aspects of evaluation that it has not been possible to address here. However, these are covered in other texts on supervision (see, for example, Wampold & Holloway, 1997) and can also be found in general textbooks on evaluation (Rossi *et al.*, 2003; Shadish *et al.*, 2000). For these reasons, I have chosen to emphasise what I believe to be a fresh and feasible avenue to the evaluation of supervision.

9

Concluding Supervision

Introduction

Clinical supervision is an 'essential' ingredient in modern mental health care (Department of Health, 2008, p.29). Not only is it essential in order to foster the practice and regulation of professionals, it is also essential in terms of achieving good clinical outcomes (Layard, 2005). The most convincing demonstrations to date of these popular beliefs has come from meta-analyses of dozens of controlled clinical outcome studies, analyses which examined the effectiveness of collaborative care for depressed patients in primary care (Bower *et al.*, 2006; Gilbody *et al.*, 2006). Utilising regression analyses, these authors were able to demonstrate that 'the use of regular and planned supervision of the case manager, usually by a psychiatrist, was related to a more positive clinical outcome' (Gilbody *et al.*, 2006, p.2317). The finding that the case managers with a mental health background and regular specialist supervision contributed significantly to the outcomes suggested to the authors that expertise was important, which carries implications for effective supervision within initiatives like Improving Access to Psychological Therapies (IAPT). These good clinical outcomes appeared to be mediated by the effect that this supervision had on the therapeutic alliance, and on adherence to the biopsychosocial treatment model. This is made all the more impressive by the failure of the therapy itself (or anti-depressive medication) to contribute significantly to the overall reduction in depression.

This heartening affirmation of high-quality supervision encourages further scrutiny of the factors that help to make it effective. Therefore, in this final chapter, I will list the 12 main principles that have been addressed within the book, summarising the essential points that have been made in relation to each, based on the research and expert consensus that have been reviewed.

Appropriately, this kind of pause to take stock represents the basis of reflection, an essential part of learning from experience. As well as being central to supervision, it is also part of critical thinking, a cognitive process 'that is focused on deciding what to believe or do' (Ennis, 1985, p.45). This seems especially fitting at the close of this book. Therefore, in addition to providing these principles as a summary, I will offer a critical commentary on some particularly prominent and vexatious issues, such as the current status of Kolb's (1984) account of experiential learning, so that we might be better placed to decide what we know and how we should behave. The specific business of bringing supervision sessions to a conclusion will also be addressed, as one of these commentaries.

Principles of EBCS

1. Take due account of the context in which supervision is practised

The knowledge-base, relevant history, governmental policy, and the framework adopted by individuals in addressing supervision are prominent amongst the myriad factors that moderate supervision. The behaviour of the supervisor and supervisee will surely be a function of their personal characteristics, in the context that they operate, and the interaction between the two (Lewin, 1951). Ignore the context at your peril!

Commentary: These characteristics are an explicit part of the context for EBCS and the augmented CBT model, as set out in Figure 3.3 (in Chapter 3). An example of something that we should believe about supervision is that the individual characteristics of supervisor and supervisee will create a micro-context for one another, significantly shaping what unfolds within the proximal and more distal contextual factors (e.g. social support and national healthcare policies, respectively).

On the negative side of individual differences we can consider the example of the alliance, where there is reason to suspect that unintentional biases, relating to characteristics such as colour, may interfere with the quality of the mutual involvement, contributing to the disproportionately high levels of dropout from therapy (Vasquez, 2007). An example cited is how some people of colour may experience slights and offences so regularly that (together with cultural values) they will tend to 'edit' their negative reactions to the working alliance. This may limit mutual awareness of a rupture, reducing any repair effort, with the consequence that the effectiveness of supervision is compromised. Others may react with super-sensitivity to any implication of criticism or rejection, possibly to the point where one party or the other discontinues. The action implications include assessing and monitoring the supervisory relationship and taking extra care in seeking mutual feedback. This can contribute to the development of cultural empathy, including mutual awareness of individually expressive, often subtle, response styles (e.g. posture; eye contact, or voice tone). Other implications are to give greater emphasis to reflecting openly on the supervision process, exploring relevant perspectives and experiences in an honest, respectful way, and facilitating the expression of feelings.

A further example cited by Vasquez (2007) is the phenomenon of 'microaggression', in which cross-cultural interactions 'convey attitudes of dominance, superiority, and denigration: that a person with privilege is better than the person of colour, who is less intelligent, capable, worthy, and so forth' (pp.880–881). Microaggression may arise in relation to any such individual differences, and Vasquez notes the examples of gender, age, sexual orientation, socio-economic status, religious or disability status.

2. Adopt a problem-solving cycle

Whether within an individual supervision session or as part of the process of delivering a training programme, it is important to have a clear and shared sense of direction, based on collaborative goal-setting. Link this systematically to the methods that are deployed in pursuit of these goals, and also link to regular measurement, so that there is corrective feedback. In essence, apply the scientific method in your routine practice. An example is developed below, under principle 5. As set out in Table 9.2, supervision is itself treated as a problem-solving cycle of activities, in order to consider how supervision might best vary in relation to different levels of competence in the supervisee.

3. Draw critically on what is known

There are many damning reviews of supervision, but they may have failed 'to see the wood for the trees'. By adopting more selective approaches, such as the best evidence synthesis review strategy, we can define a clear and helpful basis for competent practice. If this is sensitively wedded to what professionals believe, then intelligent, evidence-based approaches become viable. But individual supervisors also need to be critically engaged in their consumption of the knowledge-base in supervision, as in questioning the adequacy of the methodology and in generating alternative interpretations of the findings (Ellis, 1991). The story is told of how the Buddha would write down prominently 'This is not the truth', before speaking. Similarly, supervisors need to see for themselves what is true, through exercising their critical faculties.

4. Clarify your model of practice

It is essential in practice (and in research) to be as specific as possible about the ideas that are guiding one's work. By making comparisons with closely competing and widely divergent models you can help this specification effort. As described at several stages within this book, the CBT model has tantalising overlaps with EBCS. Consideration of these, together with the guiding principles and history of CBT, led to the view that EBCS represents an augmented CBT supervision model.

Commentary: The majority of respondents to a survey about CBT supervision did not respond to the item about their model, perhaps indicating a lack of clarity (Townend *et al.*, 2002). If true, this is hardly surprising, as there are dozens of models, and insufficient training or research to help supervisors to define and differentiate them. For instance, only 13 per cent of those in the Townend *et al.* (2002) survey had received CBT model-specific training. Even when the models are relatively well defined, close comparison with neighbouring approaches can be tricky, as there can be differences in terminology, foci, levels of analysis, and so forth.

A case in point, commenced in Chapter 3, is between CBT and EBCS. There I asserted that one of the few differences between these models was that, whilst both approaches advocated experiential learning (especially role-play and the reviewing of therapy tapes), the CBT one was not actually implemented with fidelity. To test this opinion (see Chapter 3 for the basis for this assumption), I have listed the 10 main testable statements made about CBT supervision in the most-cited (authoritative) available summaries of the model (Liese & Beck, 1997; Padesky, 1996). Examining their 'beliefs and assumptions' about this behaviour seemed like an appropriate approach within CBT, leading to some reflexive data-collection and reality-checking. All known empirical analyses of CBT supervision were therefore checked, to ascertain to what extent their findings provided confirmatory or falsifying information. These studies consisted of seven experiments and two surveys: Bambling *et al.* (2006); Heaven *et al.* (2006); James *et al.* (2008); Milne and James (2002); Milne *et al.* (2002); Milne and Westerman (2001); Reichelt *et al.* (2003); Townend *et al.* (2002) and Tyler *et al.* (2000), respectively. Table 9.1 furnishes the results, which suggest that my sceptical assumption of poor fidelity is broadly valid: in the key dimension (D: The Methods) the two relevant beliefs are 7 and 8, and the data suggest that, on average, these experiential methods occurred on only 9 per cent of observed occasions. Similarly, the general level of fidelity to the CBT model is poor: my reading of the results is that 7 of the 10 beliefs (as represented by Liese & Beck, 1997; and Padesky, 1996) were falsified by this limited available evidence, with one 'tie' (belief 1). In conclusion, as Townend *et al.* (2002) put it, 'adherence to this approach is at best limited' (p.496).

I also asserted in Chapter 3 that EBCS made more use of these experiential methods. The relevant data with which to test this claim are drawn from the intervention phases of the two relevant and matched experimental studies (i.e. where there was an attempt to increase the frequency of the same supervision activities subsumed under the category of 'experiential', under the same conditions: Milne & James, 2002; Milne & Westerman, 2001). Although there was no increase in the use of therapy tapes (there was actually a decrease during EBCS), the use of role-plays increased substantially (from a mean of 7 to 19.4 within the EBCS condition), making an average overall increase of 25 per cent. I conclude from this that EBCS probably does utilise experiential methods more frequently than CBT.

This is, of course, only a rough and ready comparison, based on my own assumptions (e.g. that the baselines reflected CBT supervision), and on one rather conventional notion of CBT. But orthodoxy can be surprisingly elusive: according to Liese and Beck (1997), CBT supervision should attend to transference and counter-transference. Conversely, dynamic psychotherapy supervision within a major research study actually included CBT-congruent methods (including the use of tapes; teaching case conceptualisation; evaluative feedback: Binder & Strupp, 1997). Therefore, it seems clear that there are different definitions of the boundaries between CBT and traditionally distinct approaches to supervision. In this context, EBCS seems much closer to schema-focused CBT (Greenwald & Young, 1998). Although there exists

Table 9.1 Evidence of poor fidelity in existing observations of CBT supervision

Supervision dimensions	Assumptions and beliefs	Observational evidence related to these beliefs (i.e. data as a reality check)
A – The Model	1. CT supervision parallels the therapy (Padesky, 1996, p.281)	'Outcomes of grounded theory analysis (10 consecutive supervision tapes from 1 supervisor receiving consultancy) mapped on very closely to the revised CT scale' (Milne, Pilkington, Gracie, & James, 2003; p.198) CT Supervision 'less structured and active than therapy' (Townend et al., 2002, p.485); and the majority of respondents (59%) didn't describe their supervision model.
B – The Objectives	2. Mastering cognitive therapy (Padesky, 1996, p.281)	Extensive use of questioning (James & Milne; 2002, pp.32–33). No data in the other studies.
C – The Content	3. Prevent 'drift' away from standard cognitive therapy (Liese & Beck, 1997, p.114)	'Cognitive Therapy was appropriate' (Milne et al., 2003, p.200). No data in other studies.
D – The Methods	4. Structure should be as per cognitive therapy (Liese & Beck, 1997, p.120) (including agenda-setting, review of homework, eliciting feedback)	'Managing' (including agenda setting) observed on only 1% of (baseline) occasions (Milne & James, 2002, p.64; 3% frequency observed in Milne & Westerman, 2001, p.457)
	5. Review case conceptualisations, utilise basic counselling skills, use CBT techniques (this one, and beliefs/assertions 6–7, 9–10 are also from Liese & Beck, 1997	Formulation the most frequent focus in supervision (94% of respondents affirmed this topic, in Townend et al. (2002, p.491)

	6. Weekly supervision (60 minutes)	60 Minutes per fortnight (Milne & Westerman, 2001, p. 447); by contrast, mean duration of 136 minutes per month reported in Townend *et al*, 2002, p. 489)
	7. Review therapy tapes ('essential', Liese & Beck, 1997, p.123)	18% of respondents reported reviewing tapes (Townend *et al.*, 2002, p.492). Tapes reviewed on only 6% of observed (baseline) occasions (Milne & James, 2002, p.64); and on 20% of (baseline) occasions in a related study (Milne & Westerman, 2001, p.451).
	8. Include role-plays (Padesky, 1996, p.281)	19% reported using role-plays in a survey (Townend *et al.*, 2002, p.492–493). Only observed on 7% of (baseline) interactions in Milne & James (2002, p.63); and 0% in Milne & Westerman, (2001, p.451).
E – Use of feedback and evaluation	9. Elicit feedback	Not reported in Townend *et al.* (2002). Feedback observed on only 3% of (baseline) occasions in both (Milne & James, 2002, p.64), and Milne & Westerman (2001, p.451)
	10. Provide feedback based on instruments assessing therapist competence (pp.123–125)	Not reported in Townend *et al.* (2002). Note: supervisors can be trained to use CTS-R fairly reliably: (Reichelt *et al.* (2003).

some blurring of boundaries, hopefully the present account at least serves as an example of how one can go about clarifying one's model of supervision practice. In terms of the bigger question, i.e. whether EBCS and CBT models are fundamentally the same model (when both are implemented with fidelity, when potentially trivial differences of foci, terminology, levels of analysis, and so forth are taken into account; and when the full spectrum of CBT approaches are considered), I have opted to go for the 'augmented' position: one of extending and strengthening the current accounts of CBT supervision.

5. Integrate theory with practice

A clear model is an enormous aid to practice, guiding the supervisor in the first instance, and providing inspiration to figure out solutions when problems arise. By contrast, appeals to an 'eclectic' approach may be tempting, but surely cannot represent the basis for informed practice or for enlightened research. A major theory within supervision is the developmental model, and there have been numerous attempts to relate this to practice.

Commentary: As discussed in Chapter 2, the idea of development permeates discussions of supervision, whether the focus is on the supervisee or the supervisor. Development is essentially a metaphor for the business of adapting successfully to varying demands throughout our careers. This may simply take the form of adjusting to the kinds of changes that come with time, such as becoming a more experienced trainee or a senior practitioner. Alternatively, the need to adapt may be driven by the workplace environment. A case in point in the UK at the time of writing is a Department of Health initiative, Improving Access to Psychological Therapies (IAPT). This has been referred to as a 'revolution in the delivery of psychological therapy services over the next decade' (Turpin, 2007, p.8). This governmental initiative is intended to deliver psychological therapy to 900,000 more people with anxiety and depression than current services and therapists achieve. It is meant to result in 25,000 fewer people on sickness benefits, thanks to 3500 newly trained psychological therapists, providing evidence-based treatments (see special issue of *Clinical Psychology Forum*, January, 2008, for details). This initiative has clear and unprecedented implications for the training and supervision of these new psychological therapists. Specifically, the initiative envisages a new kind of therapist, referred to as a 'low intensity' therapist, who is to receive a year of work-based, heavily supervised training.

This training will focus on CBT. The kind of demand for supervision that the initiative requires has been outlined by Richards and Suckling (2008) who noted, for instance, the need to shift supervision from its traditional emphasis on a therapist-driven agenda to a focus on a service-driven agenda, revolving around clinical outcomes. Also, up to 20 patients may need to be supervised per case manager per week, placing even more pressure on the supervisor to adopt a business-like model. As Richards and Suckling (2008) note, one of the novel pressures this creates on supervisors to adapt their supervision is that they find it 'difficult to give … low intensity advice to case managers when they themselves are operating from a … high intensity clinical paradigm' (p.14).

According to developmental models from general psychology, this kind of initiative creates a pressure on supervisors and the training and service systems to adapt, and three dimensions are emphasised, those of 'selection', 'optimisation' and 'compensation' (SOC). Respectively, these refer to specifying fresh goals in a changing context (including altering priorities and adapting standards); to shifting the means through which we try to achieve these goals (e.g. shifting our attention, effort, time or skills); and to monitoring the success of these optimisation efforts, so that any problems in achieving the new goals are addressed (e.g. through increased effort, allocating more time, or activating unused skills or resources) (Baltes, 1997).

In terms of the supervision literature (see Chapter 2), there are many models which adopt a developmental framework to try to capture this SOC process. Perhaps the most frequently cited is the Integrated Developmental Model (Stoltenberg, 1981). As noted in Chapter 2, the IDM recognises four developmental levels, proceeding from the novice level (characterised by high anxiety and low competence) through to the so-called integrated level (where the supervisee becomes competent across the duties of the post, within a personalised model of practice). Latterly, Ronnestad and Skovholt (2003) have revised the Stoltenberg (1981) developmental model in a form that makes it far more compatible with the IAPT initiative. According to them, six phases of development can be distinguished:

Phase 1: Lay helper (this recognises that even novice therapists will have some basic helping skills, e.g. based on social support).

Phase 2: Novice student (an exciting time but one coloured with dependence, vulnerability, anxiety and fragile self-confidence).

Phase 3: Advanced student (development of initial competence within a conservative, cautious approach).

Phase 4: Novice professional phase (the newly qualified therapist may be free of the demands of the training programme but may still feel poorly prepared for the workplace; initial development of personalised approach).

Phase 5: Experienced professional (greater attention to a personally valued, comfortable style, more flexible and personalised approaches; greater ability to judge the required degree of effort).

Phase 6: Senior professional (people with 20 or more years of experience are expected to have developed highly individualised and specialised approaches, with significant felt competence; and a growing scepticism about one's capacity to influence change).

This kind of developmental, multi-phase model implies flexible, developing patterns of supervision in order to meet the changing needs of the supervisee over time. There appears to be only a small literature that addresses the issue of developmental or flexible styles of supervision in relation to this kind of therapist development (e.g. Dennin & Ellis, 2003; Grant & Schofield, 2007; Temple & Bowers, 1998). To illustrate, corresponding to phases 5 and 6 of the Ronnestad and Skovholt (2003) phases, Dennin and Ellis (2003) argue for an approach labelled 'self-supervision', namely a process whereby senior professionals work relatively independently, directing their own professional development far more than would occur at earlier stages of development. However, the scant empirical literature on whether such developmentally informed supervision matters is far from clear cut in its support for such a multi-phase approach. For example, Shanfield *et al.* (1992), in their observational analysis of excellence amongst 34 supervisors, found that it was the core conditions of supervision that carried the greatest amount of variance. For example, empathy from the supervisor accounted for 72 per cent of the variance in rater-perceived excellence, and when empathy was dropped from the analysis an experiential orientation accounted for 60 per cent of the variance in the ratings of excellence. Moreover, they found that their supervisors appeared 'not to change significantly with different ... (therapists) ... or across different years of ... training' (p.355). In their opinion, Shanfield *et al.* (1992) viewed their results as supporting earlier observations that supervisors judged to be at the higher end of excellence tended to use the same recurring methods: 'supervisors judged to be excellent were empathic and focused on the immediate concerns of the trainee. They had an experiential orientation and tailored their comments to the residents concerns ... they were teachers who reflected with residents on their actions as therapists and supervisees' (p.355). Similarly, an empirical analysis based on supervisees' perceptions of supervision interventions over time indicated the importance of empathy and a practical clinical focus (Rabinowitz *et al.*, 1986): 'The most important supervision issues and interventions endorsed across the semester, regardless of experience level (of the supervisee), appeared to be those related to supervisory support, treatment planning, and seeking advice and direction' (p.297). In a more recent, rigorous evaluation of supervision, Bambling *et al.* (2006) compared the clinical effectiveness and working alliances of unsupervised therapists (who were treating 127 clients with a diagnosis of major depression) with therapists receiving either supervision with a focus on skill development or a focus on the process aspects of supervision. Although their fidelity assessments were able to show that these different conditions were implemented faithfully (self-rated adherence within the conditions were significantly different), they found that both of the supervision conditions had superior alliance and clinical outcomes to no supervision. But no difference was obtained between the two forms of supervision (process-focused supervision emphasised relational and insight techniques of alliance management; the skills-focus was based on CBT techniques). They concluded that 'the equivalence of effect may indicate that the effectiveness of this supervision rests on a general focus on alliance or influence of common factors' (p.327). In keeping with this emphasis on general or common factors, within the IAPT initiative there have been statements of the competencies required of supervisees (Roth & Pilling, 2008) and of the core competencies required of supervisors, at least within a CBT approach (Richards & Freeston, 2007). This emphasis is reflected within competence approaches to supervision (e.g. Falender & Shafranske, 2004).

Therefore, there appear to be two perspectives on how supervision needs to be delivered across the professional career-span. The professional consensus/expertise view is one that advocates a range of supervision approaches, whereas the available evidence would appear to point more to the flexible, developmentally appropriate application of some core approaches to supervision. In practice, it may be relatively straightforward to integrate these different perspectives. Table 9.2 is an attempt at an integration, adopting some fundamental psychological concepts. Specifically, one can think about the changing needs of the supervisee in terms of a continuum of competence, and Table 9.2 adopts perhaps the most widely known of these, the Dreyfus and Dreyfus (1986) model of skills acquisition. This suggests a taxonomy that ranges from the novice to the expert. This represents the

Table 9.2   A developmental matrix, relating levels of competence to problem-solving activities in supervision

Supervisee's competence level	Problem-solving cycle in supervision				
	Objectives (problems tackled; duties)	Problem formulation (and option selection)	Supervision methods (intervention)	Feedback and evaluation	Planning (tactics and strategy)
1. Novice (e.g. trainee low-intensity worker/ assistant psychologist; 'research applicator': consumption and implementation: C&I)	As per 'generic supervision' (GS), especially alliance building + maintenance and specific training outcomes (e.g. highly structured/ limited therapy; guideline adherence).	Agreeing learning contract, strongly influenced by service needs/tasks. Basic case conceptualisation.	Generic supervision (GS); plus specifics: apprenticeship (shaping/moulding) model, featuring a strong scaffolding (e.g. dictating objectives); close client monitoring/marked outcome orientation and a didactic/prescriptive style (e.g. structure++; instructing; modelling), fostering reflection and conceptualisation	High frequency of positive, warm feedback; build strengths and weaknesses awareness; benchmark against basic competencies and simple outcomes. Facilitate supervisee's ability to provide feedback.	Aim to complete training successfully (including study habits for high progression rates). 'By-the-book' developmental stages.
2. Advanced beginner (e.g. Masters-level, low-complexity worker; associate psychologist; 'empirical clinician': research C,I, and production: effectiveness (E1) and effects (E2).	GS and specific continuing professional development (CPD) to update & extend clinical work. Some prioritisation and negotiation of duties.	Maintaining motivation for learning new techniques; retention in post/ career development. Formulaic case formulation.	GS plus: balancing prescriptive style with some autonomy; doubts and concerns require attention, as too may subterfuge/'game-playing.' Coaching model, featuring clearly scaffolded experiential learning, fostering experimenting (e.g. elementary theory–practice integration) and reflection. Facilitating joint problem-solving.	Balance of positive/warm feedback with gentle challenge (e.g. efficiencies/improved outcomes, initial assessment of theoretical knowledge underpinning interventions (e.g. simple multiple choice questions (MCQs)), basic personalised measures of confidence in practice).	Become solid, confident clinician, with modestly distinct identity (e.g. specific therapeutic style/ angle). Embedded in service system.

3. Competent practitioner (e.g. Doctorate-level, trainee high-complexity worker; 'scholar-practitioner': research C,I, & P: E1,2 & efficacy piloting – E3a)	GS and training (e.g. CPD on interpersonal issues and clinical problem-solving skills; wide range of clients).	Novel case conceptualisation; time-management.	GS plus: doubts and concerns not disabling (stable; self-aware, if indecisive); enhanced clinical proficiency (skills and approaches). Journeying/mentoring model, featuring problem-based learning, process deliberations and professional growth aspirations, fostering reflection and modest use of learning cycle (e.g. to cover integration of 2–3 theories with practice).	Self-monitoring (SM) of outcomes; subtle reflection (SR) (e.g. value-based and drawing on several different theoretical models). Frequent challenge. Detailed benchmark against specific skill descriptors; self-benchmarking against skilled and effective colleagues (fidelity of skills assessed; professional publication outlets).	Develop into integrative or specialised clinician, with some interesting ideas. Aware of clinical developments and implications, and able to evolve own clinical tactics; reluctant to engage with service context/policy initiatives; limited capacity to plan strategically.
4. Proficient practitioner (e.g. high-complexity worker; 'scientist-practitioner': CIP & collaboration locally on E1,E2 and E3a)	GS and CPD (e.g. therapeutic style and professional identity; advanced problem-solving skills: autonomously determined attention to all manner of clinical problems, individual and systemic – e.g. addressing team issues and specific, supervisee-determined objectives).	Complex case conceptualisation; balancing competing demands.	GS plus: Doubts and concerns a stimulus for review and progress. Collegial/travelling model, featuring experiencing for personal–professional development, and significant use of learning cycle to guide highly personalised development of clinical automaticity and exploration. Can use own reactions as spur to insight/development, acknowledging multiple theoretical connections. Minimal scaffolding.	SM & SR, including higher-order integration of complex phenomena despite significant difficulties (e.g. developing novel re-formulations of cases/distress, whilst under pressure). Robust, seasoned clinician. Benchmark against professional practice, high-fidelity indicators (e.g. gifted therapists' 'masterclasses'; scientific journals of low impact).	Well-reasoned and imaginative ideas for advancing therapy (own and others: e.g. writes guidelines). Highly effective clinician. Aware of service and professional context with ability to predict evolving policies & practices, formulating sound plans & exercising leadership (e.g. workshop design and delivery).

(cont'd)

Table 9.2 (cont'd)

		Problem-solving cycle in supervision			
Supervisee's competence level	Objectives (problems tackled; duties)	Problem formulation (and option selection)	Supervision methods (intervention)	Feedback and evaluation	Planning (tactics and strategy)
5. Expert (e.g. consultant-level therapist; 'clinical scientist': CIP & collaboration nationally on E1–3b: efficacy trials)	GS and educational outcomes (e.g. improve local/ national outcome measurement system; create new techniques for use in system; autonomous/ independent stance – e.g. re-prioritising; seeking challenge).	Formulating system weaknesses and generating own, highly challenging, service-oriented goals. Adapting standards; modelling new solutions.	GS plus: Collegial/growing model, featuring fluent, sophisticated, novel use of learning cycle (e.g. generating new, viable ideas/plans) and self-supervision. Self-aware and accepting. In-depth attention to service context.	SM & SR, including novel insights into team/system operation; public challenge and disagreement (e.g. new treatments); rugged, gritty individual; benchmark against best other services processes and outcomes, (outcome benchmarking; high impact research literature).	Sensitive vigilance, used to anticipate, design and implement new clinical services (including expert rationale/persuasion) including new systems for delivering those services (e.g. fresh ways to train and develop staff), to succeed in fast-changing context.

first column of Table 9.2, and I have added some details regarding what kinds of training they might require, how they might be labelled (e.g. 'Scholar-practitioner': Milne & Paxton, 1998), alongside their involvement in R&D. Along the top of this matrix in Table 9.2 I have added the problem-solving cycle (Hayes, 1989). Finally, within each of the cells that are formed by these competence and problem-solving dimensions, I have listed general supervision (GS), to capture the implication from the above empirical research that flexible, SOC approaches to supervision may go a long way to allowing supervisors to solve problems across the competence spectrum. Additionally, the cells within Table 9.2 articulate specific, developmentally attuned approaches to supervision. These are set out in terms of the broad theory of supervision (e.g. shaping, guiding or travelling), and the kinds of objectives that would be relevant alongside the competencies that supervisors might be expected to require in relation to each combination of competence and problem-solving activity.

To illustrate this thinking, let us take the example of the proficient practitioner, level 4 on the competence taxonomy. Within the IAPT initiative, this therapist is expected to work with the more complex clinical presentations in a low-volume way, following a scientist-practitioner orientation. They will have a significant involvement in R&D. Like all other levels of proficiency, this experienced therapist will still require general supervision, featuring collaborative goal-setting and careful attention to alliance-building and its maintenance. In addition, this kind of therapist will have objectives concerning advanced problem-solving skills that may relate to self-generated clinical problems of a wide variety, for example occurring at the system level (e.g. problematic team functioning). In terms of the way that supervision helps this therapist to formulate such problems, multiple and complex models would be expected to be discussed in supervision, drawn largely from the theoretical and empirical literature. Subtle awareness of competing demands and the different contextual pressures that exist in relation to solving these kinds of problems will also feature. The methods of intervention used within supervision (column 4 in Table 9.2) will feature a more collegial relationship between the supervisor and supervisee, where the supervisor is perceived as analogous to the guide, facilitating the travelling experience of the supervisee. They will embrace doubts and concerns openly, and attend to the supervisee's personal professional development, etc. Self-monitoring and attention to clinical outcomes will feature relatively strongly at this level of competence, and indeed one of the activities discussed within supervision may be implementing systems of outcome feedback with other colleagues (see Harmon *et al.*, 2007; Worthen & Lambert, 2007). Clinicians at this level of proficiency will be inclined to benchmark their own clinical outcomes against the best available within professional practice, and use interventions with the highest possible fidelity. They will benchmark activities (like developing local outcome systems) against publication in scientific journals, with an emphasis on practitioner issues. Finally, in the last column of Table 9.2 it is recognised that the proficient practitioner will have soundly reasoned and creative ideas about how therapy could be improved (e.g. contributing to the development of new, more efficient therapies). This level of competence is also associated with a much keener awareness of the service policies and professional context of such work, meaning that their contribution is soundly informed and more likely to succeed. They may exercise this leadership by running workshops for more junior colleagues.

In summary, the debate about how supervision should be modified in relation to different kinds of therapists, their different activities, and their career development has been tackled within an integrative, competence-based, developmental approach, as summarised within Table 9.2. This argues for both a general supervisory (GS) role, featuring the normal supervision cycle steps (alliance-building, collaborative goal-setting, etc.), alongside some specific, developmentally tailored supervision approaches. This carries implications for how we organise supervision within services, and how we address developments (such as the IAPT one), as well as indicating how we might train and support such supervisors.

6. Verify assumptions

Although the ideas in this book have support from research, theory and expert consensus, it is incumbent upon professional supervisors to gather their own data and verify for themselves whether or not important features hold up in their own context (based on the kind of critical engagement outlined in principle 3). An experimental orientation affords a way of developing supervision, as reflected in this poem:

> The road to wisdom?
> Well, it's plain and simple to express:
> Err and err and err again,
> But less and less, and less (Aldwin, 2007, p.viii)

Commentary: A particularly fascinating example of verification is the business of understanding cause and effect. For instance, within Chapter 3 it was proposed that we could understand supervision by applying the causal reasoning from the therapy literature on process–outcome relations, including mechanistic notions like 'mediator' and 'mechanism'. Such assumptions may well be faulty, even in relation to therapy. Even if accurate, as assumptions about the way things are, they carry important implications, and it is wise to be aware of these. One assumption is materialism, which regards matter as the sole basis of reality, and so tries to explain cause and effect as resulting from the interaction of matter. This is completely plausible in relation to medicine, where biological substrates and physical systems are tangible, but where psychological phenomena are involved then the assumption is far less reasonable. Indeed, whereas in medicine there is a shared understanding of illness, and only a few treatments, in psychotherapy there are three dominant but widely differing explanatory systems (cognitive-behavioural, humanistic and psychodynamic), spawning a vast range of therapies. Furthermore, these are thought to achieve their results based on completely different change phenomena, ranging from specifiable ingredients/mechanisms within a scientific/materialist paradigm, to mentalistic/magical concepts, like remoralisation and instilling hope (Wampold, 2007). A popular example of the latter is mindfulness, which assumes that there is no discrete, linear cause and effect, but rather that 'everything is interconnected, interacted and integrated', as per whole, complex systems (Sagumura *et al.*, 2007). Indeed, they note, Zen Buddhism goes so far as to deny all kinds of conceptualisation, and so is opposed to scientific and even Western assumptions about causality. A position that I find helpful in this bewildering context is to view change as resulting from many concurrent causes, varying in their salience, and only partly explaining outcomes (Elliott, 2002). To clarify this process scientifically will require sophisticated approaches, such as dynamic causal modelling (Friston *et al.*, 2003).

7. Critical engagement

It is important that the ideas within this book, and your own applications of any of this material, are treated in a scholarly, critical fashion. After all, evidence-based clinical supervision is a process of gaining knowledge (i.e. erring less, through this problem-solving strategy), as well as a statement of what is known at any one point in time (e.g. the supervision guidelines that accompany this book: www.wiley.com/go/milne).

Commentary: To illustrate, I wish to re-analyse Kolb's (1984) model of experiential learning, as this has underpinned the book (it is also regarded as central to other approaches, such as CBT supervision: Lewis, 2005). Over the years, I have outlined Kolb's account within many workshops for supervisors and have been struck by its intuitive appeal to the participants. Even in published summaries it is rare to find authors questioning its validity. It has also served researchers well, as a basis for understanding, measuring and manipulating experiential learning. However, there are a number of important criticisms that should be borne in mind when considering Kolb's model (summarised in Chapter 3). Table 9.3 notes the main concerns, drawing on some published and unpublished criticisms.

To pick out a few instances from this table, from the perspective of the supervisee, Kolb's (1984) account of experiential learning is based on a vague construct (experience) and underplays other forms of learning (e.g. rote learning and learning by association). Although the learning modes are clearly distinguished and given equal weight, this does not reflect the dominance of reflection in the supervision (and CPD) literature. From the supervisor's perspective, the model can be criticised for being insufficiently contextualised, placing far too much emphasis on cognitive learning though a suspiciously neat set of intra-psychic stages. It is also reductionistic, distilling the complex business of experiential learning in humans down to a simple, linear and quantifiable process. It is argued that this distorts reality.

One of the contributors to Table 9.3 is Webb (2006), who has logically analysed the intellectual and scientific roots of the model, severely questioning its assumptions. In particular, she questions whether the four modes are indeed separate and distinct, and whether they are all required for learning to take place. She also questions Kolb's account of learning as a tension- and conflict-filled process, seeing this as a mis-application of the original meaning of dialectic, resulting in inherent inconsistencies and contradictions (e.g. inconsistent use of original terms and the integration of contradictory streams of intellectual thought). Consequently, she believes that the experiential learning model as described by Kolb (1984) lacks construct validity, and can only be remedied by adopting one stream of intellectual thought and sticking rigorously to its principles and assumptions, or by abandoning the model altogether, or by justifying the inconsistencies within the present account.

Criticisms of this kind (and the others summarised in Table 9.3) are not easily surmounted or ignored. Yet, on the other hand, Kolb's account of experiential learning plainly has face validity (i.e. it is highly acceptable to

Table 9.3 Criticisms of and corrections to Kolb's (1984) account of experiential learning

Criticisms	Corrections
From the supervisee's perspective:	
• 'Experience' is a vague construct, and Kolb's (1984) adoption of key concepts lacks fidelity (i.e. original meanings modified).	• Experience, along with the other learning modes, is operationalised within observational instruments, such as 'Teachers' PETS'. Meaning of terms admittedly started with Kolb, but then modified, in relation to applied psychology literature, as set out in the construction of Teachers' PETS' (Milne *et al.*, 2002).
• All four modes of learning from experience are given equal weight (though 'reflection' is usually the most popular and widely recognised mode).	• Evidence-based supervision (EBCS) does indeed give them equal weight in principle, but recognises that supervisors/supervisees have their preferences. Observations of EBCS indicate that reflection does indeed dominate (see, e.g. Milne & James, 2002).
• Is each mode really just another aspect of the same learning process?	• Is this another example of the 'different levels of analysis' problem? If so, then yes, at the more general level of adaptation, these modes are all part of learning from experience; but they differ when micro-analysed, which can be a great help to the learner.
• Ignores 'higher' learning (such as meta-cognition), power relationships, and unconscious processes.	• EBCS is broader, founded in the literature and on expert consensus, making it recognise these realities explicitly (see the definition within Milne, 2007, as summarised in Chapter 1; see Chapter 4 and the 'rupture–repair cycle).
From the supervisors perspective:	
• The model lacks context (e.g. organizational system; history).	• Modern accounts of supervision are strongly embedded in their context, as in the many accounts of moderating factors (see Chapters 2 and 3), and this is explicit within EBCS (see Principle 1 above).

(cont'd)

Table 9.3 (cont'd)

Criticisms	Corrections
• It is reductionistic, too narrowly psychological (especially about cognitive learning, and in presenting a neat set of stages), and assumes a rational, linear, quantifiable process. All four modes are not necessary for experiential learning to occur.	• The emphasis on experiencing and experimenting in EBCS corrects this cognitive bias; there is no appeal to neat stages, or to a linear process (and indeed a micro-analytic pilot study suggested a highly fluid interaction amongst stages/modes of learning; Milne, Sheikh, Haines et al., 2006). But EBCS is avowedly reductionistic and does indeed assume that quantification is vital (a consequence of adopting a scientific approach), though within a tolerant, post-positivist approach, including qualitative data, from multiple perspectives. EBCS assumes that optimal experiential learning does depend on the full use of the learning modes, but it is recognised that some successful experiential learning can occur whilst operating within one mode (e.g. through carefully considered reflection).
• Few empirical validations equates to a weak evidence-base (though extravagant claims are made: 'a theory of life and everything').	• At least as operationalised within EBCS, there are some promising validations of experiential learning (see Chapter 3 and earlier in this chapter), and claims are restricted to staff development.
• The model lacks construct validity – e.g. the 'dialectic tension' is not a viable logical mechanism.	• As per the foregoing, the pure and more 'magical' claims of Kolb (1984) are not part of EBCS, though there does appear to be something important within this thinking, as in the 'destabilisation–development' episode.

Source: Criticisms are based on: Holman *et al.* (1997); Kayes (2002); Miettinen (2002); Reynolds (1997); Vince (1998); and Webb (2006).

consumers, such as supervisors attending workshops), it is a practical way to structure supervision, and scientifically it has the merit of suggesting how some critical aspects of supervision can be examined empirically. On this logic, it seems to me that Kolb (1984) is worth reformulating, through a process of empirical development. To take Webb's (2006) suggestion, I wonder whether the optimal way to do this is to adopt one stream of thought (i.e. one coherent model), applying this with internal consistency and rigour.

In this spirit, I have added a 'corrections' column to Table 9.3. As I write these rejoinders, I realise that there was some disquiet about Kolb's (1984) account from the outset of the EBCS research in which I was involved. For example, we were uncomfortable with the breadth and ambiguity of the 'experimenting' mode, and so tried to delineate it, 'for practical purposes and conceptual clarity', from 'experiencing' (Milne *et al.*, 2002, p.189). Thus, on the one hand we might argue that we can address Webb's (2006) searching criticisms due to the ways in which the Kolb (1984) has been reformulated within EBCS, an internally consistent, rigorous approach. But in so doing we need also to recognise that something of Kolb's (1984) thinking is either abandoned or reformulated, making EBCS something that is 'guided' by his integrative theory of experiential learning, rather than representing a direct operationalisation of his work. Thus, in place of Kolb's (1984) problematic definitions we introduce contemporary ones, within science-informed models (e.g. Bennett-Levy's 2006 account of reflection).

8. Build and maintain the supervisory alliance

This much-endorsed principle lies at the heart of supervision, regardless of the model. It is thought to sit at the interface of supervisor and supervisee input, determining the resultant outcomes (as indicated by the old idea of 'the analytic pact'). It centres on agreeing the goals of supervision, followed by mutual engagement in pursuing them, and an emergent emotional bond. But the evidence for the role of the alliance in supervision is surprisingly minimal, and is marked by complex interactions with other variables (as is true in clinical research). A case in point is whether the bond is a cause or effect, with some reason to believe that it grows as a consequence of the goal-setting and collaboration. Another illustration of the complexity is transactional 'game-playing', which can confuse the supervisor and the researcher alike. Supervisors should therefore treat the alliance as the foundation for their work, but a foundation that needs regular maintenance (e.g. ensuring the 'rupture–repair' cycle succeeds). A critical phase in the alliance is the management of endings, which is now discussed.

Commentary: It is surprising to find that the business of bringing supervision sessions to an end is virtually ignored in texts and research, given its prominence in the therapy literature and its obvious potential significance as the end of what may have been an important relationship. Ending therapy, for example, can leave patients feeling abandoned, hopeless and betrayed, whilst their therapists may feel frustrated, sad, guilty and unsure about their competence (including how best to address endings: see Anthony & Pagano, 1998, for a case study; and Baum, 2006, for the results of a survey).

Unfortunately, such issues do not appear to be addressed within the supervision literature. For instance, even the events (episodes) approach excludes endings from its list of seven 'critical events', the 'most common and challenging incidents that arise in psychotherapy supervision' (Ladany *et al.*, 2005, p.19). Similarly, when Chambers and Cutcliffe (2001) searched the literature, they found that not one of the 275 papers they located dealt with issues of endings in their titles or key words. Thankfully, this oversight is corrected in the Bernard and Goodyear (2004) text, though the lack of attention to endings is again noted. They opined that some form of mutual debriefing was missing in 'most' routine supervision (p.207), despite being a natural stage in the process. They note that it is recognised as such in group supervision, where it is referred to as 'adjourning'. This tends to cover farewells, the handing-over of unfinished cases/work (often including incomplete reports/paperwork), recognition of successes, and some direction about addressing weaknesses subsequently (e.g. an improvement plan). If appropriate, it would also subsume mutual evaluation. Lomax *et al.* (2005) agree with this agenda, adding that the termination phase should include clarification of the supervisor's future availability, recognition of achievements and disappointments, a special 'celebratory' final session and a suitable closure event (they advocate an informal lunch meeting).

Given that one possible part of such endings is that a trainee is informed that they have failed to demonstrate the requisite competencies to receive a pass mark (or may have their placement terminated early, or may even be advised to leave the profession), it seems evident that the conclusion of supervision can be a highly challenging event for all concerned. Korinek and Kimball (2003) review a number of such tense 'conflicts', drawing on the marital and family therapy literature for ways to resolve them effectively (e.g. conflict over the goals of supervision, as in the supervisor's tendency to insist on the supervisee's personal and professional growth, versus the supervisee's focus on passing, and on gaining the qualification with the minimum of effort or risk). They urge supervisors to work preventively, as in specifying relevant objectives within the contract, and the regular provision of mutual feedback, and they also add some ways of resolving conflicts when these cannot be prevented (e.g. access to a consultant).

More commonly, supervision ends affirmatively, with a dominant sense of achievement and partnership (during my training, I had the habit of thanking my supervisors with a bottle of champagne, as this seemed like an appropriate way to say 'thanks, and farewell'). Based on a survey of 55 experienced social worker supervisors in Israel, Baum (2007) also recoded positive feelings, including satisfaction with their trainees' progress, pride in their contribution to this development, and a sense of gratification and fulfilment. But although the slight majority ($N = 28$) recounted such affirmative feelings, 24 also reported more uncomfortable feelings (including sadness over ending a productive relationship; frustration over the incompleteness of the experience; relief from the supervisees' demands). Echoing the reports immediately above, these supervisors also expressed concerns about their own ability and performance ($N = 39$), and half reported concerns over professional issues (e.g. 22 were unhappy about not knowing how best to end supervision). These reports are especially remarkable because these supervisors appeared to be carefully selected, and exceptionally well prepared and supported in this role. In less impressive systems, others may be more likely to feel redundant, rejected and even 'bereaved', and so struggle to let go of the supervisee appropriately. In noting these possibilities, Chambers and Cutcliffe (2001) propose that healthy endings can be promoted by having supported, negotiated and gradual endings (no wrench of sudden loss), where the supervisee retains some control, and where both work towards a sense of closure. The latter should, they propose, include the supervisors being genuine about their feelings, so modelling a healthy response (e.g. reviewing the journey; celebrating success; recognising loose ends). As a result, the participants should feel a sense that this stage of the professional journey is complete, and a readiness to get on with the next one.

9. Utilise the full supervision cycle

As in related interventions like staff training and therapy, it is sometimes tempting to proceed quickly to the 'heart' of the business, the supervision interventions (e.g. instructing or questioning). But a principled, psychologically informed approach requires that the supervisor exercises just as much care and attention over the educational needs assessment stage, the collaborative setting of learning objectives, and the evaluation of progress. These interdependent steps are best construed as necessary elements within a system, with attention to one inevitably influencing the others. As an expression of the dynamic nature of this system, even within a supervisory hour the effective supervisor will tend to complete a 'lap' of this cycle (possibly including a couple of steps back or across the cycle).

10. Engage the supervisee as a collaborator

We must quickly re-emphasise that this onus on the supervisor merely reflects the understanding that he/she is the formally designated and natural leader. In reality, the supervisee necessarily plays a vital role, at every step in what is after all a joint process. As noted under principle 8, whist this is generally a straightforward pact or alliance, with the supervisee possibly even the more energised of the partners (at least within CPD supervision), there can be tensions and complications. This is now illustrated with an example from my own experience, when I was acting as a Consultant to an experienced CBT supervisor (Caroline Leck). This consultancy was within our joint programme of action research, and entailed that I listened to her supervision tapes weekly. I noticed that one of her supervisees was exceptionally unforthcoming and uncooperative, creating a tedious and stupefying atmosphere, one that almost put me to sleep whilst listening to their tapes. This can be considered a transactional 'game', designed to reduce the effective functioning of the supervisor. In going along with this game, the supervisor is colluding with a supervisee-led process in which functions such as threat-reduction (e.g. not allowing one's competence to be judged) are being managed, to the possible detriment of the patient (Kadushin, 1968).

In order to help Caroline to make sense of this experience, the procedure described in 'self-reflection' (Bennett-Levy & Thwaites, 2007) was utilised within one of our consultancy sessions. Their six-stage process model for dealing with relationship difficulties within a CBT framework was applied, in order to make sense of this problematic relationship. The stages are: focused attention, where the problem is framed as a question; the reconstruction of the experience; clarifying the emotions, thoughts and

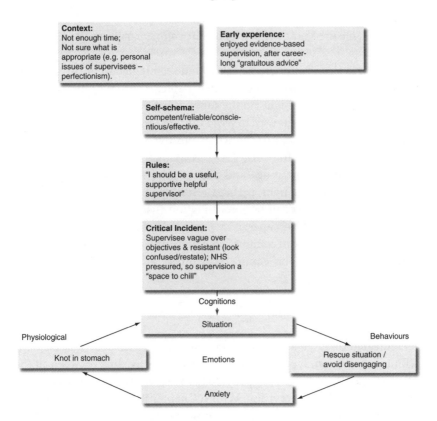

Figure 9.1 A CBT formulation of game-playing in supervision (i.e. collusion), resulting from consultant-facilitated self-reflection, self-practice

behaviours that accompanied the experience; trying to make sense of what was occurring (an interpersonal conceptualisation); role-play and the rehearsal of ways to deal with the supervisee using the new strategies; and trying out these strategies as homework. This process is summarised in Milne, Leck and Choudhri (2008).

In relation to the fourth of these stages, conceptualizing the experience, we felt it was appropriate to adopt the kind of CBT formulation that Caroline used routinely within her clinical and supervisory work, only this time it was applied reflexively, to her experience of this unresponsive supervisee. Figure 9.1 provides a summary of this formulation, which hopefully illustrates how one might address, in a suitably empowering way, problems in engaging the supervisee.

11. Ensure that there is support for your supervision efforts

This example also illustrates one valued but seemingly rare form of supervision for the supervisor, consultancy. Chapter 7 listed a range of other ways that a consultant might aid the supervisor (Table 7.2). I note that one of the earliest instruments used to try to capture consultancy had the related item of 'validation' within it, defined as positive summaries, emphasising agreement (Bergan & Tombari, 1975). Although some 10 other support options were listed, the range and adequacy of support for supervisors generally appears to be poor, perhaps resulting in what appears to be the relatively high frequency of peer consultation (usually referred to as 'peer supervision'). In this vein, supervisors may need to invent their own support mechanisms, preferably in conjunction with course organisers or employers, and draw on their personal coping repertoires.

12. Evaluate supervision

As indicated in Table 9.2 above, evaluation is another necessary element within supervision. It provides an essential corrective link between all the other elements, and it should provide the kind of information needed to adjust and develop supervision. Within Chapter 8 the fidelity framework was introduced as a unifying device, drawing together some complementary aspects of evaluation to address the basic questions in any problem-solving process (e.g. 'What is the right thing to do?'; 'Was it done right?'). Evaluation is conventionally placed last in summaries of this process, so it a fitting point at which to conclude this review of the book. However, in my final thoughts below, I will apply these questions to this book.

Concluding Thoughts

In this book I set out to provide supervisors (and those who work with them, especially supervisees, tutors and researchers) with a fresh, evidence-based account of clinical supervision that could 'compute' (Watkins, 1997). I have tried to infuse this account with a critical, scholarly style, so that the available material was suitably refined and balanced. Additionally, I wished to bolster and enliven this summary of other people's work with findings and examples from the programme of applied research that I and my colleagues in the north-east of England have been engaged in for the past few years. This was intended to isolate some fundamental principles of supervision, partly to clarify what we know, and partly to apply these so as to try to advance supervision, to address what is not yet known.

Therefore, this was not intended to be a completely neutral, disinterested review of the field, but rather the version you might expect from a committed scientist-practitioner, someone who has spent the past 30 years as an employee and vigorous supporter of Britain's National Health Service, written as if engaged in trying to guide supervisors (and those who support them), so that such services can develop and mental health can be fostered. Like any decisive stance, this platform brings with it some distinct biases and blind-spots, and so I wish to close by recognising some of these potential 'regimes of truth' that challenge the required open-mindedness (Davy, 2002, p.225). I am keenly aware (particularly from presenting the material to colleagues at meetings and conferences) that the delicate balance between evidence and enthusiasm can sometimes become disturbed in my case, resulting at times in what can seem to be an overly prescriptive and opinionated account. It is therefore appropriate to acknowledge that my EBCS model is but one perspective, one that can readily be construed as 'arrogant and imperious', like CBT (Richards, 2007). My apologies if the book has at times appeared to have taken on that kind of unappealing stance: please attribute it to my enthusiasm getting the better of my judgement. I trust that you will correct this imbalance with your own critical engagement. In time, careful evaluations will, no doubt, also moderate my enthusiasm.

As a case in point, a major part of my approach has been to base these principles, and the associated supervision practices, on a series of systematic reviews of the research literature (e.g. Milne & James, 2000; Milne, 2007). The reviews were of a particularly optimistic, constructive kind, namely the best evidence synthesis (BES; Petticrew & Roberts, 2006). This is an example where imbalance and attendant collegial resistance may arise, directed at the ironic possibility that the BES yields an unacceptably biased account of 'what is the right thing to do'. In particular, there is a concern that, by carefully excluding unsuccessful manipulations of supervision, some important (possibly even contrary) information is lost, leading to faulty conclusions about what to believe and do. This strikes me as a logical possibility, but one that I believe awaits more sophisticated evaluations of supervision before being entertained seriously (e.g. dismantling studies, which systematically tease apart the relative value of the different components in supervision; and comparative evaluations, such as that by Bambling *et al.*, 2006). In the meantime, as it is rare for unsuccessful studies (of anything) to be published, it is difficult to know how one might draw out the relevant comparison.

At least this pragmatic stance carries what would appear to be an insignificant risk of doing the wrong thing, unlike therapies like boot camps for conduct disorder, or attachment therapy (Lilienfeld, 2007). One of my lasting motivations for trying to get things right are those seriously biased accounts of what matters in supervision. I refer to positions that seem to exagerate the importance of one factor, such as the relationship (e.g. 'Good supervision, like love, we believe, cannot be taught': Hawkins & Shohet, 2000, p.195). But I am also energised by sweeping generalisations, ones that characterise the supervision literature as sadly wanting (e.g. Ellis *et al.*, 1996), and by Watkins' (1997) appeal to make supervision compute.

A related drive is to create an improved approach to supervision, one suited to the modern healthcare system and to dedicated groups of professionals. This should draw on the best-available evidence (top-down), moderated by expert consensus (bottom-up). In short, there needs to be well-grounded innovation within health services, a devilishly difficult but hugely important objective. This would support new technologies, like real-time, computer-assisted training (Rosenberg, 2006), and wed them to intelligent innovation strategies, involving methods like 'trialability' (i.e. providing innovation adopters with the option of experimenting with new methods: Greenhalgh *et al.*, 2004). This will allow us to respond better to changes in the healthcare system, like the advent of 'low-intensity' therapists, as featured in Table 9.2 (Richards & Suckling, 2008).

Of course, my preferred innovation, EBCS, should itself be subjected to further experimentation. When related to the 'pyramid of research knowledge' (Milne *et al.*, 2007), it can be seen that, at best, EBCS has progressed from the 'knowledge synthesis' stage (i.e. where the available knowledge is synthesised and guidelines are developed), through the 'mapping and modelling' stage, to some 'pilot investigations'. This work should next be replicated, and then, if promising, progressed on to the stages of 'definitive investigation' and 'long-term implementation'. With Ellis (1991), I favour a 'scientific agenda' (p.248), which is based on 'vigorously testing theoretical propositions about what supervision techniques will result in what outcomes' (p.246). This raises the question as to whether it is valid to refer to EBCS as 'evidence-based' at this stage. Am I being rather too liberal in my use of the term? The popular definition of evidence-based practice is that it is: 'the conscientious, explicit, and judicious use of current best evidence in making decisions about the care of patients' (Sackett *et al.*, 1996, p.71). On this logic, clinical expertise should be combined with the 'best available external clinical evidence from systematic research' (p.71), evidence that is not restricted to randomised controlled trials (RCTs) and other experimental designs. In this sense EBCS appears to satisfy the definition of EBP, though the research evidence only approximates to 'systematic' if one regards EBCS as an assembly of various foundations of well-established psychological knowledge (e.g. the evidence justifying the learning needs assessment from the education literature; goal-setting from the training literature; learning from experimental psychology). This definition is less anchored in rigorous research evidence and more concerned with an evidence-based approach to one's work. On this view, EBP is a process of career-long learning, in which such evidence as can be located is critically appraised and applied to answerable questions about our clinical practice, leading to evaluation of our performance (Sackett *et al.*, 1996). On this definition, EBP is an approach to professional practice that is intended to limit the problems associated with relying on one's initial training for an evidence-base, an approach that encourages a healthy engagement with the full EBP spectrum (as per Figure 3.4) as an antidote to complacency and inconsistency. EBCS clearly satisfies this definition, attempting as it does to close the gap between the knowledge-base and supervisory practice, in the tradition of the scientist-practitioner. If pursued, it will naturally lead to evaluation against the ultimate criterion, the RCT, to which we now turn.

There is a second and more exacting definition of EBP, one which requires not just the 'best available' evidence but the successful completion of the most rigorous and large-scale research. As expressed by Roth *et al.* (1996), EBP is initially a broad developmental process that works to combine information from diverse sources, including small-scale, rigorous research (e.g. they endorse the $n = 1$ design as part of this development work), clinical consensus, CPD, audits, and so forth (see Figure 3.4). But, according to them, these various EBP-related activities are merely part of the necessary work which ultimately needs to lead to 'formal evaluation', to research that 'conforms to the most rigorous standards of enquiry' (p.49), which they appear to regard as the RCT. Then, once research with high internal validity has demonstrated efficacy, service-based evaluations can address external validity and implementation issues. On this definition it is harder to assert that EBCS is 'evidence-based', at least insofar as it has not yet been subjected to an explicit RCT.

Therefore, on this exacting logic we need to ask: what is the status of EBCS? Following the NICE approach (NICE, 2007), such evidence as exists at any one time is graded against an 8-step hierarchy of research rigour, ranging from expert consensus up to the RCT. In turn, the recommendations that then emerge within NICE guidelines draw on this classification of the evidence to grade all the included evidence on a 3-point scale (A = at least one RCT, in good quality literature addressing the specific recommendation, without extrapolation; B = no RCTs, but good clinical studies; C = expert consensus, in the absence of good quality studies). In my opinion, EBCS merits the 'B' grading, as there are several high-quality systematic reviews of controlled research in supervision, a few RCTs that test EBCS assumptions, and some well-conducted case–control type research that is either explicit or highly related (i.e. research where there is a moderate probability that the relationship is causal). I feel reassured that this position is bolstered by extrapolation to those assembled parallel literatures, which would surely support one or more 'A' gradings.

But in practice, as Roth *et al.* (1996) note, 'few if any psychotherapies have been programmatically taken through this full cycle', and so they recognise that 'It would be impractical and indeed unnecessary to insist that research findings should be integrated across all these levels before being applied to clinical guidelines and standards of practice' (p.50). Indeed, the shortcomings in research 'are overcome through interpretation', as per expert judgement and systematic consensus-building. Therefore, I conclude that my use of the term EBCS is appropriate, and is consistent with current best practice. However, as is hopefully evident from my emphasis on R&D, it is of course highly desirable for RCTs (and other forms of rigorous research) to be undertaken on EBCS, to advance it beyond its present intermediate evidence-based status. The material within this book should facilitate such progress. In the meantime, supervisors should exercise careful judgement about the application of the material within this book, and should evaluate this work.

Leaving aside the definition of EBP, these promising developments are indeed heartening. In something I wrote over 20 years ago (Milne, 1986), I noted the likelihood that much supervision was 'superstitious', in the sense that supervisors probably engaged in many functionally irrelevant activities, owing to inadequate training and feedback. Even then I was advocating better training and evaluation, as a way to 'make things compute' (Watkins, 1997)! Now there is a widespread recognition of the need for supervision, and a number of effective options for replacing superstition with applied science. Even the reflections in this chapter indicate that what we now know about supervision is considerably advanced since the 1980s, and so knowing what to do in your own supervision is thankfully more straightforward. It is deeply satisfying for me to witness this progress. I hope that this book has also conveyed to you a new way of making the profound business of clinical supervision compute.

References

Agnew-Davies, R., Stiles, W.B., Hardy, G.E., Barkham, M. & Shapiro, D.A. (1998). Alliance structure assessed by the Agnew relationship measure (ARM). *British Journal of Clinical Psychology, 37*, 155–172.

Aldwin, C.M. (2007). *Stress, coping and development.* New York: Guilford Press.

Alliger, G.M., Tannenbaum, S.I., Bennett, J.R., Traver, H. & Shotland, A. (1997). A meta-analysis of the relations among training criteria. *Personnel Psychology, 50*, 341–358.

Anthony, S. & Pagano, G. (1998). The therapeutic potential for growth during the termination process. *Clinical Social Work Journal, 26*, 281–296.

American Psychological Association. (2002). *Guidelines on multicultural education, training, research, practice, and organizational change for psychologists.* Washington, DC: APA.

American Psychological Association. (2005). Determination and documentation of the need of practice guidelines. *American Psychologist, 60*, 976–978.

Armstrong, P.V. & Freeston, M.H. (2005). Conceptualising and formulating cognitive therapy supervision. In N. Tarrier (Ed.) *Case formulation in cognitive-behaviour therapy.* New York: Brunner-Routledge.

Ayers, T.D. (1987). Stakeholders as partners in evaluation: A stakeholder-collaborative approach. *Evaluation and Programme Planning, 10*, 263–271.

Bahrick, A.S. (1990). Role induction for counsellor trainees: Effects on the supervisory working alliance. *Dissertation Abstracts International, 51*, 1484B (University microfilms No. 90-14, 392).

Baker, S.B., Daniels, T.G. & Greeley, A.T. (1990). Systematic training of graduate level counsellors: Narrative and meta-analytic reviews of three major programmes. *The Counselling Psychologist, 18*, 355–421.

Baltes, P.B. (1997). On the incomplete architecture of human ontogeny. *American Psychologist, 52*, 366–380.

Baltes, P.B., Lindenberger, U. & Staudinger, U.M. (1998). Lifespan theory in developmental psychology. In W. Damon & R.M. Lerner (Eds.) *Handbook of child psychology* (5th edn, pp.1029–1144). New York: Wiley.

Baltimore, M.L. & Crutchfield, L.B. (2003). *Clinical supervisor training: An interactive CD ROM training programme for the helping professions.* London: Allyn & Bacon.

Bambling, M., King, R., Raue, P., Schweitzer, R. & Lambert, W. (2006). Clinical supervision: Its influence on client-rated working alliance and client symptom reduction in the brief treatment of major depression. *Psychotherapy Research*, 16, 317–331.

Barker, C., Pistrang, N. & Elliott, R. (2002). *Research methods in clinical psychology: An introduction for students and practitioners* (2nd edn). Chichester: Wiley.

Barkham, M., Evans, C., Margison, F., McGrath, G., Mellor-Clark, J., Milne, D.L. *et al.* (1998). The rationale for developing and implementing core outcome batteries for routine use in service settings and psychotherapy outcome research. *Journal of Mental Health*, 7, 35–47.

Barron, R. & Kenny, D. (1986). The moderator–mediator variable distinction in social psychological research: Conceptual, strategic and statistical considerations. *Journal of Personality and Social Psychology*, 51, 1173–1182.

Barrow, M. & Domingo, R.A. (1997). The effectiveness of training clinical supervisors in conducting the supervisory conference. *The Clinical Supervisor*, 16, 55–78.

Baum, N. (2006). End-of-year treatment termination: Responses of social work student trainees. *British Journal of Social Work*, 36, 639–656.

Baum, N. (2007). Field supervisors' feelings and concerns at the termination of the supervisory relationship. *British Journal of Social Work*, 37, 1095–1112.

Bebbington, P.E., Marsden, L. & Brewin, C.R. (1997). The need for psychiatric treatment in the general population: The Camberwell Needs for Care Survey. *Psychological Medicine*, 27, 821–834.

Beck, A.T., Rush, J.A, Shaw, B.F. & Emery, G. (1979). *Cognitive therapy of depression.* New York: Guilford Press.

Beck, A., Steer, R. & Garbin, M. (1987). *Psychometric properties of the Beck Depression Inventory: 25 years of evaluation. A handbook for practitioners.* London: Pearson Education.

Beinart, H. (2004). Models of supervision and the supervisory relationship and the evidence base. In I. Fleming & L. Steen (Eds.) *Supervision and clinical psychology: Theory, practice and perspectives* (pp.36–50). Hove: Brunner-Routledge.

Belfield, C., Thomas, H., Bullock, A., Eynon, R. & Wall, D. (2001). Measuring the effectiveness for best medical education: A discussion. *Medical Teacher*, 23, 164–170.

Bennett-Levy, J. (2006). Therapist skills: Cognitive model of their acquisition and refinement. *Behavioural and Cognitive Psychotherapy*, 34, 57–78.

Bennett-Levy, J., Lee, N., Travers, K., Pohlman, S. & Hanernik, E. (2003). Cognitive therapy from the inside: Enhancing therapists' skills through practicing what we preach. *Behavioural and Cognitive Psychotherapy*, 31, 143–158.

Bennett-Levy, J. & Thwaites, R. (2007). Self and self reflection in the therapeutic relationship; a conceptual map and practical strategies for the training, supervision and self supervision of interpersonal skills. In P. Gilbert & R.L. Leahy (Eds.) *The therapeutic relationship in the cognitive behavioural therapy* (pp.255–281). London: Routledge.

Bergan, J.R. & Tombari, M.L. (1975). The analysis of verbal interactions occurring during consultation. *Journal of School Psychology, 13*, 209–226.

Bernard, J.M. (1997). The discrimination model. In C.E. Watkins (Ed.) *Handbook of psychotherapy supervision* (pp.310–327). New York: Wiley.

Bernard, J.M. & Goodyear, R.K. (1992). *Fundamentals of clinical supervision*. Boston, MA: Allyn & Bacon.

Bernard, J.M. & Goodyear, R.K. (2004). *Fundamentals of clinical supervision* (3rd edn). London: Pearson.

Beutler, L.E. (2001). Comparisons among quality assurance systems: From outcome assessment to clinical utility. *Journal of Consulting and Clinical Psychology, 69*, 197–204.

Bhanthumnavin, D. (2000). Importance of supervisory social support and its implications for HRD in Thailand. *Psychology and Developing Societies, 12*, 155–166.

Bibring, E. (1937). The four countries conference: Discussion on control analysis. *Internal Journal of Psychoanalysis, 18*, 369–371.

Binder, J.L. (1993). Is it time to improve psychotherapy training? *Clinical Psychology Review, 13*, 301–318.

Binder, J.L. & Strupp, H.H. (1997). Supervision of psychodynamic psychotherapies. In C.E. Watkins (Ed.) *Handbook of psychotherapy supervision* (pp.44–62). New York: Wiley.

Bjork, R. (2006). *Shedding light on learning.* (This appeared in a conference report, by S. Cleland, published in *The Psychologist*, August, 463).

Blackburn, I-M., James, I.A., Milne, D.L., Baker, C., Standart, S.H., Garland, A. *et al.* (2001). The revised Cognitive Therapy Scale (CTS-R) psychometric properties. *Behavioural and Cognitive Psychotherapy, 29*, 431–446.

Bloom, B.S., Englehart, M.D., Furst, E.J., Hill, W.H. & Krathwohl D.R. (1956). *Taxonomy of educational objective, handbook I: Cognitive domain.* New York: McKay.

Bordin, E.S. (1979). The generalisability of the psychoanalytic concept of the working alliance. *Psychotherapy: Theory, Research, Practice, 16*, 252–260.

Bordin, E.S. (1983). Supervision in counselling: Contemporary models of supervision: A working alliance-based model of supervision. *The Counselling Psychologist, 11*, 35–42.

Borelli, B., Sepinwall, D., Ernst, D., Bellg, A.J., Czajkowski, S., Breger, R. *et al.* (2005). A new tool to assess treatment fidelity and evaluation of treatment fidelity across 10 years of health behaviour research. *Journal of Consulting and Clinical Psychology, 73*, 852–860.

Bouchard, M.A., Wright, J., Mathieu, M., Lalonde, F., Bergeron, G. & Toupin, J. (1980). Structured learning in teaching therapists social skills training: Acquisition, maintenance, and impact on client outcome. *Journal of Consulting and Clinical Psychology*, 48, 491–502.

Boud, D., Keogh, R. & Walker, D. (1985). *Reflection: Turning experience into learning*. London: Routledge.

Bouwen, R. & Taillieu, T.J. (2004). Multi-party collaboration as social learning for interdependence: Developing relational knowing for sustainable natural resource management. *Community and Applied Social Psychology*, 14, 137–153.

Bower, P., Gilbody, S., Richards, D, Fletcher, J. & Sutton, A. (2006). Collaborative care for depression in primary care. *British Journal of Psychiatry*, 189, 484–493.

Boyatzis, R.E. & Kolb, D.A. (1991). Assessing individuality in learning: The learning skills profile. *Educational Psychology*, 11, 279–295.

Bransford, J., Brown, A. & Cocking, R. (2000). *How people learn: Brain, mind, and experience and school*. Washington, DC: National Academy Press.

British Psychological Society. (2002). *Guidelines on clinical supervision*. Leicester: BPS.

British Psychological Society. (2003). *Policy guidelines on supervision in the practice of clinical psychology*. Leicester: BPS.

British Psychological Society. (2007). *Criteria for the accreditation of postgraduate training programmes in clinical psychology*. Retrieved 6 January 2008 from http://www.bps.org.uk/document-download-area/document-download$.cfm?file_uuid=48516386-1143-DFD0-7E99-DBB0AE131B71&ext=pdf

Brown, J.F. & Ash, B. (2001). Two heads with different tails: A look at the supervision process. *Clinical Psychology*, 2, 11–13.

Bruce, S. & Paxton, R. (2002). Ethical principles for evaluating mental health services: A critical examination. *Journal of Mental Health*, 11, 267–279.

Bruner, J.S. (1966). *Toward a theory of instruction*. Cambridge, MA: Harvard University Press.

Bryson, B. (2004). *A short history of nearly everything*. London: Black Swan.

Bryson, C. (2004). What about the workers? The expansion of higher education and the transformation of academic work. *Industrial Relations Journal*, 35, 38–57.

Busari, J.O., Scherpbier, A.J.J.A., Van der Vleuten, C.P.M. & Essed, G.G.M. (2006a). A two-day teacher-training programme for medical residents: Investigating the impact on teaching ability. *Advances in Health Sciences Education*, 11, 133–144.

Cacioppa, J.T., Berntson, G.G., Sheridan, J.F. & McClintock, M.K. (2000). Multilevel integrative analysis of human behaviour: Social neuroscience and the complementing nature of social and biological approaches. *Psychological Bulletin*, 126, 829–843.

Campbell, J.M. (2006). *Essentials of clinical supervision*. Chichester: Wiley.

Cape, J. & Barkham, M. (2002). Practice improvement methods: Conceptual base, evidence based research, and practice based recommendations. *British Journal of Clinical Psychology, 41,* 285–307.

Capra, F. (1996). *The web of life: A new scientific understanding of living systems* New York: Doubleday.

Carroll, M. (2007). Clinical psychology supervision. *Clinical Psychology Forum, 174,* 35–37.

Carroll, M. & Gilbert, M.C. (2005). *On being a supervisee: Creating learning partnerships.* London: Vukani.

Castonguay, L.G., Goldfried, M.R., Wiser, S., Raue, P.J. & Hayes, A.M. (1996). Predicting the effect of cognitive therapy for depression: A study of unique and common factors. *Journal of Consulting and Clinical Psychology, 64,* 497–504.

Chambers, M. & Cutcliffe, J.J.R. (2001). The dynamics and processes of 'ending' in clinical supervision. *British Journal of Nursing, 10,* 1403–1411.

Chen, H. (1990). *Theory-driven evaluation.* Newbury Park, CA: Sage.

Cleary, M. & Freeman, A. (2006). Fostering a culture of support in mental health settings: Alternatives to traditional models of clinical supervision. *Issues in Mental Health Nursing, 27,* 985–1000.

Clinical Psychology Forum. (2008). *Special Issue on the Improving Access to Psychological Therapies Initiative, 181.*

Cogswell, D. & Stubblefield, H. (1988). Assessing the training and staff development needs of mental health professionals. *Administration and Policy in Mental Health and Mental Health Services Research, 16,* 14–24.

Colquitt, J.A., LePine, J.A & Noe, R.A. (2000). Toward an integrative theory of training motivation: A meta-analytic path analysis of twenty years of research. *Journal of Applied Psychology, 85,* 678–707.

Concise Oxford English Dictionary. (2004). Oxford: Oxford University Press.

Corrigan, P.W. & McCracken, S.G. (1997). *Interactive staff training: Rehabilitation teams that work.* New York: Plenum.

Cowen, E.L. (1982). Help is where you find it. *American Psychologist, 37,* 385–395.

Davies, J.B. (2004). Bring on the physics revolution. *The Psychologist, 17,* 692–693.

Davies, P. (2000). Approaches to evidence based teaching. *Mental Teacher, 22,* 14–21.

Davy, J. (2002). Discursive reflections on a research agenda for clinical supervision. *Psychology and Psychotherapy: Theory, Research and Practice, 75,* 221–238.

DeBell, D.E. (1963). A critical digest of the literature on psychoanalytic supervision. *Journal of the American Psychoanalytic Association, 11,* 546–575.

Deery, R. (2004). An action research study exploring midwives' support needs and the effect of group clinical supervision. *Midwifery, 21,* 161–176.

Demchak, M. & Browder, D.M. (1990). An evaluation of the pyramid model of staff training in group homes for adults with severe handicaps. *Education and Training in Mental Retardation, 25,* 150–163.

Dennin, M.K. & Ellis, M.V. (2003). Effects of a method of self-supervision for coun-sellor trainees. *Journal of Counselling Psychology, 50,* 69–83.

Department of Health. (1993). *A vision for the future.* London: Department of Health.

Department of Health. (1998). *A first class service: Quality in the new NHS.* London: Department of Health.

Department of Health. (2000). *A health service of all the talents: Developing the NHS workforce.* London: Department of Health.

Department of Health. (2001). *Working together – learning together: A framework for life long learning for the NHS.* London: Department of Health.

Department of Health. (2004). *Organising and delivering psychological therapies.* London: Department of Health.

Department of Health. (2004a). *The ten essential shared capabilities.* London: Department of Health.

Department of Health. (2004b). *National standards, local action.* London: Department of Health.

Department of Health. (2007). *A learning and development toolkit for the whole of the mental health workforce, across both health and social care.* London: Department of Health.

Department of Health. (2008). *Improving Access to Psychological Therapies (IAPT) commissioning toolkit.* London: Department of Health.

Dewald, P.A. (1997). The process of supervision in psychoanalysis. In C.E. Watkins (Ed.) *Handbook of psychotherapy supervision* (pp.31–43). New York: Wiley.

Dewey, J. (1910). *How we think.* Lexington, NA: DC Heath.

Dewey, J. (1933). *How we think: A restatement of the relation of reflective thinking to the educative process* (Rev. edn). Boston: DC Heath.

Dewey, J. (1938). *Experience and education.* New York: Touchstone.

Dewey, J. (1955). *Democracy and education. An introduction to the philosophy of edu-cation.* New York: Macmillan.

Docchar, C. (2007). *Mapping of UK supervision courses for counsellors and psycho-therapists.* Paper presented at the 'Supervision Today' conference, British Association for Counselling and Psychotherapy, Birmingham, 4 December.

Donabedian, A. (1988). The quality of care: How can it be assessed? *Journal of the American Medical Association, 260,* 1743–1748.

Dreyfus, H.L. (1989). The Dreyfus model of skill acquisition. In J. Burke (Ed.) *Competency-based education and training.* London: Falmer Press.

Dreyfus, H.L. & Dreyfus, S.E. (1986). Mind over machine: The power of human intuition and expertise in the era of the computer. Oxford: Blackwell.

Driscoll, J. (1999). Getting the most from clinical supervision. Part I: The supervi-see. *Mental Health Practice, 2,* 28–35.

Duan, C. & Roehlke, H. (2001). A descriptive 'snapshot' of cross-racial supervision in university counseling center internships. *Journal of Multicultural Counseling and Development, 29,* 131–146.

Edwards, E., Bernard, P., Hamigan, B., Cooper, L., Adams, J., Juggessur, T. *et al.* (2006). Clinical supervision and burn out: The influence of clinical supervision for community mental health nurses. *Journal of Clinical Nursing, 15,* 1007–1015.

Efstation, J.F., Patton, M.J. & Kardish, C.M. (1990). Measuring the working alliance in counsellor supervision. *Journal of Counseling Psychology, 37,* 322–329.

Elliott, R. (2002). Hermeneutic single-case efficacy designs. *Psychotherapy Research, 12,* 1–21.

Ellis, M.V. (1991). Research in clinical supervision: Revitalizing a scientific agenda. *Counselor Education and Supervision, 30,* 238–251.

Ellis, M.V. & Douce, L.A. (2001). Group supervision of novice clinical supervisors: Eight recurring issues. *Journal of Counselling and Development, 72,* 520–525.

Ellis, M.V. & Ladany, N. (1997). Inferences concerning supervisees and clients in clinical supervision: An integrative review. In C.E. Watkins (Ed.) *Handbook of psychotherapy supervision* (pp.447–507). New York: Wiley.

Ellis, M.V., Ladany, N., Krengel, M. & Schult, D. (1996). Clinical supervision research from 1981–1993: A methodological critic. *Journal of Counselling Psychology, 43,* 35–40.

Ennis, R.H. (1985.). A logical basis for measuring critical thinking skills. *Educational Leadership, 43,* 44–48.

Faith, M. & Thayer, J.F. (2001). A dynamical systems interpretation of a dimensional model of emotion. *Scandinavian Journal of Psychology, 42,* 121–133.

Falender, C., Cornish, J.A.E., Goodyear, R., Hatcher, R., Kaslow, N.J., Leventhal, G. *et al.* (2004). Defining competencies in psychology supervision: A consensus statement. *Journal of Clinical Psychology, 60,* 771–785.

Falender, C.A. & Shafranske, E. (2004). *Clinical supervision: A competency based approach.* Washington, DC: APA.

Fall, M. & Sutton, J.M. (2004). *Clinical supervision: A handbook for practitioners.* Boston: Pearson.

Fleming, I. (2004). Training clinical psychologists as supervisors In I. Fleming & L. Steen (Eds.) *Supervision and clinical psychology: Theory, practice and perspectives* (pp.72–92). New York: Brunner-Routledge.

Fleming, I., Gone, R., Diver, A. & Fowler, B. (2007). Risk supervision in Rochdale. *Clinical Psychology Forum, 176,* 22–25.

Fleming, R.K., Oliver, J.R. & Bolton, D.M. (1996). Training supervisors to train staff: A case study in a human service organization. *Journal of Organizational Behaviour Management, 16,* 3–25.

Follette, V.M. & Batten, S. (2000). The role of emotion in psychotherapy supervision: A contextual behavioural analysis. *Cognitive and Behavioural Practice, 7,* 306–312.

Fonagy, P., Target, M., Cottrell, D., Phillips, J. & Kurtz, Z. (2002). *What works for whom? A critical review of treatments for children and adolescents.* New York: Guilford Press.

Frankel, B.R. & Piercy, F.P. (1990). The relationship among selected supervisor, therapist, and client behaviours. *Journal of Marital and Family Therapy, 16,* 407–421.

Fraser, S.W. & Greenhalgh, T. (2001). Complexity science: Coping with complexity: Educating for capability. *British Medical Journal, 323,* 799–803.

Frawley-O'Dea, M.G. & Sarnet, J.E. (2001). *The supervisory relationship: A contemporary psychodynamic approach.* New York: Guildford Press.

Fredrickson, B.L. & Losada, M.F. (2005). Positive affect and the complex dynamics of human flourishing. *American Psychologist, 60,* 678–686.

Freitas, G.J. (2002). The impact of psychotherapy supervision on client outcome: A critical examination of two decades of research. *Psychotherapy: Theory/Research/Practice/Training, 39,* 354–367.

Freud, S. (1909). Analysis of a phobia of a five year old boy. *The Pelican Freud Library (1977), Vol. 8. Case Histories 1* (pp. 169–306). Harmondsworth: Penguin.

Freud, S. (1912). *The standard edition of the complete psychological works of Sigmund Freud* (Vol. 12, pp.98–108). London: Hogarth Press.

Friedlander, M.L. & Ward, L.G. (1984). Development and validation of the supervisory styles inventory. *Journal of Counselling Psychology, 31,* 541–557.

Friedman, D. & Kaslow, N.J. (1986). The development of professional identity in psychotherapists: Six stages in supervision process. In F.W. Kaslow (Eds.) *Supervision and training: Models, dilemmas, challenges.* New York: Howarth.

Friston, K.J., Harrison, L. & Penny, W. (2003). Dynamic causal modelling. *Neuroimage, 19,* 1273–1302.

Froyd, J.E., Lambert, M.J. & Froyd, J.D. (1996). A review of practices of psychotherapy outcome measurement. *Journal of Mental Health, 5,* 11–15.

Furr, S.R. & Carroll, J.J. (2003). Critical incidents in student counselor development. *Journal of Counselling and Development, 81,* 483–489.

Gabbay, M.B., Kiemle, G. & Maguire, C. (1999). Clinical supervision for clinical psychologists: Existing provision and unmet needs. *Clinical Psychology and Psychotherapy, 6,* 404–412.

Georgiades, N.J. & Phillimore, L. (1975).The myth of the hero innovator and alternative strategies for organisational change. In C.C. Kiernan & F.P. Woodford (Eds.) *Behaviour modification with the severely retarded.* London: Associated Scientific Press.

Gilbody, S., Bower, P., Fletcher, J., Richards, D. & Sutton, A.J. (2006). Collaborative care for depression: A meta analysis and review of longer-term outcomes. *Archives of Internal Medicine, 166,* 2314–2320.

Gillmer, B. & Marckus, R. (2003). Personal professional development in clinical psychology training: Surveying reflective practice. *Clinical Psychology Forum, 27,* 20–23.

Godfrey, E., Chalder, T., Ridsdale, L., Seed, P. & Ogden, J. (2007). Investigating the active ingredients of cognitive behaviour therapy and counselling for patients with chronic fatigue in primary care: Developing a new process measure to assess treatment fidelity and predict outcome. *British Journal of Clinical Psychology, 46,* 253–272.

Goldstein, I.L. (1993). *Training in organizations: Needs assessment, development, and evaluation.* Pacific Grove, CA: Brooks/Cole.

Goldstein, I.L. & Gilliam, P. (1990). Training system issues in the year 2000. *American Psychologist, 45,* 134–43.

Gonsalvez, C.J., Oades, L.G. & Freestone, J. (2002). The objectives approach to clinical supervision: Towards integration and empirical evaluation. *Australian Psychologist, 37,* 68–77.

Goodyear, R.K. & Nelson, M.L. (1997). The major formats of psychotherapy supervision. In C.E. Watkins, Jr. (Ed.) *Handbook of psychotherapy supervision* (pp.328–344). New York: Wiley.

Grant, J.A. & Schofield, M. (2007). Career-long supervision: Realities and controversies. *Counselling and Psychotherapy Research. Special Issue on Supervision, 7,* 3–11.

Gray, I. (2006). The policy context. In L. Golding & I. Gray (Eds.) *Continuing professional development for clinical psychologists* (pp.23–46). Oxford: BPS Blackwell.

Gray, L.A., Ladany, N., Walker, J.A. & Ancis, J.R. (2001). Psychotherapy trainees' experience of counter-productive events in supervision. *Journal of Counseling Psychology, 48,* 371–383.

Green, D. (2004). Organising and evaluating supervisor training. In I. Fleming & L. Steen (Eds.) *Supervision and clinical psychology* (pp.93–107). Hove: Brunner-Routledge.

Greenburg, L.S. & Malcolm, W. (2002). Resolving unfinished business: Relating process to outcome. *Journal of Consulting and Clinical Psychology, 70,* 406–416.

Greenhalgh, T., Robert, G., Bate, P., Kyriakidou, O., MacFarlane, F. & Peacock, R. (2004). *How to spread good ideas: A systematic review of the literature on diffusion, dissemination and sustainability of innovations in health service delivery and organization.* London: University College (Report for the National Co-ordinating Centre for NHS Service Delivery and Organisation R&D: NCCSDO).

Greenspan, R., Hamfling, S., Parker, E., Primm, S. & Waldfogel, D. (1991). Supervision of experienced agency workers; a descriptive study. *The Clinical Supervisor, 9,* 31–42.

Greenwald, M. & Young, J. (1998). Schema-focussed therapy: An integrated approach to psychotherapy supervision. *Journal of Cognitive Psychotherapy, 12,* 109–126.

Grencavage, L.M. & Norcross, J.C. (1990). What are the commonalities among therapeutic common factors? *Professional Psychology: Research and Practice, 21,* 372–378.

Hall-Marley, S. (2000). *Therapist evaluation checklist. Unpublished instrument.* Reported in Falender & Shafranske (2004), pp 277–280 (Appendix L).

Hansebo, G. & Kihlgren, M. (2004). Nursing home care: Changes after supervisions. *Journal of Advanced Nursing, 45,* 269–279.

Hansen, J., Pound, R. & Petro, C. (1976). Review of research on practicum supervision. *Counsellor, Education and Supervision, 16,* 107–116.

Harden, R.M., Grant, J., Buckley, G. & Hart, I.R. (1999). Best evidence medical education. *Medical Teacher, 21,* 553–562.

Harkness, D.R. (1987). Social work supervision in community mental health: Effects of normal and client focussed supervision on client satisfaction and generalised contentment. *Dissertation Abstracts International, 49,* 1271-A.

Harkness, D. (1997). Testing interactional social work theory: A panel analysis of supervised practice and outcomes. *Clinical Supervisor, 15,* 33–50.

Harkness, D. & Poertner, J. (1989). Research and social work supervision: A conceptual review. *Social Work, 34,* 115–119.

Harmon, S.C., Lambert, M.J., Smart, D.M., Hawkins, E., Nielsen, S.L., Slade, K. *et al.* (2007). Enhancing outcome for potential treatment failures: Therapist–client feedback and clinical support tools. *Psychotherapy Research, 17,* 379–392.

Harmse, A.D. (2001). Support systems for supervisors in the social work profession. *Dissertation Abstracts International, A: The Humanities and Social Sciences, 61,* 3351.

Hart, G. (1982). *The process of clinical supervision.* Baltimore, MD: University Park Press.

Hatcher, R.L. & Lassiter, K.D. (2007). Initial training in professional psychology: The practicum competencies outline. *Training and Education in Professional Psychology, 1,* 49–63.

Hawkins, P. & Shohet, R. (2000). *Supervision in the helping professions: An individual, group and organizational approach.* Milton Keynes: Open University Press.

Hayes, H. (1991). A re-introduction to family therapy: Clarification of three schools. *Australian and New Zealand Journal of Family Therapy, 12,* 27–43.

Hayes, J.R. (1989). *The complete problem solver.* Hillsdale, NJ: Erlbaum.

Hayes, S.C., Barlow, D.H. & Nelson-Gray, R.O. (1999). *The scientist-practitioner: Research and accountability in the age of managed care.* Boston: Allyn & Bacon.

Hays, P.A. (2001). *Addressing cultural complexities in practice: A framework for clinicians and counselors.* Washington, DC: APA.

Health Professions Council. (2007). *Standards of education and training guidance.* London: HPC.

Heaven, C., Clegg, J. & Maguire, P. (2006). Transfer of communication skills training from workshop to workplace: The impact of clinical supervision. *Patient Education and Counselling, 60,* 313–325.

Henggeler, S.W., Schoenwald, S.K., Liao, J.G., Letourneau, E.J. & Edwards, D.L. (2002). Transporting efficacious treatments to field settings: The link between supervisory practices and therapist fidelity in MST programmes. *Journal of Clinical Child Psychology, 31*, 155–167.

Henry, W.P., Schacht, T.E., Strupp, H.H., Butler, S.F. & Binder, J.L. (1993). Effects of training in time-limited psychodynamic psychotherapy: Mediators of therapists' response to training. *Journal of Consulting and Clinical Psychology, 61*, 441–447.

Heppner, P.P., Kivlighan, D.M., Burnett, J.W., Berry, T.R., Goedinghaus, M., Doxsee, D.J. *et al.* (1994). Dimensions of characterise supervisor interventions delivered in context of live supervision of practical counsellors. *Journal of Counselling Psychology, 41*, 227–235.

Heppner, P.P. & Roehlke, H.J. (1984). Differences among supervisees at different levels of training; implications for a developmental model of supervision. *Journal of Counselling Psychology, 31*, 76–90.

Hess, A.K. (1987). Psychotherapy supervision: Stages, Buber and the theory of relationship. *Professional Psychology: Research and Practice, 18*, 251–259.

Hilsenroth, M.J., Defife, J.A., Blagys, D. & Ackerman, S.J. (2006). Effects of training in short-term psychodynamic psychotherapy: Changes in graduate clinician technique. *Psychotherapy Research, 16*, 295–305.

Holloway, E.L. (1984). Outcome evaluation in supervision research. *The Counselling Psychologist, 12*, 167–174.

Holloway, E.L. (1995). *Clinical supervision: A systems approach.* Thousand Oaks, CA: Sage.

Holloway, E.L. (1997). Structures for the analysis and teaching of supervision. In C.E. Watkins (Ed.) *Handbook of psychotherapy supervision* (pp.249–276). New York: Wiley.

Holloway, E.L & Neufeldt, S.A. (1995). Supervision: Its contribution to treatment efficacy. *Journal of Consulting and Clinical Psychology, 63*, 207–213.

Holloway, E.L. & Poulin, K.L. (1995). Discourse in supervision. In J. Siegfried (Ed.) *Therapeutic and everyday discourse in behaviour change: Towards micro-analysis in psychotherapy process research* (pp.245–273). Norwood: Ablex.

Holloway, E.L. & Wolleat, P.L. (1994). Supervision: The pragmatics of empowerment. *Journal of Educational and Psychological Consultation, 5*, 23–43.

Holman, D., Pavlica, K. & Thorne, R. (1997). *Re-thinking Kolb's theory of experiential learning in management education.* Management learning textbook. London: Sage.

Hook. K. & Bunce, D. (2001). Immediate learning in organisational computer training as a function of training intervention, affective reaction and session impact measures. *Applied Psychology: An International Review, 50*, 436–454.

Hundert, J. & Hopkins, B. (1992). Training supervisors in a collaborative team approach to promote peer interaction of children with disabilities in integrated pre-schools. *Journal of Applied Behaviour Analysis, 25*, 385–400.

Hyrkas, K. & Lehti, K. (2003). Continuous quality improvement through team supervision supported by continuous self-monitoring of work and systematic patient feedback. *Journal of Nursing Management, 11*, 177–188.

Inskipp, F. & Proctor, B. (1993). *Making the most of supervision: Professional development for counsellors, psychotherapists, supervisors and trainees.* London: Cascade.

Jackson, S.W. (1999). *Care of the psyche: A history of psychological healing.* London: Yale University Press.

Jacobs, D., David, P. & Meyer, D.J. (1995). *The supervisory encounter: A guide for teachers of psychodynamic psychotherapy and analysis.* New Haven, CT: Yale University Press.

James, I.A., Allen, K. & Collerton, D. (2004). A post-hoc analysis of emotions in supervision: A new methodology for examining process features. *Behavioural and Cognitive Psychotherapy, 32*, 507–513.

James, I.A., Blackburn, I-M., Milne, D.L., Freeston, M. & Armstrong, P. (2005). *Supervision Training and Assessment Rating Scale for Cognitive Therapy (STARS – CT).* Unpublished instrument, available from Ian James (ianjamesncht@ yahoo.com), The Centre for the Health of the Elderly, Newcastle General Hospital, England, NE4 6BE.

James, I.A., Blackburn, I-M., Milne, D.L. & Reichelt, F.K. (2001). Moderators of trainee therapists' competence in cognitive therapy. *British Journal of Clinical Psychology, 40*, 131–141.

James, I.A., Milne, D.L., Blackburn, I-M. & Armstrong, P. (2006). Conduction successful supervision: Novel elements towards an integrative approach. *Behavioural and Cognitive Psychotherapy, 35*, 191–200.

James, I.A., Milne, D.L. & Morse, R. (2008). Microskills of clinical supervision: Scaffolding skills. *Journal of Cognitive Psychotherapy, 22*, 29–36.

James, I.A. & Morse, R. (2007). The use of questions in cognitive behaviour therapy: Identification of question type, function and structure. *Behavioural and Cognitive Psychotherapy, 35*, 507–511.

James, W. (1890). *The principles of psychology.* New York: Holt.

Johnson, W.B. (2007). Transformational supervision: When supervisors mentor. *Professional Psychology: Research and Practice, 38*, 259–267.

Jones, J. & Hunter, D. (1995). Consensus methods for medical and health services. *British Medical Journal, 311*, 376–380.

Joyce, B. & Showers, B. (2002). *Student achievement through staff development.* Alexandra, VA: Association for Supervision and Curriculum Development.

Juwah, C., Macfarlane-Dick, D., Matthew, B., Nicol, D. & Smith, B. (2004). *Enhancing student learning though effective formative feedback.* York: The Higher Education Academy.

Kadushin, A. (1968). Games people play in supervision. *Social Work, 13*, 23–32.

Kadushin, A. (1976). *Supervision in social work.* New York: Columbia University Press.

Kagan, H. & Kagan, N.I. (1997). Interpersonal process recall: Influencing human interaction. In C.E. Watkins (Ed.) *Handbook of psychotherapy supervision* (pp.296–309). New York: Wiley.

Kaslow, N.J., Borden, K.A., Collins, F.L., Forrest, L., Illfelder-Kaye, J., Nelson, P.D., et al. (2004). Competencies conference: Future directions in education and credentialing in professional psychology. *Journal of Clinical Psychology, 60,* 699–712.

Katon, W., Von Korff, M., & Lin, E. (2001). Rethinking practitioner roles in chronic illness: The specialist primary care physician and the practice nurse. *General Hospital Psychiatry, 23,* 138–144.

Kavanagh, D.J., Spence, S.H., Strong, J., Wilson, J., Sturk, H. & Crow, N. (2003). Supervision practices in allied mental health: Relationships of supervision characteristics to perceived impact and job satisfaction. *Mental Health Services Research, 5,* 187–195.

Kavanagh, D.J., Spence, S.H., Wilson, J. & Crow, N. (2002). Achieving effective supervision. *Drug and Alcohol Review, 21,* 247–252.

Kayes, D.C. (2002). Experiential learning and its critics: Preserving the role of experience in management learning and education. *Academy of Management Learning and Education, 1,* 137–149.

Kazdin, A.E. (1998). *Research design in clinical psychology.* Boston: Allyn & Bacon.

Kiesler, D.J. (1983). The 1982 interpersonal circle: A taxonomy for complementarity in human transactions. *Psychological Review, 90,* 185–214.

Kilburg, R.R. & Diedrich, R.C. (2007). *The wisdom of coaching: Essential papers in consulting psychology for a world of change.* Washington, DC: APA.

Kilminster, S.M. & Jolly, B.C. (2000). Effective supervision in clinical practice settings: A literature review. *Medical Education, 34,* 827–840.

Kirkpatrick, D.L. (1967). Evaluation of training. In R.L. Craig & L.R. Bittel (Eds.) *Training and development handbook* (pp.87–112). New York: McGraw-Hill.

Klein, M.H, Mathieu-Coughlan, P.L. & Kiesler, D.J. (1986). The experiencing scale. In L.S. Greenberg & W.M. Pinsof (Eds.) *The psychotherapy process: A research handbook* (pp.21–71). New York: Guilford Press.

Knapp, M.R.J. (1997). Economic evaluations and interventions for children and adolescents with metal health problems. *Journal of Child Psychology and Psychiatry, 38,* 3–25.

Knapp, S. & Vandecreek, L. (1997). Ethical and legal aspects of clinical supervision. In C.E. Watkins (Ed.) *Handbook of psychotherapy supervision* (pp.589–602). New York: Wiley.

Knapp, S.J. & VandeCreek, L.D. (2006). *Practical ethics for psychologists: A positive approach.* Washington, DC: APA.

Knowles, M. (1990). *The adult learner: A neglected species.* Houston, TX: Gulf Publishing Company.

Kolb, D.A. (1984). *Experiential learning: Experience as the source of learning and development.* Englewood Cliffs, NJ: Prentice-Hall.

Korinek, A.W. & Kimball, T.G. (2003). Managing and resolving conflict in the supervisory system. *Contemporary Family Therapy, 25,* 295–310.

Kovacs, V. (1936). Training and control analysis. *International Journal of Psychoanalysis, 17,* 346–354.

Kraemer, H.C., Wilson, G.T., Fairburn, C.G. & Agras, W.S. (2002). Mediators and moderators of treatment effects in RCT-S. *Archives of General Psychiatry, 59,* 877–883.

Kraiger, K., Ford, J.K. & Salas, E. (1993). Application of cognitive skills-based and effective theories of learning outcomes to new methods of training evaluation. *Journal of Applied Psychology, 78,* 311–328.

Krasner, R.F., Howard, K.I. & Brown, A.S. (1998). The acquisition of psychotherapeutic skills: An empirical study *Journal of Clinical Psychology, 54,* 895–903.

Krathwohl, D.R., Bloom, B.S. & Masia, B.B. (1964). *Taxonomy of educational objectives. The classification of educational goals, handbook II: Affective domain.* New York: McKay.

Kruger, J. & Dunning, D. (1999). Unskilled and unaware of it: How difficulties in recognising one's own incompetence lead to inflated self assessments. *Journal of Personality and Social Psychology, 77,* 1121–1134.

Ladany, N (2002). Psychotherapy supervision: How dressed is the emperor? *Psychotherapy Bulletin, 37,* 14–18.

Ladany, N., Ellis, M.V. & Friedlander, M.L. (1999). The supervisory working alliance, trainee self-efficacy and satisfaction. *Journal of Counseling and Development, 77,* 447–455.

Ladany, N., Friedlander, M.L. & Nelson, M.L. (2005). *Critical events in psychotherapy supervision: An interpersonal approach.* Washington, DC: American Psychological Association.

Ladany, N., Hill, C.E., Corbett, M.M. & Nutt, E.A. (1996). Nature, extent, and importance of what psychotherapy trainees do not disclose to their supervisors. *Journal of Counselling Psychology, 43,* 10–24.

Laireiter, A-R. & Willutzki, U. (2003). Self reflection and self practice in training of cognitive behavioural therapy: An overview. *Clinical Psychology and Psychotherapy, 10,* 19–30.

Lambert, M.J. (1980). Research and the supervisory process. In A.K. Hess (Ed.) *Psychotherapy supervision: Theory, research and practice* (pp.423–450). New York: Wiley.

Lambert, N.J. (1992). Psychotherapy outcome research: Implications for integrative and eclectic therapists. In, J.C. Norcross & M.R. Goldfreed (Eds.) *Psychotherapy integration* (pp.94–129). New York: Basic Books.

Lambert, N.J. (2005). Early response in psychotherapy; further evidence for the importance of confactors rather than placebo effects. *Journal of Clinical Psychology, 61,* 855–869.

Lambert, N.J. & Bergin, A.E. (1994). The effectiveness of psychotherapy. In A.E Burgin & S.L. Garfield (Eds.) *Handbook on psychotherapy and behaviour change* (4th edn, pp.143–189). New York: Wiley.

Lambert, N.J. & Ogles, B.M. (1997). The effectiveness of psychotherapy supervision. In C.E. Watkins (Ed.) *Handbook of psychotherapy supervision* (pp.421–446). New York: Wiley.

Latham, M. (2006). *Supervisor and training accreditation* (Training Newsletter, February, p.3). Accrington: British Association of Behavioural and Cognitive Psychotherapies (BABCP).

Lavender, A. & Thompson, L. (2000). Attracting newly qualified clinical psychologists to NHS Trusts. *Clinical Psychology Forum, 139*, 35–40.

Lawrence, R.M. (1910). *Primitive psychotherapy and quackery.* London: Constable.

Layard, R. (2005). *Therapy for all on the NHS.* Sainsbury Centre Lecture, 6 September. London: Sainsbury Centre.

Lazarus, R.S. & Folkman, S. (1984). *Stress, appraisal, and coping.* New York: Springer.

Leary, T. (1957). *Interpersonal diagnosis of personality.* New York: Ronald Press.

Lehrman-Waterman, D. & Ladany, N. (2001). Development and validation of the evaluation process within supervision inventory. *Journal of Counselling Psychology, 48*, 168–177.

Lerner, R.M. (1998). Theories of human development: Contemporary perspectives. In W. Damon & R.M. Lerner (Eds.) *Handbook of child psychology* (5th edn, pp.1029–1144). New York: Wiley.

Lewin, K. (1951). *Field theory in social science.* New York: Harper.

Lewis, K. (2005). *The supervision of cognitive and behavioural psychotherapists.* *BABCP Magazine*, Supervision Supplement, 33. Accrington: BABCP.

Liese, B.S. & Alford, B.A. (1998). Recent advances in cognitive therapy supervision. *Journal of Cognitive Psychotherapy, 12*, 91–94.

Liese, B.S. & Beck, J.S. (1997). Cognitive therapy supervision. In C.E. Watkins (Ed.) *Handbook of psychotherapy supervision* (pp.114–133). New York: Wiley.

Lilienfeld, S.O. (2007). Psychological treatments that cause harm. *Perspectives in Psychological Science, 2*, 53–70.

Lister, P.G. & Crisp, B.R. (2005). Clinical supervision in child protection for community nurses. *Child Abuse Review, 14*, 57–72.

Loganbill, C., Hardy, E. & Delworth, U. (1982). Supervision: A conceptual model. *Counseling Psychologist, 10*, 3–42.

Lomax, J.W., Andrews, L.B., Burruss, J.W. & Moorey, S. (2005). Psychotherapy supervision. In *Oxford Textbook of Psychotherapy* (pp.495–503). Oxford: Oxford University Press.

Lovell, C.W. (2002). Development and disequilibration: Predicting councillor trainee gain and loss scores on the Supervisee Levels Questionnaire. *Journal of Adult Development, 9*, 235–240.

Lucock, M.P., Hall, P. & Noble, R. (2006). A survey of influences on the practice of psychotherapists and clinical psychologists in training in the UK. *Clinical Psychology and Psychotherapy, 13,* 123–130.

Lyons, J.S., Howard, K.I., O'Mahoney, M.T. & Lish, J.D. (1997). *The measurement and management of clinical outcomes in mental health.* Chichester: Wiley.

Lyth, G.M. (2000). Clinical supervision: A concept analysis. *Journal of Advanced Nursing, 31,* 722–729.

Machado, A. & Silva, F.J. (2007). Toward a richer view of the scientific method. *American Psychologist, 62,* 671–681.

Mager, R.F. (1984). *Preparing instructional objectives.* Belmont, CA: Pitman Learning.

Marks, I. (1998). Overcoming obstacles to routine outcome measurement. *British Journal of Psychiatry, 173,* 281–286.

McIntosh, N., Dircks, A., Fitzpatrick, J. & Shuman, C. (2006). Games in clinical genetic counselling supervision. *Journal of Genetic Counselling, 15,* 225–243.

McMahon, N. & Simons, R. (2004). Supervision training for professional councillors: An exploratory study. *Councillor Education and Supervision, 43,* 301–309.

Methot, L.L., Williams, W.L., Cummings, A. & Bradshaw, B. (1996). Measuring the effects of a manager's supervisor training programme through the generalised performance of managers, supervisors, front line staff and clients in a human service setting. *Journal of Organizational Behavioural Management, 16,* 3–34.

Miller, W.R., Yahne, C.E., Moyers, T.B., Martinez, J. & Pirritano, M. (2004). A randomized trial of methods to help clinicians learn motivational interviewing. *Journal of Consulting and Clinical Psychology, 72,* 1050–1062.

Milne, D.L. (1986). *Training behaviour therapists: Methods, evaluation, and implementation with parent, nurses and teachers.* London: Croom-Helm.

Milne, D. (1991). Why supervise? A survey of costs and benefits. *Clinical Psychology Forum, April,* 27–29.

Milne, D. (1998). Clinical supervision: Time to reconstruct or to retrench? *Clinical Psychology and Psychotherapy, 5,* 199–203.

Milne, D.L. (2007). An empirical definition of clinical supervision, *British Journal of Clinical Psychology, 46,* 437–447.

Milne, D.L. (2007a). CPD workshop for new clinical supervisors: A tutor's guide. Unpublished document, available from (www.wiley.com/go/milne).

Milne, D.L. (2007b). Developing clinical supervision through reasoned analogies with therapy. *Clinical Psychology and Psychotherapy, 13,* 215–222.

Milne, D.L. (2007c). Evaluation of staff development: The essential 'SCOPPE'. *Journal of Mental Health, 16,* 389–400.

Milne, D.L. (2008). Evaluating and enhancing supervision: An experiential model. In C. Falender & E. Shafranske (Eds.) *Clinical supervision: A competency-based approach – casebook.* Washington, DC: APA.

Milne, D.L. (2008a). CBT supervision: From reflexivity to specialisation. *Behavioural and Cognitive Psychotherapy* (in press).

Milne, D.L. (2008b). Manualised supervisor training: A pilot study. Unpublished research report, available from the author.

Milne, D.L., Aylott, H., Dunkerley, C., Wharton, S. & Fitzpatrick, H. (2008). *Towards evidence-based training for clinical supervisors: A systematic review.* Manuscript in preparation, available from the first author.

Milne, D.L., Aylott, H., Fitzpatrick, H. & Ellis, M.V. (2008). How does clinical supervision work? Using a Best Evidence Synthesis approach to construct a basic model of supervision. (in press: *The Clinical Supervisor*).

Milne, D.L., Freeston, M., Paxton, R., James, I.A., Cooper, M. & Knibbs, J. (2007). A new pyramid of research knowledge for the NHS. *Journal of Mental Health, 16,* 1–11.

Milne, D. & Gracie, J. (2001). The role of the supervisee: 20 ways to facilitate clinical supervision. *Clinical Psychology, 5,* 13–15.

Milne, D. & James, I. (2000). A systematic review of effective cognitive-behavioural supervision. *British Journal of Clinical Psychology, 39,* 111–27.

Milne, D.L. & James, I.A. (2002). The observed impact of training on competence in clinical supervision. *British Journal of Clinical Psychology, 41,* 55–72.

Milne, D. & James, I. (2005). Clinical supervision: 10 tests of the tandem model. *Clinical Psychology Forum, 151,* 6–9.

Milne, D.L., James, I.A., Keegan, D. & Dudley, M. (2002). Teachers' PETS: A new observational measure of experiential training interactions. *Clinical Psychology and Psychotherapy, 9,* 187–199.

Milne, D.L., Keegan, D., Westerman, C. & Dudley, M. (2000). Systematic process and outcome evaluation of brief staff training in psychosocial interventions for severe mental illness. *Journal of Behaviour Therapy and Experimental Psychiatry, 31,* 87–101.

Milne, D.L., Leck, C., Procter, R, Ramm, L. Weetman, J.R., Wilkinson, J. *et al.* (2008). Evaluating the fidelity of clinical supervision. MS under editorial review, available from the first author.

Milne, D.L., Leck, C. & Choudhri, N. (2008). Collusion in clinical supervision: Review & case study in self-reflection. *MS under editorial review.*

Milne, D.L., Lombardo, C., Kennedy, E., Freeston, M. & Day, A. (2008). Zooming in on clinical supervision. *Behavioural and Cognitive Psychotherapy, 36,* 619–624.

Milne, D.L. & Oliver, V. (2000). Flexible formats of clinical supervision: Description, evaluation and implementation. *Journal of Mental Health, 9,* 291–304.

Milne, D. & Noone, S. (1996). *Teaching and training for non-teachers.* Leicester: BPS.

Milne, D.L. & Paxton, R. (1998). A psychological re-analysis of the scientist-practitioner model. *Clinical Psychology and Psychotherapy, 5,* 216–230.

Milne, D.L., Pilkington, J., Gracie, J. & James, I.A. (2003). Transferring skills from supervision to therapy: A qualitative and quantitative N=1 analysis. *Behavioural and Cognitive Psychotherapy, 31,* 193–202.

Milne, D.L., Reichelt, K. & Wood, E. (2001). Implementing HoNOS: An eight-stage approach. *Clinical Psychology and Psychotherapy, 8*, 106–116.

Milne, D.L., Sheikh, Haines, C. & Kennedy, E. (2006). Reflective practice in clinical supervision. Paper presented at the Joint Clinical Conference, Ambleside, July.

Milne, D.L. & Westerman, C. (2001). Evidence-based clinical supervision: Rationale and illustration. *Clinical Psychology and Psychotherapy, 8*, 444–445.

Mithaug, D.E., Mithaug, D.K., Agran, M., Martin, J.E. & Wehmeyer, M.L. (2003). *Self-determined learning theory: Construction, verification and evaluation.* London: Lawrence-Erlbaum.

Moos, R.H. (1993). *Coping responses inventory: CRI – adult form. Professional manual.* Odessa, FL: Psychological Assessment Resources.

Morgan, B. (1997). *The S___ word: What teachers consider important in the supervision of paraeducators.* Paper presented at 16th Annual Conference on the Training and Employment of the Paraprofessional Workforce in Education, Los Angeles.

Moseley, D., Baumfield, V., Elliott, J., Higgins, S., Miller, J. & Newton D.P. (2005). *Frameworks for thinking: A handbook for teachers and learning.* Cambridge: Cambridge University Press.

Nathan, P.E., Stuart, S.P. & Dolan, S.L. (2000). Research on psychotherapy efficacy and effectiveness: Between Scylla and Charybdis? *Psychological Bulletin, 128*, 964–981.

National Health Service. (1998). *Our healthier nation.* London: Department of Health.

Nel, P.W. (2006). Trainee perspectives on their family therapy training. *Journal of Family Therapy, 28*, 307–328.

Nelson, M.L. & Friedlander, M.L. (2001). A close look at conflictual supervisory relationships: The trainee's perspective. *Journal of Counseling Psychology, 48*, 384–395.

Nelson, M.L. & Holloway, E.L. (1990). Relation of gender to power and involvement is supervision. *Journal of Counseling Psychology, 37*, 473–481.

Neufeldt, S.A. (1994). Use of a manual to train supervisors. *Councillor Education and Supervision, 33*, 327–336.

Newman, C.F. (1998). Therapeutic and supervisory relationships in CBT: Similarities and differences. *Journal of Cognitive Psychotherapy, 12*, 95–108.

Newman, D., Griffin, P. & Cole, M. (1989). *The construction zone – working for cognitive change in school.* Cambridge: Cambridge University Press.

Nice (2007). *Guidelines Manual.* London: National Institute for Health and Clinical Excellence.

Norcross, J.C. (2001). Empirically supported therapy relationships: Summary report of the division 29 task force. *Psychotherapy, 38*, 4.

Norcross, J.C. (2002). *Psychotherapy relationships that work.* Oxford: Oxford University Press.

Norcross, J.C. & Halgin, R.P. (1997). Integrative approaches to psychotherapy supervision. In C.E. Watkins (Ed.) *Handbook of psychotherapy supervision* (pp.203–222). New York: Wiley.

Norman, G. (2001). Editorial – best evidence medical education and perversity of humans as subjects. *Advances in Health Sciences Education*, 6, 1–3.

Oakley, A., Strange, V., Bonell, C., Allen, E. & Stephenson, J. (2007). Process evaluation in randomised controlled trials of complex interventions. *British Medical Journal*, 332, 413–416.

Olsen, S. & Neale, G. (2005). Clinical leadership in the provision of hospital care. *British Medical Journal*, 330, 1219–1220.

Orlinsky, D.E. & Ronnestad, M.H. (2005). *How psychotherapists develop: A study of therapeutic work and professional growth*. Washington, DC: APA.

Padesky, C.A. (1996). Developing cognitive therapist competency: Teaching and supervision models. In P.M. Salkovskis (Ed.) *Frontiers of cognitive therapy* (pp.266–292). London: Guilford Press.

Palomo, M. (2004). *Development and validation of a questionnaire measure of supervisory relationship (SRQ)*. Unpublished Doctorate thesis, Doctorate in Clinical Psychology Programme, Oxford University.

Parker, R.M. & Thomas, K.R. (1980). Fads, flaws, fallacies and foolishness in evaluation of rehabilitation programmes. *Journal of Rehabilitation*, 46, 32–34.

Parry, G. (2000). Developing treatment choice guidelines in psychotherapy. *Journal of Mental Health*, 9, 273–281.

Patton, M.J. & Kivlighan, D.M. (1997). Relevance of the supervisory alliance to the counselling alliance and to treatment adherence in counsellor training. *Journal of Counseling Psychology*, 44, 108–115.

Pearson, Q.M. (2004). Getting the most out of clinical supervision: Strategies for mental health. *Journal of Mental Health Counseling*, 26, 361–373.

Penman, R. (1980). *Communication processes and relationships*. London: Academic Press.

Perris, C. (1994). Supervising cognitive psychotherapy and training supervisors. *Journal of Cognitive Psychotherapy*, 8, 83–103.

Petticrew, M. & Roberts, H. (2006). *Systematic reviews in the social sciences: A practical guide*. Oxford: Blackwell.

Pickering, M.J. (2006). The dance of dialogue. *The Psychologist*, 19, 734–737.

Popper, K.R. (1972). *Conjectures and refutations: The growth of scientific knowledge*. London: Routledge & Kegan Paul.

Pretorius, W.M. (2006). Cognitive-behavioural therapy supervision: Recommended practice. *Behavioural and Cognitive Psychotherapy*, 34, 413–420.

Proctor, B. (1988). A cooperative exercise in accountability. In M. Marken & M. Payne (Eds.) *Enabling and ensuring* (pp.21–34). Leicester: Leicester National Youth Bureau and Council for Education and Training in Youth and Community Work.

Proctor, B. (1992). On being a trainer and supervision for counselling. In P. Hawkins & R. Shohet (Eds.) *Supervision in the helping professions*. Milton Keynes: Open University Press.

Proctor, B. (2000). *Group supervision*. London: Sage.

Proctor, B & Inskipp, F. (2001). Group supervision. In J. Scaife (Ed.) *Supervision in the mental health professions: A practitioner's guide* (pp.99–121) Hove: Brunner-Routledge.

Quality Assurance Agency. (2005). *Major healthcare review: University of Newcastle upon Tyne and Northumberland, Tyne and Wear NHS trust*. Retrieved 30 October 2007 from http://www.qaa.ac.uk/reviews/health/Newcastle06.pdf

Rabinowitz, F.E, Heppner, P.P. & Roehlke, H.J. (1986). Descriptive study of process and outcome variables of supervision over time. *Journal of Counseling Psychology, 33*, 292–300.

Reichelt, F.K., James, I.A. & Blackburn, I-M. (2003). Impact of training on rating competence in cognitive therapy. *Journal of Behaviour Therapy and Experimental Psychiatry, 34*, 87–99.

Reid, D.H, Parsons, M.B., Lattimore, L.P., Towery, D.L. & Reade K.K. (2005). Improving staff performance through clinician application of outcome management. *Research in Developmental Disabilities, 26*, 101–116.

Reid, D.H., Rotholz, D.A., Parsons, M.B., Morris, L., Braswell, B.A., Green, C. *et al.* (2003). Training human service supervisors in aspects of PBS: Evaluation of a statewide, performance based program. *Journal of Positive Behavior Interventions, 5*, 35–46.

Reilly, C.E. (2000). The role of emotion in cognitive therapy, cognitive therapists, and supervision. *Cognitive and Behavioural Practice, 7*, 343–345.

Reis, H.T., Collins, W.A. & Berscheid, E. (2000). The relationship context of human behavior and development. *Psychological Bulletin, 126*, 844–872.

Reynolds, M. (1997). Learning styles: A critique. *Management Learning, 28*, 115–133.

Richards, D. (2007). Arrogant, inflexible, remote and imperious: Is this what's wrong with CBT? *British Association for Behavioural and Cognitive Psychotherapy Magazine, 35*, 12–13.

Richards, D.A. (2008). *Clinical case supervision in high-volume CBT environments*. Paper presented at the BABCP Spring Conference, University of Westminster, London, 18 April.

Richards, D.A. & Freeston, M.H. (2007). Scoping supervision competencies: Discussion document, originally presented at the Improving Access to Psychological Therapies competencies workforce meeting, January 2007. Available from d.l.milne@ncl.ac.uk

Richards, D.A. & Suckling, R. (2008). Improving Access to Psychological Therapy: The Doncaster demonstration site organisational model. *Clinical Psychology Forum, 181*, 9–16.

Rigazio-DiGilio, S.A., Daniels, T.G. & Ivey, A.E. (1997). Systemic cognitive-developmental supervision: A developmental-integrative approach to psychotherapy supervision. In C.E. Watkins (Ed.) *Handbook of psychotherapy supervision* (pp.233–248). New York: Wiley.

Ronen, T. & Rosenbaum, M. (1998). Beyond direct verbal instructions in cognitive behavioural supervision. *Cognitive and Behavioural Practice, 5,* 7–23.

Ronnestad, M.H. & Skovholt, T.M. (2003). The journey of the counsellor and therapist: Research findings and perspectives on professional development. *Journal of Career Development, 30,* 5–44.

Rosenberg, J.I. (2006). Real-time training: Transfer of knowledge through computer-mediated, real-time feedback. *Professional Psychology: Research and Practice, 37,* 539–546.

Rossi, P.H., Freeman, H.E. & Lipsey, M.W. (2003). *Evaluation: A systematic approach* (7th edn). Thousand Oaks, CA: Sage.

Roth, A. & Fonagy, P. (1996). *What works for whom? A critical review of psychotherapy research.* New York: Guilford Press.

Roth, A., Fonagy, P. & Parry, G. (1996). Psychotherapy research, funding & evidence-based practice. In A. Roth & P. Fonagy (Eds,). *What works for whom?* (pp.37–56). New York: Guilford Press.

Roth, A. & Pilling, S. (2007). Clinical practice and the CBT competence framework: An update for clinical and counselling psychologists. *Clinical Psychology Forum, 179,* 53–55 (framework available from: www.ucl.ac.uk/CORE/).

Roth, A.D. & Pilling, S. (2008). Using an evidence-based methodology to identify the competencies required to deliver effective cognitive and behavioural therapy for depression and anxiety disorders. *Behavioural and Cognitive Psychotherapy, 36,* 129–147.

Russell, R.K. & Petrie, T. (1994). Issues in training effective supervisors. *Applied and Preventive Psychology, 3,* 27–42.

Russell, R.K., Crimmings, A.M. & Lint, R.W. (1984). Counsellor training and supervision: Theory and research. In S.D. Brown & R.W. Lint (Eds.) *Handbook of counselling psychology* (pp.625–681). New York: Wiley.

Sackett, D.L., Rosenberg, W.M.C., Gray, J.A.M. & Richardson, W.S. (1996). Evidence-based medicine: What it is & what it isn't. *British Medical Journal, 312,* 71–2.

Safran, J.D. & Muran, J.C. (2000). *Negotiating the therapeutic alliance: A relational treatment guide.* New York: Guilford Press.

Safran, J.D & Segal, Z.V. (1990). *Interpersonal process in cognitive therapy.* New York: Basic Books.

Sagumura, G., Haruki, Y. & Koshikawa, F. (2007). Building more solid bridges between Buddhism and Western psychology. *American Psychologist, 62,* 1080–1081.

Salzberger-Wittenberg, I., Henry, G. & Osborne, E. (1983). *The emotional experience of learning and teaching.* London: Routledge.

Scaife, J. (2001). *Supervision in the mental health professions: A practitioner's guide.* Hove: Brunner-Routledge.

Schindler, N.J. & Talen, M.R. (1994). Focus supervision: Management format for supervision practices. *Professional psychology: Research and practice, 25,* 304–306.

Shadish, W.R., Cook, T.D. & Campbell, D.T. (2000). *Experimental and quasi-experimental designs for generalised causal inference.* New York: Houghton Mifflin.

Shakow, D. (2007). *Clinical psychology as science and profession.* London: Aldine Transaction.

Shanfield, S.B., Matthews, K.L. & Hetherly, V. (1993). What do excellent psychotherapy supervisors do? *American Journal of Psychiatry, 150,* 1081–1084.

Shanfield, S.B., Mohl, P.C., Matthews, K.L. & Hetherly, V. (1989). A reliability assessment of the psychotherapy supervisory inventory. *American Journal of Psychiatry, 146,* 1447–1450.

Shanfield, S.B., Mohl, P.C., Matthews, K.L. & Hetherly, V. (1992). Quantitative assessment of the behaviour of psychotherapy supervisors. *American Journal of Psychiatry, 149,* 352–357.

Shapiro, D.A. (1995). Finding out how psychotherapies help people change. *Psychotherapy Research, 5,* 1–21.

Sheckley, B.G., Allen, G. & Keeton, M.T. (1993). Adult learning as a recursive process. *The Journal of Cooperative Education, 28,* 56–67.

Shore, B.A., Iwata, B.A., Vollmer, T.R., Lerman, D.C. & Zarcone, J.R. (1995). Pyramidal staff training in the extension of treatment for severe behaviour disorders. *Journal of Applied Behaviour Analysis, 28,* 323–332.

Siegler, R.S. (1995). How does change occur: A microgenetic study of number conservation. *Cognitive Psychology, 28,* 225–273.

Siegler, R.S. (2002). Microgenetic studies of self-explanation. In N. Granott & J. Parziale (Eds.) *Microdevelopment: Transition processes in development and learning* (pp.31–58). Cambridge, MA: Cambridge University Press.

Skovholt, T.M. & Ronnestad, M.H. (1992). Themes in therapist and counsellor development. *Journal of Counseling and Development, 70,* 505–515.

Smith, R. (1998). All changed, changed utterly. *British Medical Journal, 316,* 1917–1918.

Solomon, P. (1992). Learning contracts in clinical education: Evaluation by clinical supervisors. *Medical Teacher, 14,* 205–210.

Spence, S.H., Wilson, J., Kavanagh, D., Strong, J. & Worrall, L. (2001). Clinical supervision in four mental health professions: A review of the evidence. *Behaviour Change, 18,* 135–155.

Stallard, P., Utwin, O., Goddard, M. & Hibbert, S. (2007). The availability of cognitive behaviour therapy within specialist child and adolescent mental health services (CAMHS): A national survey. *Behavioural and Cognitive Psychotherapy, 35,* 501–505.

Stein, D.M. & Lambert, M.J. (1995). Graduate training in psychotherapy: Are therapy outcomes enhanced? *Journal of Consulting and Clinical Psychology*, *63*, 182–196.

Stiles, W.B., Elliott, R., Llewelyn, S.P., Firth-Cozens, J.A., Margison, F.A. & Shapiro, D. (1990). Assimilation of problematic experiences by clients in psychotherapy. *Psychotherapy: Theory, research, practice and training*, *27*, 411–420.

Stiles, W.B. & Shapiro, D.A. (1994). Disabuse of the drug metaphor: Psychotherapy process–outcome correlations. *Journal of Consulting and Clinical Psychology*, *62*, 942–948.

Stoltenberg, C.D. (1981). Approaching supervision from a developmental perspective: The counsellor complexity model. *Journal of Counseling and Development*, *72*, 131–138.

Stoltenberg, C.D. & Delworth, U. (1987). *Supervising counselors and therapists*. San Francisco, CA: Jossey-Bass.

Stoltenberg, C.D. & McNeill, B.W. (1997). Clinical supervision from a developmental perspective: Research and practice. In C.E. Watkins (Ed.) *Handbook of psychotherapy supervision* (pp.184–202). New York: Wiley.

Stoltenberg, C.D., McNeill, B.W. & Crethar, H.C. (1994). Changes in supervision as counselors and therapists gain experience: A review. *Professional Psychology: Research and Practice*, *25*, 416–449.

Strauss, S. (1993). Theories of learning and development for academics and educators. *Educational Psychologist*, *28*, 191–203.

Sue, D.W. & Torino, G.C. (2005). Racial/cultural competence: Awareness, knowledge and skill. In R.T. Carter (Ed.) *Handbook of racial/cultural psychology and counselling: Training and Practice* (pp.3–18). New York: Wiley.

Sugarman, L. (1986). *Lifespan development: Concepts, theories and interventions*. New York: Methuen.

Suzuki, D.T. (1934). *The training of the Zen Buddhist monk*. New York: Globe Press.

Talen, M.R. & Schindler, N. (1993). Goal-directed supervision plans. *The Clinical Supervisor*, *11*, 77–98.

Temple, S. & Bowers, W.A. (1998). Supervising cognitive therapists from diverse fields. *Journal of Cognitive Psychotherapy*, *12*, 139–151.

Tharenou, P. (2001). The relationship of training motivation to participation in training and development. *Journal of Organizational Psychology*, *74*, 599–621.

Thelen, E. & Smith, L.B. (1998). Dynamic systems theories. In W. Damon & R. Lerner (Eds.) *Handbook of child psychology: Vol. 1. Theoretical models of child development* (pp.563–634). New York: Wiley.

Thorn, B.E. (2007). Evidence-based practice in psychology. *Journal of Clinical Psychology*, *63*, 607–609.

Tight, M. (1996). *Key concepts in adult education and training*. London: Routledge.

Townend, M. (2004). *Supervision contracts in cognitive behavioural psychotherapy*. BABCP: Accrington.

Townend, M., Iannetta, L. & Freeston, M.H. (2002). Clinical supervision in practice; a survey of UK cognitive behavioural psychotherapists accredited by the BABCP. *Behavioural and Cognitive Psychotherapy, 30*, 485–450.

Tracey, T.J.G. (2002). Stages of counseling and therapy: An examination of complementarity and the working alliance. In G.S. Tryon (Ed). *Counselling based on process research: Applying what we know* (pp.265–297). Boston: Allyn & Bacon.

Triantafillou, N. (1997). A solution-focused approach to mental health supervision. *Journal of Systemic Therapies, 16*, 305–328.

Turpin, G. (2007). *Improving access to psychological therapies: Briefing paper.* Leicester: BPS.

Tyler, J.D., Sloan, L.L. & King, A.R. (2000). Psychotherapy supervision practices of academic faculty: A national survey. *Psychotherapy, 37*, 98–101.

Vasquez, M.J.T. (2007). Cultural differences and the therapeutic alliance: An evidence-based analysis. *American Psychologist, 62*, 878–885.

Veloski, J., Boex, J.R., Grasberger, M.J., Evans, A. & Wolfson, D.B. (2006). Systematic review of the literature on assessment, feedback and physicians' clinical performance. *Medical Teacher, 28*, 117–128.

Vermunt, J.D. & Verloop, N. (1999). Congruence and friction between learning and teaching. *Learning and Instruction, 9*, 257–280.

Vespia, K.M., Heckman-Stone, C. & Delworth, U. (2002). Describing and facilitating effective supervision behaviour in counselling trainees. *Psychotherapy: Theory/Research/Practice/Training, 39*, 50–65.

Vygotsky, L.S. (1978). *Mind in society: The development of higher psychological processes.* Cambridge, MA: Harvard University Press.

Wampold, B.E. (2007). Psychotherapy: The humanistic (and effective) treatment. *American Psychologist, 62*, 857–873.

Wampold, B.E., David, B. & Good, R.H. (1990). Hypothesis validity of clinical research. *Journal of Consulting and Clinical Psychology, 58*, 360–367.

Wampold, B.E. & Holloway, E.L. (1997). Methodology, design and evaluation in psychotherapy supervision research. In C.E. Watkins (Ed.) *Handbook of psychotherapy supervision* (pp.11–30). New York: Wiley.

Warr, P.B. (1980). An introduction to models in psychological research. In A.J. Chapman & D.M. Jones (Eds.) *Models of man* (pp.291–310). Leicester: BPS.

Warr, P. & Downing, J. (2000). Learning strategies, learning anxiety and knowledge acquisition. *British Journal of Psychology, 91*, 311–333.

Watkins, C.E. (1995). Psychotherapy supervisor development: On musings, models, and metaphor. *Journal of Psychotherapy Practice and Research, 4*, 150–158.

Watkins, C.E. (Ed.) (1997). *Handbook of psychotherapy supervision.* New York: Wiley.

Watson, J.D. (1999). *The double helix: A personal account of the discovery of the structure of DNA.* London: Penguin.

Webb, N. (2006). *A definitive critique of experiential learning theory.* Retrieved 5 December 2006 from http://cc.wiresu.edu/nmnweb

Wells, A. (1997). *Cognitive therapy of anxiety disorders.* Chichester: Wiley.

West, M.A. & Farr, J.L. (1989). Innovation at work: Psychological perspectives. *Social Behaviour, 4,* 15–30.

Whaley, A.L. & Davis, K.E. (2007). Cultural competence and evidence based practice in mental health services: A complimentary perspective. *American Psychologist, 62,* 563–574.

Wheeler, S. (2004). A review of supervisor training in the UK. In I. Fleming & L. Steen (Eds.) *Supervision and clinical psychology: Theory, practice and perspectives* (pp.15–35). New York: Brunner-Routledge.

Wheeler, S. & King, D. (2000). Do counselling supervisors want or need to have their supervision supervised? An exploratory study. *British Journal of Guidance and Counselling, 28,* 279–290.

Wheeler, S. & Richards, K. (2007). The impact of clinical supervision on counsellors and therapists, their practice and their clients. A systematic review of the literature. *Counselling and Psychotherapy Research, 7,* 54–65.

Wilkes, M. & Bligh, J. (1999). Evaluating educational interventions. *British Medical Journal, 318,* 1269–1272.

Winstanley, J. (2000). Manchester Clinical Supervision Scale. *Nursing Standard, 14,* 31–32.

Witmer, L. (1907). Clinical psychology. *The Psychological Clinic, 1,* 1–9.

Wood, J.A.V., Miller, T.W. & Hargrove, D.S. (2005). Clinical supervision in rural settings: A telehealth model. *Professional Psychology: Research and Practice, 36,* 173–179.

Worthen, V.E. & Isakson, R.L. (2000). *Supervision outcomes survey: Unpublished scale.* Reported in Falender & Shafranske (2004), pp.271–272, Appendix J.

Worthen, V.E. & Lambert, M.J. (2007). Outcome-oriented supervision: Advantages of adding systematic client tracking to supportive consultations. *Counselling and Psychotherapy Research, 7,* 48–53.

Worthington, E.L. (1987). Changes in supervision as counsellors and supervisors gain experience. *Professional Psychology: Research and Practice, 18,* 189–208.

York University. (2007). Patient Case Management Information System. Department of Health Sciences, York University.

Zorga, S. (2002). Supervision: The process of life long learning in social and educational professions. *Journal of Inter Professional Care, 16,* 265–276.

Index